Essays in
PUBLIC
FINANCE and
FINANCIAL
MANAGEMENT

Essays in PUBLIC FINANCE and FINANCIAL MANAGEMENT

State and Local Perspectives

Edited by
John E. Petersen and
Catherine Lavigne Spain
with the assistance of Martharose F. Laffey

Government Finance Research Center
Washington, D.C.

CHATHAM HOUSE PUBLISHERS, INC.
Chatham, New Jersey

Essays in PUBLIC FINANCE and FINANCIAL MANAGEMENT

State and Local Perspectives

CHATHAM HOUSE PUBLISHERS, INC.
Box One, Chatham, New Jersey 07928

This book was prepared with the support of National Science Foundation Grant APR 77-20340. However, any opinions, findings, conclusions and/or recommendations herein are those of the authors and do not necessarily reflect the views of the National Science Foundation.

Library of Congress Cataloging in Publication Data

Main entry under title:

Essays in public finance and financial management.

1. Consists of the essays first published in State and local government finance and financial management published by Government Finance Research Center, Washington in 1978.
    Includes bibliographical references.
    1. Finance, Public—United States—States—Addresses, essays, lectures. 2. Local finance—United States—Addresses, essays, lectures. 3. Intergovernmental fiscal relations—United States—Addresses, essays, lectures. I. Petersen, John E. II. Spain, Catherine Lavigne.
HJ275.S682   1979   336'.013   79–24847
ISBN 0–934540–03–9

Manufactured in the United States of America
10 9 8 7 6 5 4 3 2 1

Contents

Foreword

This collection of essays constitutes a unique contribution to scholarship in the state-local government finance and financial management fields. Unlike the typical journal survey that analyzes a relatively narrow band of research, each of these commissioned surveys stakes out a fairly broad field and in combination they represent a definitive status report on current fiscal research.

The essayists were aided in their task by having descriptions of current projects from a national survey of researchers, governmental agencies, and philanthropic foundations conducted by the Government Finance Research Center of the Municipal Finance Officers Association and supported by a National Science Foundation grant.

The field of state-local finance is no exception to the adage that it is an ill wind that does not do some good. The New York City financial emergency of 1974 and the "tax revolt" of 1978 have created a brisk demand for more basic information on the workings of our diverse state-local finance systems. To be more specific, financial emergencies in New York City and Cleveland have quickened the search for new and better ways of managing local fiscal systems. In the post-Proposition 13 era, conventional assumptions that underpin our tax and spending decisions are also getting new, vigorous, and, at times, agonizing reappraisal.

State-local finance research is increasingly taking on characteristics of a high-fashion industry. Today's studies on improved financial reporting, budget control, and productivity enjoy a strong demand. Not so long ago, school finance was the fair-haired child of the researchers. Many now predict that public pension policies will claim far more attention over the next few years. Meanwhile, such "oldies but goodies" as state and local tax issues, intergovernmental grants, public finance theory, and metropolitan fiscal disparities should continue to maintain a substantial research presence.

Because this volume of essays cuts across the entire spectrum of state-local finance topics, it should prove valuable to those working at the cutting edge on new issues as well as to those who need a quick fix on the latest findings in the more traditional areas of policy concern.

I hope that this systematic review of the public finance literature will not turn out to be a "one shot" affair. A periodic update stands out as the best compliment for this noteworthy effort.

John Shannon
Assistant Director, Taxation and Finance
U.S. Advisory Commission on
Intergovernmental Relations

Introduction

State and local government finance is an area of pressure and ferment. The changing economic circumstances of many states and localities, as well as popular attitudes, have encouraged a reassessment of the appropriate and feasible roles of these governments as providers of services and determiners of how they should be financed. The state and local sector has become highly significant in recent years.

In the last three decades, state and local expenditures have increased dramatically as a percentage of the gross national product, growing from 10 percent in 1950 to 17 percent in 1978. Federal aid has supported state-local growth; such aid has increased from $2.3 billion in 1950 to an estimated $82 billion in 1979, and now represents somewhat over 25 percent of all state-local receipts. Also, employment in the state-local sector has grown faster than in any other major part of the economy during the last twenty years, moving from 4 million full-time employees in 1955 to 12 million fully employed by 1978. Thus, in 1980, approximately one out of every eight persons employed works for state or local government.

One consequence of this growth has been a heightened interest in the financial operations and responsibilities of state and local governments. The desire to better understand these governments as financial entities has led to a proliferation of studies over a wide range of subjects. To organize and place these efforts into focus is an ambitious but highly worthwhile activity.

This collection of essays provides an overview of research activities in the major financial and problem areas of state and local government finance. The essays not only provide a reference point for current research but also represent a valuable contribution to defining the state of the art over a vast array of disciplines and problems.

The essays in this volume were originally published as part of a compendium of current research in the field of state and local government finance and financial management. The compendium was created under a grant from the National Science Foundation as part of a project to develop comprehensive pictures of research work that had been undertaken since 1974.

The charge to the authors commissioned to write the essays was to help readers locate the mainstream of research in the subject area, identify where it seemed to be (or should be) heading, and assess its significance for policy and practice. Beyond that, the essayists were free to integrate, emphasize and editorialize as they saw fit.

The research reviewed spans both public finance and financial management. Public finance finds as its habitat the study of how public funds are collected, stored and used, and the relationship of these activities to other sectors of the economy. Financial management is more immediately concerned with how the money-handling processes function as parts of governmental organizations and influence their behavior as corporate entities producing public services. The two disciplines know no set boundaries, and overlaps are manifold. In addition, many studies in public finance and financial management cut across the traditional lines of functional areas and activities such as revenues, expenditures and budgeting and address particular topics, such as education finance and urban fiscal studies.

Although each essayist is active in public finance, as a group they bring a diversity of disciplines to the subject. Despite their varied professional interests, however, the essayists struck a common theme in their reviews of current research: the need for more research that is applicable to policy and practice.

In the first essay, Robert D. Ebel reviews research and policy developments in state and local taxation. Ebel underscores the importance for policy makers and tax practitioners of having an understanding of the basic economic factors that characterize a government's fiscal system. This is, he emphasizes, the need to understand background conditions and trends that establish the policy framework. By definition, these policy-framework studies are ongoing because of the dynamic environment in which revenue decisions are made. Therefore, the research that exists may be no more than an "old truth" or an outdated time-slice of research efforts.

In the wake of Proposition 13, Robert T. Deacon observes in his review of the literature on public expenditures that our current understanding of governmental processes may be rudimentary but that recent trends in the development of new ideas and the integration of old ones gives some reason for optimism. Specifically, Deacon cites the absence of a consistent theory of public expenditure determination as the primary cause of the divergent research activities.

In his essay on public budgeting, Edward A. Lehan traces the American experience in this field, spanning three quarters of a century. He talks about the transition from the original emphasis on the coordination and control features of budgeting to the broader policy-making and economic potentials of the budget idea. Lehan underscores the schizophrenia of the budgetary world, in which a wide rift exists between the realities of day-to-day budget preparation and control and the ideal, goal-oriented models featured in the literature and the classroom.

In his review of capital budgeting, Michael J. White observes that researchers have neglected capital budgeting in recent years. He notes that this elusive subject lacks clear definitions, organized traditions of inquiry, conceptual boundaries, standard questions and reliable data sets.

Ronald W. Forbes points out that effective and efficient cash management has been the focus of research and application in the public sector for many years. Nevertheless, the cash management function has become increasingly important because of rapid increases in both the level and the volatility of interest rates. Opportunities for research to promote further gains in efficiency and explore the interrelationships between cash management and other govermental decision processes have flourished.

In his essay on debt management, John E. Petersen relates the growing interest in research in state and local government debt policy and management to the New York fiscal crisis of the mid-1970s and its impact on the municipal securities market. Petersen identifies new areas of research introduced during this period—investor information needs, disclosure methods and fiscal condition indicators—and discusses other topics that have been and continue to be of interest to researchers, such as the structure of investor demands, the efficiency of tax exemption, technical innovations in the design and marketing of debt instruments and new kinds and uses of borrowing.

Bernard Jump suggests that one of the ironies of state and local public finance and financial management research is that public employment, which accounts for the single largest operating expenditure in most general-purpose governments, has until recently been given so little attention by public finance specialists. Jump acknowledges that public employment, collective bargaining and compensation research have made substantial strides during the 1970s. But much remains to be done—beginning with the elimination of major data inadequacies.

In his review of accounting, auditing and financial reporting, James M. Williams also attributes heightened interest in these areas to the New York fiscal crisis. He notes that many observers were prompted to scrutinize the financial management practices of state and local governments and question their accounting systems, auditing practices, and reporting mechanisms. Driven by concerns over the quality of the state of the art and desirable improvements, new research on the need for more uniform accounting principles and auditing standards has emerged. How to meet them forms another problem. Williams characterizes the research performed to date in public accounting as minuscule and sporadic, but sees it increasing in recent years. In his review of the literature, Williams finds cause for optimism because interest in the issues is great and growing all the time. Research responds best to increased attention and resources—a situation that now obtains for governmental accounting.

George F. Break suggests that if fiscal research is stimulated by rapid growth in the programs to be studied, intergovernmental finance should be basking in the warm glow of expert attention. Since the adoption of federal revenue sharing in 1972, researchers have been increasingly turning their attention to grant programs. Harkening to a statement by Henry Aaron regarding research on intergovernmental finance, Break notes that much work must still be done because few findings that bear on enduring issues of public policy can be expected to remain generally accepted for very long.

Harold A. Hovey looks at intergovernmental finance research at the state-local level. He finds that although these intergovernmental financial relationships are key research topics, the subject matter has not developed much of a literature when compared with federal grant programs. He cites a number of reasons for this state of affairs, among which is the unavailability of research money to look at purely state-local matters. The literature that does exist tends to be anecdotal rather than quantitative treatments and often is parochial, based upon limited data. Hovey finds that the research undertaken is often developed to fill the policy-making needs of a single state, taking the form of testimony, task force reports, or staff reports, and is seldom disseminated beyond the state in which it is created. Generalizing, tapping the experiences of one state to the benefit of others, should be a primary objective.

William H. Oakland reports that the literature on state and local finance theory, unlike that of most areas discussed in this book, is tremendously diverse. Oakland chooses to focus his piece on a summary of the state of the art and recent contributions in three broad areas: the optimal structure of government for the delivery of state and local public services, the theory of the expenditure behavior of a state or local government unit, and the incidence of state and local property taxes.

Although effective fiscal planning is one of the most pressing needs of state and local governments, Roy W. Bahl describes the state of the art in revenue and expenditure forecasting as primitive. He suggests that because the problems associated with forecasting revenues and expenditures—particularly expenditures and, especially, at the local government level—are formidable, there has been a paucity of research on the subject. Bahl explores the problems in detail and outlines the obstacles to better forecasting.

In his essay on the state-local sector and the economy, Robert W. Rafuse addresses two sets of issues that have been the objects of intermittent attention in the professional literature for decades: the overall cyclical behavior of the sector and the existence of regional disparities in employment, income and fiscal levels. Rafuse points out that only in the very recent past have these areas become subjects of national policy debate and matters of major concern to researchers. He identifies the lack of national-income-account data on a disaggregated basis as a serious deterrent to the analysis of fiscal and economic issues at the subnational level. This problem notwithstanding, Rafuse finds that researchers have demonstrated ingenuity and have produced a veritable explosion of studies, analyses and occasional polemics on the general subject of subnational disparities in state-local economic and fiscal behavior.

Allan Odden reviews the extensive literature found in the school finance area by analyzing the issues recognized by state policy makers and school finance scholars within the broader context of local, state and federal public finance and intergovernmental fiscal relations. The issues include school finance equalization, collective bargaining and teacher retirement systems, tax and expenditure limitations and urban school finance.

Philip M. Dearborn, in his survey of urban fiscal problems, notes that recent years have been fertile ones for those involved in urban fiscal analysis. Attention has been focused on improved understanding of how cities manage their fiscal affairs with special emphasis on the problems of analyzing current financial conditions and isolating the factors that predict future problems. Dearborn notes, however, that while analysis and understanding of the financial conditions in cities has improved, there is still no dependable monitoring system that can give assurance about the health of all cities.

Nancy S. Hayward tells us that the implications for state and local governments of the U.S. "productivity crisis" are significant as the cost of delivering public services continues to rise and pressures to reduce the tax burden increase. Hayward finds that, in the past, governmental productivity has been only indirectly addressed by most researchers. Noting that the commitment to such study in the public sector is significantly greater than it has ever been, she identifies directions for new productivity research.

The essays in this book are extensive, and within their individual subject areas, comprehensive. But the book is not conclusive. Public finance continues to change rapidly, often in reaction to the changing desires and resources of the society. As these essays were being completed, the eruption of Proposition 13 took place as California voters decided to slash and cap the local property tax in that state. The startling change in local government revenue sources brought corresponding alterations in state-local relations, budgeting practices and debt-financing techniques, to mention a few.

Taxpayer dissatisfaction and a growing mood of conservatism swept the country, leaving few zones of public finance unshaken. New attention focused on the optimal size and design of the public sector, ways to measure and enhance its performance and—most prominently—how its growth could be checked through a variety of externally mandated tax and expenditure limitations. Thus, new currency and urgency came to those research areas involving alternative means of financing public services, more economy in government and processes by which to control the public budget more tightly. As the fight over where to reduce and how to allocate the shrinking budget becomes even more bitter, questions of the equity of alternative actions and their long-term implications for government finance are sure to become increasingly important.

While the early tremors of Proposition 13 rocked first the state and local sector, the federal government was soon to feel the aftershock. Under pressure to balance the federal budget and halt wasteful and inflationary spending, federal budget-makers began to search for ways to cut back outlays. Major candidates for reduction can be found in the vast array of aid programs to state and local governments that have accumulated over the years. But the other side of the coin is that many cities and states have grown highly dependent on federal assistance. Thus, a dilemma for intergovernmental finance: reductions at the federal level promise to tighten the budgetary squeeze on governments already faced with constrained tax bases.

Other enduring themes continue to roll. The financial viability of the nation's older cities and regions—and local vs. state vs. national responsibility to improve it—remain at issue. Public employee pensions present difficult to measure but demonstrably huge future drains on government resources. A decade of inflation has made increasingly important, but also more difficult, fiscal forecasting. Long-standing commitments to clean up the environment, to improve public transit and to provide a host of other conveniences, benefits and protections to the individual have come to be increasingly burdensome. Perhaps they will prove to be unachievable when subjected to increasingly tight-fisted budgets. In an era of slower growth, the demographics of an aging population will no doubt reshape the desired package of public services.

This collection of essays serves as a milestone of how these and other problems in public finance are being studied today. We believe they serve as a useful point of departure for those who seek to understand the role and uses of research in analyzing issues and formulating and implementing those policies that will continue to emerge in the future.

Essays in
PUBLIC
FINANCE and
FINANCIAL
MANAGEMENT

Research and Policy Developments: Major Types of State and Local Taxes

One of the most significant developments in fiscal federalism in recent years has been the growth in the state and local sector. Since 1960, state and local expenditures on a national income accounts basis have increased at an annual rate of 10.5 percent, compared to a 9.3-percent increase in federal expenditures.[1] Although much of this expenditure growth has been financed by federal aid, the subnational governments have also relied increasingly on their own resources. Between 1962 and 1974, state and local expenditures from own sources increased three and a half times—from $58,252 million to $165,898 million.

This growth of state and local governments has led to an increase in their political clout and national economic impact. Not only have the statehouses and city halls generated a large employment constituency, but their growing share of the national product has heightened awareness of the national importance of the fiscal health of both the sector as a whole and states and cities individually.

Another result of this growth is, of course, that state and local governments must find new revenues. This requires both looking for new sources of financing and using existing tax and revenue devices more intensively. But, as existing revenue sources are used more intensively, there is danger that their inherent structural defects may become intolerable.[2] Moreover, as the level of total tax revenues has increased, new questions have arisen as to the role these taxes play in achieving the often contradictory goals of overall tax equity, neutrality, simplicity, and private-sector growth.

As a result of these developments, it is of critical importance that policy makers, administrators, and researchers alike not only reexamine the old "truths" concerning the nature and effects of state and local taxation, but also make the effort to exchange information in order to improve state and local fiscal systems. The purpose of this paper is to contribute to that effort. In particular, it summarizes several policy and research developments in the major tax categories of property, general business, personal income, and sales and excises. Included in this fourth category is a discussion of new developments in the taxation of natural resources.

The Tax Base

One of the safest observations to make regarding the financial situation of local

Robert D. Ebel is Professor of Economics at the University of the District of Columbia. The author wishes to thank Michael Bell, Catherine Kweit, John Shannon, Will Myers, Joan Towles, and Jonathan Rowe for comments on an earlier draft of this paper. Joan Towles also assisted in the literature search.

governments is that the long-run outlook is one of continued fiscal strain—a factor which appears to be generally true for large (e.g., central city) and small jurisdictions alike.[3] The severity of this strain will vary among jurisdictions and will depend on such factors as the macroeconomics of the national economy, the continuation of existing intergovernmental expenditure and grant arrangements, and the ability of certain groups of voters to successfully express their dissatisfaction with local political policies[4] by voting against their governments' pleas for increased financial support.

Though most of this concern regarding budgetary strain has been directed to local governments, the states will not be isolated from its effects. True, the states have been able to take on an increased share of state and local expenditures in recent years.[5] However, this trend cannot be expected to continue, particularly if inflation continues in the range of six to seven percent in the next few years.[6] The current fiscal surpluses of the state/local sector are not an indication of the long-run fiscal position of these governments.[7]

Accordingly, in order to make informed decisions regarding state and local budget issues, it is important that policy makers and tax practitioners have an understanding of the basic economic factors that characterize the fiscal system as a whole. That is, it is necessary to understand the background conditions and trends which establish the policy framework. The concern here goes well beyond technical problems of revenue forecasting. What is at issue is the ability of state and local governments to generate sufficient revenues to provide funds for the maintenance of the scope and quality of their existing program structures, as well as to provide the revenues to finance growing expenditure demands.

There are several types of policy-framework studies. For convenience here they are divided into three categories: city fiscal emergencies; tax yield—economic-base linkages; and fiscal capacity and effort. The first two of these focus on local government. The third deals with state revenue systems.

Emergencies

In 1973, two years preceeding the New York City "crisis," the U.S. Advisory Commission on Intergovernmental Relations (ACIR) published its report on defining city financial emergencies and provided a list of historically identified characteristics of a municipality on the brink of an emergency. The director of that report, Philip M. Dearborn, has subsequently updated and expanded several of those indicators focusing on liquidity measures which provide insights into the financial condition of general obligation credits, the treatment of debt-service revenues and budget performance measures which serve as predictors of future fiscal problems.[8]

A similar emergency-indicators approach has also been examined by Elizabeth Dickson.[9] In a report financed by the U.S. Department of Housing and Urban Development, Dickson examines several indicators of local fiscal trends. These include measures of revenue capacity (tax-base stagnation, tax-base comparisons with neighboring jurisdictions), expenditures (growth, real-wage maintenance), and state aid and tax-base sharing. For each of these indicators the performance of a sample of large U.S. cities is tested.

Economic-Base Linkages: The City

Changes in the structure of the urban economic base and the resulting performance of tax yields are at the heart of the urban fiscal problem. While each of these topics has been separately examined, little research has been done establishing a link between the city's changing economic structure and its revenue system.

In response to this need, Roy Bahl and David Greytak have developed a model which can be used to empirically link the changing level and composition (e.g., by commuting patterns, industrial mix) of the city's employment base to both its existing revenue system and proposed changes in that system. This analysis was originally applied to New York City, but has been extended elsewhere.[10] No attempt is made to

2

answer the question of which particular tax or group of taxes is "best" according to the several criteria (e.g., neutrality, equity, administration) of judging a revenue system. Rather, the analysis focuses only on the long-run revenue productivity of the tax system and its alternatives. Such an isolated focus, however, provides a critically important piece of information to policy makers and tax practitioners. A city council member may design the most equitable neutral tax package imaginable; but unless the package can generate needed revenues over time, it will have little practical benefit.

Fiscal Capacity and Effort

Ever since ACIR published its 1962 tax-capacity study which developed the representative tax system approach,[11] one conventional measure of the fiscal status of a subnational government has been its revenue capacity and effort. For example, since 1967 the Southern Regional Education Board (SREB) has annually reported on this aspect of tax performance for the states and their various subdivisions.[12] The study provides measures of actual and potential tax collections, and then compares these measures in order to determine which states are overutilizing or underutilizing their relative ability to collect taxes.

A forthcoming study by Kent Halstead also provides state-by-state rankings using the ACIR approach. However, this report adds two other types of information.[13] First, the recent trends (1967–75) are presented in addition to this conventional one-year-at-a-time comparison. The purpose of looking at the trend is to differentiate between governments which may have equal "representative" tax yields but which may have different rates of growth in their capacities. Second, the report explores, on a limited basis, measures of fiscal "need" according to various program indices (e.g., poverty, school enrollments, housing conditions). These need indicators are then adjusted by a price index of public-sector wages.

Property Taxation

The local property tax continues to be a major focus of state and local tax research. The reasons are familiar, ranging from the fact that not only is the tax among the most visible of state and local revenue devices, often creating cash-flow problems for property owners, but also that the tax accounts for the overwhelming percentage of local tax revenues (81.5 percent in 1976).[14]

In spite of the recent dramatic success of the Jarvis-Gann initiative in reducing California property taxes, and the subsequent attacks—at least in rhetoric—on the tax in other parts of the nation, heavy local reliance on the property tax relative to other revenue sources will continue. This is true for at least four reasons.

First, duplicating a Jarvis-Gann rollback elsewhere is unlikely. Not only was California's fiscal situation unusual among the states, (having property taxes 40 percent above the national average in 1976, plus a state surplus of $5 billion for the next fiscal year), but the "solution" is uncommon. Only 15 states have initiative mechanisms by which voters can place constitutional amendments on the ballot, and in six of these the procedure is much more difficult than in California.[15] A more likely response is that the California vote will give support to the recent trend by both state and local governments to enact expenditure and tax restrictions in the form of state limits on local property tax rates and levies and full-disclosure laws, state expenditure constraints,[16] and personal income tax indexation.[17]

Second, for many local governments the property tax is the only broad-based levy for which institutional tools and administrative bureaucracies are well developed.

Third, research is giving support to those who have been arguing that the tax has an undeservedly bad reputation for structural defects and inequities. Supporters of the tax (i.e., defenders against tax-base erosion) point out that not only does the tax provide the best method by which one can tax unrealized capital gains,[18] but that traditional arguments that the tax is generally regressive have been undermined by recent research.[19]

3

Finally, the property tax has been shown to have the greatest potential of any state or local tax source for revenue growth during inflation—i.e., to automatically generate tax-base increases (property values) which are proportionately greater than the change in the general price level.[20] Such a finding is likely to make the tax increasingly attractive to local governments which must cope with the long-run tendency toward fiscal imbalance.[21]

It should be emphasized here that the focus of this latter point is on the revenue potential. Because of both its unique administrative and institutional characteristics and its ready susceptibility to *ad hoc* political manipulation, potential and actual tax collections are not likely to be equal. Although property values may be rising rapidly, practical considerations minimize corresponding tax-yield increases. These considerations include time lags between the market change in the value of the property and its assessment for tax purposes, the likely (and politically unpopular) tax-burden redistribution effects of assessing property at its current market value,[22] and the erosion of the tax base by various property tax relief devices such as tax-rate limits,[23] freezing assessments and/or tax levels, and requiring that certain types of property (e.g., agricultural land[24] and open space[25]) be valued at their present actual rather than at their "highest and best use," or market value.

Homeowner Tax Relief

Property tax relief differs from reform in that it generally accepts the current property tax structure as given and then targets certain groups of taxpayers for reduced tax burdens. There have been several recent studies evaluating the major alternative mechanisms for tax relief. Perhaps the most comprehensive of these have been provided by Aaron, Gold, and ABT Associates in a report prepared for the U.S. Department of Housing and Urban Development (HUD).[26] The HUD report focused on programs designed to provide reduced tax burdens for the elderly, but is nevertheless sufficiently analytical to give insight into the issue of general tax relief.

Four alternative approaches—the tax freeze, tax deferral, homestead exemption, and circuit breaker—are evaluated for their distribution effects, revenue implications, and administrative characteristics. Of these devices, low marks must be given to the tax freeze, which is vertically inequitable and inefficient, and the homeowner exemption, which violates horizontal and vertical equity criteria because it cannot be well targeted. Although tax deferral is politically unpopular since it is often perceived as a threat to home ownership, it is getting increasingly favorable attention.[27] The deferral is ranked high on equity since all deferred taxes must be repaid when a new owner takes title, on neutrality because it minimizes government interference with private housing decisions, and on revenue productivity grounds.

Of all the tax relief devices, the circuit breaker has received the greatest amount of attention. Already the second most used tool (the homestead exemption is first), it is gaining rapid acceptance throughout the country. Although basically two variants of the circuit breaker can be identified—the threshold and sliding-scale approaches—in practice the form of the circuit breaker is so diverse that generalizations on its performance are difficult to make.[28]

The circuit breaker's proponents point to the relative ease with which it can be targeted to low-income taxpayers regardless of their housing-tenure status. Moreover, in most places the circuit breaker has the practical advantage of being state-funded.

The criticisms are growing, however. Among the more important of these are that:
- As structured in many states, the tax has become so cumbersome from a compliance standpoint that the practical result is that relief fails to fully reach those for whom it is intended;
- It provides aid that rises with the wealth of the recipient; and
- It may create vertical inequities in light of recent evidence that property tax is becoming a progressive levy.[29]

4

Classification

Under a classified real property tax, different types of property are taxed at different rates.[30] It may be implemented by assessing property in different classes at different percentages of market value, or by applying different tax rates to different classes. In either case, the distinguishing characteristic of a classified property tax is that the effective tax rate (the tax paid on a property as a percentage of its market value) is different for different classes of property. For real property, classes are defined by use, with the initial distinction usually being made between commercial and residential real estate.

In evaluating the relative merits of increasing revenues via a classified tax versus an increase in a uniform levy, two fundamental questions arise: What are (1) the distributional consequences and (2) the non-neutral effects (if any)?

The answer to the first of these is largely determined by the change in rents once the classified tax induces a switch of land from commercial to residential use. In general, the extra property tax burden of the classified tax will be shared by consumers of commercial enterprises and commercial landowners. As a result of this second effect, land will be transferred from commercial to residential use—i.e., that type of real estate which is earning a highest return. The expanded supply of residential land will drive down the price of residential real estate, and this process will occur until the returns in commercial and residential real estate are equalized.

Thus, three groups of individuals who will be affected differently by the tax increase can be distinguished. First, the customers of commercial establishments will be worse off because the price they pay for the goods and services must be higher to offset the increased rent that those establishments pay for real estate. Second, the occupants of the jurisdiction's housing will be better off because the rents they pay will be lower. Third, the economic position of landowners (both residential and commercial) will be worsened because the rent of land will be lower.[31]

The extent to which private economic decisions are distorted also depends on the elasticity of demand for commercial property relative to that of residential property. If the demand for commercial real estate is very sensitive to tax-induced price changes vis-à-vis the demand for residential real estate, there will be a significant reduction in demand for commercial real estate which could only be absorbed in the residential sector by a substantial reduction in land rents. In this case, strict neutrality criteria would favor the continuance of the current uniform property tax. If the demand for commercial real estate is not sensitive to tax-induced price changes, one would expect only modest changes in land rents. Here the neutrality criteria would favor substituting classification for an equal yield increase in the uniform property tax.

Whatever this outcome, however, the uniformity vs. classified choice presents policy makers with a difficult set of policy trade-offs. As indicated above, in a jurisdiction which is heavily rental oriented and which is characterized by a relatively inelastic demand for land, there is a clear element of tax relief from classification. However, it should also be noted that classification has its drawbacks. Three criticisms are of particular importance and must be weighed in any policy decision.

1. Classification is a crude and inefficient tool for residential property tax relief. If such relief is desirable, there are superior methods which should be used.
2. Inherent in the adoption of a classified property tax are additional administrative problems in the assessment procedure created by the need to equitably determine the use to which the property is put. This burden becomes even more severe in attempting to determine the proper allocation for mixed-use property.
3. There is no objective point at which classification should stop with respect to either the commercial-residential rate differential or the number of property classes to be established.

Who Pays?

A central issue in the property tax is that of where the burden of the tax ultimately falls.[32] The real property tax base includes both land and capital improvements. Economists generally agree that a tax on land results in a decrease in its return and a capital loss to the owner of the land at the time the tax is imposed (or increased). That is, as a result of the fixed supply of land, potential renters need bid no more for the land than they did before the imposition of the property tax. And, since the owners of the land must pay the tax, the potential net rental income is reduced. Thus, potential buyers will bid less for the land. It turns out that the reduction in the value of the land would be exactly equal to the (increased) property tax liability capitalized at the appropriate rate.

The situation for the tax on the improvements component of real property is more complicated. According to the "traditional" approach, the property tax is viewed as an excise tax on capital which slows the rate of investment in the taxed good—e.g., new structures and rehabilitation. This restriction of supply continues until the after-tax rate of return is equal to the rate of return before the tax. Thus, the property tax tends to be largely borne by users, with the assumption usually being made that property taxes on residential structures are distributed according to housing expenditures and taxes on other structures distributed by general consumption patterns.

Under the "new" theory, the property tax is viewed as having two portions. The first is that which is common to all jurisdictions—i.e., a nationwide component. In this case it is assumed that the supply of capital cannot be altered by the national tax and, thus, the tax falls on capital owners. And, since capital ownership is concentrated in the high-income groups, this portion of the tax tends to be progressive in terms of tax burden.

The second portion of the property tax is the differential between a given jurisdiction's rate and the average national rate. This differential portion may be treated as a tax on different sectors (taxed versus untaxed) of capital. If capital is highly mobile, then the theory suggests that resources will shift from the taxed to untaxed sectors until the after-tax rates of return in both sectors are equal. Stated differently, investors will direct their resources to jurisdictions with high tax rates only if the before-tax return compensates them for the higher property tax. Who will "pay" for securing these higher returns? It depends on local market and factor conditions. Laborers may accept lower wages, consumers higher prices, and/or landowners lower rents. The exact pattern will be a function of the local economy.[33]

Which view provides the best policy guideline? That depends on the question being examined.[34] If the concern is a change in the national average property tax rate, e.g., a federal revenue replacement for the tax, then the new view that the change will impact on capital owners is appropriate. However, if the concern is a change in the local property tax as an isolated event, then the traditional view, focusing on excise tax effects, provides the better framework. Thus, the two "views" are, in fact, complementary and not competing.

Despite the reaffirmation of the traditional view as a guide to local policy decisions, it does not necessarily follow that the property tax will be regressive. This is true for two reasons. First, as noted above, tax shifting is a function of local market conditions. Second, the measure of burden will vary according to definition of income used in tax burden estimates. Some recent empirical work has indicated that if property tax burdens are allocated to long-term average income rather than annual money income, the regressivity of the property tax largely vanishes even if the traditional theory of tax incidence is retained.[35] Property tax bills, meanwhile, come due in the short run.

Finally, it should be recalled that conclusions about the regressivity of property taxes are a function of the administration of the tax. To the extent that there is an assessment bias in favor of high-valued properties, the local property tax is more regressive than the theory suggests.[36]

Site-Value Taxation

Site-value taxation refers to that form of a real property tax which is levied only on the value of the land. Total improvement value is excluded from the tax base and is therefore totally exempt from taxation. This is in contrast to the current "uniform" real property tax which taxes land and improvements at the same rate. To illustrate how a site-value tax would work *vis-à-vis* the current uniform tax, assume that there are three residential lots side by side and all have the same value. The first has a well-maintained house on it; the second has a similar home, but very run-down; the third is vacant. Under the present property tax, the tax rate is applied to the sum of the land value plus the building value. Thus, the first home carries the highest assessment and the highest tax; the blighted home pays a substantially lower tax; and the unused lot is charged least of all. With site-value taxation, each of these properties is charged an identical amount because it is assumed the lots are equally attractive and, therefore, of equal value.

Advocates of site-value taxation see the tax as a substitute for the current real property tax on land and improvements. The argument is that the current tax on improvements has non-neutral effects on investment decisions resulting in:

o The extended utilization of buildings beyond the point at which they should be replaced;

o Disincentives for maintenance or improvement of the capital improvements; and

o The substitution of land for capital causing low density development—urban sprawl and leapfrog development.

Although the site-value tax has been used in Australia and New Zealand (with disagreement as to its success),[37] the tax has never gained much political support in the United States. Hawaii enacted a modified site-value tax in 1963. The idea was to start in 1966 by taxing buildings at 90 percent of the land tax rate and then reduce the building factor by 10 percent every two years until it was 40 percent of the land rate. However, political decisions kept that factor from ever going below 70 percent, and the state repealed the differential tax effective July 1978. The major reason given for repeal was that the tax was cumbersome to comply with and to administer, and that there was no evidence that the graded property tax worked.[38] A recent study of the Hawaii experience, however, indicates that had the state actually given site-value taxation a chance, it would have significantly increased the degree of capital intensity in the production function.[39]

The site-value tax has also received mixed reviews elsewhere. It has been recommended for serious consideration in New York City,[40] but rejected by a special tax study commission in the District of Columbia.[41] The New York report argued in favor of its incentive effects on improvements. The District's commission also recognized that a site-value tax would accelerate the development of some underutilized land. However, it also concluded that these incentives are overemphasized and that there are nontax policies (zoning, facilitation of land assembly, reducing government red tape) that are likely to be more effective in achieving the site-value tax goal which do not have the significant tax-burden shifts and wealth changes which are associated with the tax.

Also of concern are the legal obstacles to the adoption of such a tax policy. After a comprehensive review of the relevant case law, Oliver Oldman and Mary Miles Teachout[42] have concluded that none of the present methods of land value assessment could withstand court appeal by an aggrieved taxpayer, because none adequately establishes (according to the criteria employed by courts) the market value of the land underlying individual properties. Indeed, such practical obstacles of accurate and legally acceptable assessments have figured prominently in Great Britain's debate over adoption of the tax. In 1976, a special Parliamentary Committee on Local Government Finance concluded that there is considerable doubt whether the evidence of land sales would be adequately and evenly distributed to produce consistent assessments. These difficulties would mean that there would be considerable scope for challenge, appeal, and litigation. Difficulties would also arise because of the absence of policy and of decisions from the courts. A new range of law and practice would have to be developed.[43]

These legal and operational issues are certainly of paramount importance to any jurisdiction in which the site-value tax is being proposed. However, such concern should not necessarily become an excuse for rejecting the site-value tax out of hand. As Oldman and Teachout also argue, legal and administrative remedies are potentially available which make the tax operational.

Tax-Exempt Property

Approximately one-third of all property in the U.S. is exempt from property taxation. And that property is worth about $800 billion. Seventy percent of it belongs to governments. Of the other 30 percent, over half is owned by religious groups. The remainder goes to schools, cemeteries, museums, and various charitable organizations ostensibly operating in the social interest.[44]

The exempt property is not, however, distributed evenly. Urban areas generally have more exempt property than suburban areas, and the federal land presence (primarily the Forest Service system and Bureau of Land Management lands) has impacted heavily on some Western states.[45]

In 1976, the Congress passed the Payments-in-lieu-of-Taxes Act which provides for annual payments to local governments impacted by several land categories.[46] The act added a flat per-acre payment system to the traditional U.S. approach of sharing with county governments revenues generated from the federal lands. However, the issue of the effect of federal holdings on the states is unsettled. In a forthcoming report, the ACIR concludes that there is no significant relationship between the extensiveness of federal land and per capita tax measures or expenditure levels.[47]

The cities are also becoming increasingly concerned with the exempt-property problem. In several of the largest cities in the Eastern U.S., where exemption is well guarded by tradition and long-term political interests, the total value of exempt property may exceed taxable property values.[48] Accordingly, some states and localities are beginning to focus attention on the local tax-base erosion resulting from institutional exemption.

Last year, the New Jersey Legislature enacted legislation requiring the state to make in-lieu tax payments to municipalities for state-held property. The Connecticut Legislature has just passed a law requiring the state to compensate localities for property tax losses due to the exempt status of universities and hospitals. Two other cities, Omaha and Washington, D.C., have recently received special reports recommending a form of payment in-lieu of taxes. Finally, following up on the 1976 congressional action to aid the nonurban area with in-lieu payment, Michael E. Bell has suggested five alternative methods of computing a similar federal payment to the cities.[49]

Business Taxation

Measuring The Tax Base

One of the most controversial areas in state corporate income in recent years deals with whether a multinational enterprise (worldwide combination) should be taxed by the states as if the parent corporation and its affiliates are separate entities or a combined (unitary) operation.[50] This issue became quite important in June of 1978 when the U.S. Senate deleted from a United States-United Kingdom treaty a provision which would have prohibited the states from taking into account the overseas operations of U.K. based firms in the determination of the amount of total corporate income subject to state apportionment. That is, the provision would have disallowed state use of the unitary approach.

Initially this treaty prohibition would have applied only to U.K. firms. However, several states and state lobby organizations argued that had such a provision

8

been accepted by the Senate, it would have been likely to be extended through other treaties and legislation to all multinational (including U.S.) firms. Further, opponents of the provision argued that foreign treaties were inappropriate instruments for determining state taxing authority.

The case for using the separate-entity approach rather than the unitary concept has found strong domestic support of several business groups which have organized through the Committee on State Taxation (COST) of the Council of State Chambers of Commerce. Accordingly, despite the Senate's action, the controversy over defining the total tax base of worldwide combinations will continue; but, this time it will be in the legislative (congressional) arena.

Under the separate-entity concept, affiliates of a multistate parent are each treated as having a separate economic and legal status for state tax purposes. This requires that (a) each firm keep books on an affiliate-by-affiliate basis; (b) intercompany transactions (e.g., between the manufacturing and marketing divisions of the multicorporate enterprise) be adjusted as if made on an arms-length basis, and (c) the profit or loss status of each affiliate be deemed an event independent of the actions of the corporate whole.

The approach seems straightforward. Not only does it have the virtue of geographical neutrality, but, to the extent that arms-length prices are ascertainable, it minimizes the likelihood of double taxation.

Some recent research concludes however, that the practical merits of the separate-entity approach are so superficial, and its defects so serious, as to require the abandonment of the separate-entity approach in favor of the conceptually more attractive unitary method. The technical criticisms are adequately detailed elsewhere.[51] In general, they can be summarized as follows:

o The system is expensive to taxpayer and tax administrator alike.
o It is unduly complex, primarily due to the need to construct imputed prices of goods and services sold between affiliates. The complexity stems from the practical reality that data on comparable arms-length transactions are often just not available.
o The approach ignores the economic reality that multicorporate entities can reduce their costs through the advantages of economies of scale, central management, advertising, reduced transactions costs, quantity discounts and access to capital markets.
o The amount of the tax paid depends on the form of corporate operation through which business is done. By simply shifting from a branch operation to a subsidiary form, a firm can change how its total operations are treated.

The unitary approach views a group of affiliates as a single business which, for reasons of legal convenience, are divided into separate incorporated subsidiaries. Thus, it is designed to pierce this legal veil and treat all the corporations which are under common ownership and management in the production, distribution, and marketing of a commodity as an interdependent whole.

Once total income is so determined, that income is apportioned between a given state and other jurisdictions by formula apportionment. However, the use of a formula does not necessarily mean that the business is being taxed on a unitary basis. Rather, the firm may be filing as a single corporation operating in several jurisdictions.

California, Oregon, and Alaska are the only states which apply the unitary concept as a general policy, although the Multistate Tax Commission has instructions from fourteen of its member states to audit using unitary rules. Several other states permit multistate and/or multinational corporations to file on a permissive basis.

Although the unitary approach is conceptually superior to separate accounting in its treatment of the multicorporate enterprise, it is not without its practical problems. The most serious of these problems has been developing objective standards, especially for diversified firms, for determining the boundaries of a unitary business in a combined report. For example, California, the best known of the unitary states, has

9

been repeatedly attacked as having a system that is unevenly applied and conducive to costly controversy and litigation resulting from too wide an area of administrative discretion.

Although such criticism may have merit, it does not follow that the unitary theory cannot be administered even-handedly. In fact, several operational and objective rules have been prepared to address this concern. These solutions range from grouping affiliates according to industry or product characteristics such as those used in the detailed Standard Industrial Classification (SIC) system or the Federal Trade Commission's "line of business" codes, to defining control of an affiliate as meaning ownership of a specified percentage of a corporation's voting stock.[52]

Uniformity

In addition to determining how broadly total corporate taxable income should be measured, state policy makers must resolve the issues of their interpretation of tax laws and the method of formula apportionment to be used. In the last 10 years, there has been considerable movement toward uniformity among the states in both these areas. Increased agreement among the states has been particularly notable with respect to (a) the adoption of the Uniform Division of Income for Tax Purposes Act (UDITPA) and the Multistate Tax Commission's guidelines on interpreting the act; (b) the use of federal taxable income for determining the tax base; (c) the use of the federal asset depreciation range; and (d) agreement upon the equally weighted three-factor (property, payrolls, sales) formula in apportioning multistate income.[53]

The trend toward apportionment uniformity may be weakening, however, as some states begin to manipulate their formulas in order to provide locational incentives to "home" industries. For example, the State of Iowa, with the active support of the Iowa Manufacturers Association, has long used a sales-only formula. However, an Illinois firm, Moorman Manufacturing Company, disregarded the one-factor approach and computed its Iowa income on the basis of the equally weighted three-factor formula which was used by the State of Illinois. For fiscal 1949–1960 this was done with Iowa's permission. Then, from 1961–1964 the firm complied with the statutory formula. Since 1965, however, the firm has reverted to the three-factor formula—without Iowa's consent—arguing that the sales-only formula (1) resulted in duplicative taxation and (2) that Iowa was, in fact, taxing profits due to out-of-state (Illinois) activities.

In 1976, Iowa trial court agreed with Moorman, declaring that the Iowa single-factor approach discriminated against interstate commerce. Subsequently, however, the Iowa Supreme Court upheld the constitutionality of the approach, rejecting the argument of manufacturers who were headquartered out-of-state, but who sell in Iowa, that the formula "provides local business with a direct commercial advantage not so enjoyed by interstate business."[54]

Last June, the U.S. Supreme Court, dividing 6 to 3, upheld the Iowa Supreme Court. Specifically, it declared that not only is the existence of duplicative taxation "speculative," but that, even assuming some overlap, it cannot be constitutionally argued that Iowa, rather than Illinois, is "at fault."[55]

The decision has at least two important implications for the interstate apportionment of corporate income in general. First, it suggests that groups such as the multistate tax compact will have to increase their efforts to effect apportionment uniformity among the corporate income tax states. Failure to accomplish uniformity voluntarily may result in new pressures for federal legislation. Second, it gives a go-ahead signal for other states to depart from the equally weighted three-factor formula, thus dampening the recent gains towards uniform treatment—despite the fact that single-factor formulas are anachronistic relics of the early days of state income taxation.

Three states—Florida, New York and Massachusetts—have taken a more subtle approach in emphasizing the role of their marketplace in interstate commerce by requiring a double weighting of the sales component in the three-factor formula. This double weighting of sales has also been given serious consideration in New Jersey ("exports are treated favorably relative to imports") and the District of Columbia ("to provide incentives for investment . . .").[56]

Minnesota and Wisconsin place special emphasis on their sales components by offering optional apportionment formulas. A firm operating in Minnesota may use either the equal weight three-factor approach or a formula which weights sales by 70 percent, property by 15 percent, and payroll by 15 percent. This alternative primarily serves as a tax break for domestic firms. Wisconsin business taxpayers have the option of using the double sales weighting described above or using a two-factor approach of 66-2/3 percent to sales and 33-1/3 percent to either payrolls or property.

Locational Incentives

Recent research on the role of various tax concessions to business supports the view that not only do state and local fiscal incentives play a relatively minor role in the business location/expansion decisions[57] (demographic changes, labor costs, sites, energy costs, and local government red-tape minimization, and a whole range of federal tax and nontax programs are the significant variables),[58] but also that the increase in the fiscal-resource base of the local community often is outweighed by increased costs of providing new services to the industry and the community.[59] Moreover, fiscal incentives often reduce overall economic efficiency and impose uncompensated, but nevertheless real, costs of congestion and pollution on local residents.[60]

Some evidence exists that, at best, tax incentives are more likely to have an influence on intraregional rather than interregional locational decisions.[61] However, one extensive empirical study of the impact of intraurban tax differentials in the Washington, D.C., metropolitan area (which for tax purposes consists of three states: Virginia, Maryland, and the District of Columbia) found that tax differentials, though they clearly exist, are ranked lower than any other economic factor in the jurisdictional selection process.[62] As a result, the study concluded that a tax policy designed to attract business would be ineffective and unwise.

Another study which focused on the intraregional/interregional issue took an even stronger policy position. In examining a range of state financial incentive programs for industry, Hellman, Wassall and Falk concluded that what gains do accrue from an incentive program are often enjoyed at the expense of neighboring jurisdictions. Accordingly, they recommended that if the states do not start coordinating their tax programs in order to minimize the losses due to incentive programs of individual jurisdictions, Congress should consider making certain intraregional programs illegal.[63]

Two caveats should be noted regarding such findings. First, the evidence above refers to general state/local fiscal policy. A particular firm with specific marginal investments in question may react favorably to an incentive.[64] Second, the findings may demonstrate that over time competing jurisdictions with similar economic structures have acted to minimize tax differences because large tax-level differences may result in some loss of business activity. Perhaps more research will shed light on these two issues. But while the search goes on for the optimal incentive, it is undoubtedly good policy for states and localities to avoid eroding their tax bases in an effort to "attract business" in spite of the pleas of some business groups.

Value Added Tax and Principles of Taxing Business

The ACIR is beginning a series of reports on the topic of state economic growth and tax competition among the states. The first volume[65] of this series accomplishes two objectives. First, it examines in detail one of the most significant innovations in state and local finance, the application by Michigan of the value added tax (VAT) as a replacement for more traditional forms of business taxes.[66] Second, the report uses the Michigan experience to launch a discussion of a set of principles for taxation of business activity in the state and local economy.

11

Because of the differing structural and economic conditions among the states, the ACIR does not make any recommendation for widespread use of the VAT. The Commission nevertheless goes on to develop certain general principles derived from the Michigan experiment. These provide state business taxation guidelines needed to achieve the objectives of tax uniformity and nondiscrimination. These criteria include adopting a broader base than profits, while recognizing that some ability-to-pay safeguards may be required; expensing of capital investment as preferable to granting of special tax concessions; avoiding an excessive variety of business taxes; and requiring that all businesses, whether they realize profits or not, make some tax contribution for the services provided to them by state government.

Joint Tax Audits

Last February the U.S. Supreme Court upheld the validity of the Multistate Tax Compact and its administrative division, the Multistate Tax Commission (MTC).[67] The 7-to-2 decision ended a five-year effort by 16 major U.S. corporations to limit the MTC's ability to engage in joint audits on behalf of its 19 member states. In challenging the MTC, the appellants, all threatened by audits by the Commission, disputed the tax on the basis of violation of the U.S. Constitution's compact clause (the states in the audit program needed to obtain the consent of Congress), the Commerce clause (MTC was encroaching on congressional power), and the Fourteenth amendment (appellants are denied due process and equal protection).

It is quite likely that had the MTC lost, its entire organizational future would have been in serious jeopardy. With the favorable ruling, however, states which were uncertain about MTC membership may now be induced to join the joint-audit program.

Personal Income Taxation

Recent and ongoing research on general topics of state and local income taxation has ranged from discussions of tax simplification, the effects of personal taxes on location decisions (for total personal taxes) and tax administration, to analyses of specific state income taxes and the effects of indexation of personal income taxes. For purposes here, the first three of these issues are summarized below.

Simplification

Most taxpayers complete their federal income taxes before beginning their state returns. Or, at the very least, they keep their records primarily on the basis of the federal law. Accordingly, simplification of state income taxes essentially means conformity with the federal structure.[68]

There are four degrees of income tax conformity. Three states have *complete conformity*. Under this approach, a taxpayer computes his state tax due simply by applying a fixed percentage rate to his federal income tax due. Eight states have *substantial conformity*, which requires taxpayers to apply state tax rates to their federal taxable income. With the *moderate conformity* employed by 21 states, a state accepts the federal definition of adjusted gross income but then defines its own set of personal exemptions, deductions, tax rates, and credits against the tax. The District of Columbia and eight states are currently either *low conformity* or nonconforming jurisdictions.

Complete conformity or "piggybacking" would produce the greatest degree of tax simplification for taxpayers and administrators alike. For example, taxpayers in Rhode Island compute their tax liability by making just a few entries on a 4-inch by 8-inch card. And, due to a provision in the Tax Reform Act of 1976, any complete conformity state can have the Internal Revenue Service collect its tax—at federal expense. Such simplifcation, however, has its price in reduced state policy-making flexibility.

Because complete conformity must, by definition, be on a "moving basis," involving automatic adoption of federal tax base changes, states are subject to unexpected changes in income tax revenues due to changes in the federal code. For example, the federal government can pass significant tax cuts at the end of a year, with the cuts effective retroactively to the beginning of that year. This reduces federal tax liabilities for the full year and, thereby, state tax liabilities as well. These revenue losses, in turn, can cause severe fiscal strains at the state level if the state legislature is unable to counteract the federal change.

Another price of conformity results from the fact that the state is required to accept both the federal progressive tax rate schedule and the IRS definition of what is to be excluded from and included in the income tax base. For example, in order to qualify for federal collection, a state may not employ a property tax relief credit, such as a circuit breaker. However, income tax credits for sales taxes paid and for income taxes paid to other state/local jurisdictions are permitted.

A state which adopts substantial conformance can also qualify for the federal collection of its taxes, and at the same time make an optional adjustment to its tax base by applying different tax rates to the tax preference items subject to the federal "minimum tax." Thus, substantial conformance achieves most of the taxpayer simplification achieved by complete conformity. However, it still leaves the jurisdiction exposed to end-of-the-year changes in federal taxable income due to increases in the personal exemption or the standard deduction permitted on federal tax returns, and denies for federal collection purposes the use of property tax circuit breakers.

Moderate conformance permits a state to establish its own personal exemption, standard deduction, and tax rate schedule. The state can also establish its own rules for itemized deductions. Moreover, it greatly reduces the possibility that changes in federal tax law, particularly at the end of the year, will have an adverse impact on state revenues. But one cost of moderate conformity is that under current law it disqualifies the state for federal collection of its tax.

Location

Very little has been written recently on the specific role of state and local government policies (e.g., income tax levels) on the residential location decision. Instead, most residential location analysis has focused on general residential mobility patterns and the identification of desirable and undesirable housing characteristics. Individual factors generally found to be primary determinants usually include quality and costs of transportation services, proximity to employment, jurisdictional familiarity, and housing costs (including taxes and expectations of property value changes) and conditions (interior layout, size, external setting), and community reputation and image (an elusive, perhaps even subconscious, selection factor).

A 1977 economic survey of the Washington, D.C., metropolitan area ranked various residential location factors of persons who were recent movers in either the District of Columbia or the Maryland and Virginia suburbs.[70] The study revealed that for owners and renters alike, the residential selection process was determined largely on the basis of proximity to job (63 percent of owners responding; 63 percent of renters); a desire to be near friends and family (31 percent; 34 percent); community reputation (25 percent; 19 percent); and nontax economic factors such as housing costs (17 percent; 16 percent). In fact, only 1 percent of owners and 2 percent of renters considered local taxes as of primary importance. Most interviewed (77 percent; 90 percent) indicated that they did not even seriously take interjurisdictional tax differences into account in the location decision.

Such findings of a particular area should, of course, be interpreted with caution. The ability to generalize such findings depends on (a) whether interjurisdictional tax level and/or distribution differences are, in fact, significant,[71] and (b) the personal characteristics of the movers themselves (e.g., their family status, job expectations). Nevertheless, as was noted in the discussion of the impact of tax inducements on business activity, the evidence indicates that pleas for lower state and local taxes on locational grounds should be viewed with great skepticism.

Administration

The 1959 study by Clara Penniman and Walter Heller, *State Income Tax Administration,* is currently being revised, with publication expected sometime in 1979.[72] Although many findings are, of course, tentative, a "20 years later" description will show that:
- o Now every income state, rather than only 10, has payroll withholding;
- o Most have current payment for other personal income taxes;
- o Computers are a necessity for most states and have radicaly changed what is (or at least could be) done;
- o Structurally there is much more functional integration within the major tax agency, with more taxes being administered centrally; and
- o Insufficient auditing, little intelligence work of a sophisticated type, and substantial delays in tax collections frequently indicate inadequate resources and insufficient attention to cost/benefit analysis in the state budget decision for tax departments.

Sales and Excise Taxes

General Sales Tax

General sales taxes have maintained their place as the primary producer of state revenues since 1970 and, in addition, have increased their relative importance among the major taxes examined in this report.[73] The general acceptability of the sales tax stems from its relative simplicity of collection, cyclical revenue stability, and, if broad based, ability to generate large revenues at low rates. But, as currently used in the U.S., the tax has several structural defects. These range from the relatively "minor" problems of the failure of some states to tax rentals of tangible personal property to exemptions for new and/or expanded industries. Not so minor, due to their prevalence, are the equity and neutrality problems associated with the definition of the size of the sales tax base. Two such issues are discussed here: the extension of the sales tax to food and to all services.[74]

Few tax issues seem to be as controversial, and as subject to misunderstanding, as the choice between over-the-counter sales tax exemption for food (and often medicines) purchased for home consumption versus an income tax credit for sales taxes paid. Under the exemption, as used in 22 states, that part of the sales tax which would normally be passed forward to the consumer is simply not charged at the time of purchase.

With the credit used in seven states, the sales tax is applied to food and nonfood items alike, but then the equivalent of part or all of the sales tax on the food portion is returned at the end of the year in the form of a lump-sum reduction in income taxes, or a rebate in the event that there is an insufficient income tax liability.

The primary justification for each approach is to reduce the regressivity of the sales tax. And both methods are generally successful. The exemption tends to make the sales tax proportional for most income classes. However, it still permits sales tax regressivity at the very low income levels, partly because many poor must still consume restaurant food which is almost never exempt.

The credit also achieves the antiregressivity effect, if it is used by those for whom it is intended. It is this caveat—that the credit may be theoretically attractive but results in a low compliance rate—which has become a major political argument against the substitution of the credit for the exemption. New Mexico's experience, however, has demonstrated that if a government makes a serious effort to educate its low-income residents to the availability and advantage of claiming a credit, a high rate of compliance will result. In spite of its use of a cumbersome and unnecessarily broad definition of "income for credit purposes," New Mexico reports that about 70 percent of all eligible claimants are now filing for its comprehensive credit.

Once this compliance problem is solved, the credit is superior to the exemption in nearly every respect. Unlike the exemption which accrues to consumers regardless of their personal or economic status, the credit can be targeted to resident taxpayers on the basis of income level, age and/or family size. As a result, it can be designed to achieve the same antiregressivity goal as the exemption, but at a substantially lower net cost to the state. Furthermore, the credit accomplishes its equity goal with a minimum of administrative problems (e.g., defining "food" versus "nonfood" items) and non-neutral effects.

The extension of sales taxes to all services is a somewhat more complex issue. Nevertheless, the arguments for such base broadening are persuasive. These arguments include lessening the regressivity of the sales tax, since consumption of most services is concentrated in the high-income groups; minimizing the distortion of private consumer decisions in favor of tax-exempt as against taxable purchases; and facilitation of tax administration, because it is unnecessary for auditors to conduct extensive examinations of vendors who sell both taxable goods and exempt services.

This sales tax broadening may, however, present some difficult policy trade-offs to states which have interjurisdictional competition along their borders. Two issues are of particular concern. First, problems of tax enforcement and administration would be created because some service forms (especially professionals) can avoid the tax rather easily by establishing out-of-state offices for billing and other internal administrative purposes, and yet maintain "branch" offices in the neighboring state. Second, a unilateral base broadening would tend to encourage some "footloose" businesses to locate just across a state line. Again, the professional firms provide the best example.

Despite these problems it does not necessarily follow that the best policy is one of complete tax exemption for these specific services. Indeed, some economists argue that a theoretically "optimal" sales tax structure requires that sales taxes should be levied at "high" rates on those goods and services which exhibit a relatively price-inelastic demand, i.e., the quantity of the product demanded is relatively unresponsive to small price changes, and that those products with relatively price-elastic demands are candidates for "lower" rates of taxation. Thus it is argued that those services which face the most competitive market conditions should be taxed at the lowest rate. However, there is no *a priori* assumption that that rate should necessarily be a zero rate.

Taxation of Natural Resources [75]

The increasing development of energy resources in the West has created a renewed interest in the taxation of natural resources. Although resource taxation refers to levies on gas, timber, oil, and metals, the declaration by politicians and the business community that coal is the nation's energy "ace in the hole" has now given the taxation of that resource particular importance. [76]

Two major issues are of concern: minimizing the excessive tax burden due to the "front-end load" problem and preserving some of the financial benefits of today's mining of a depletable resource for future years.

The front-end load problem refers to the fact that as a mine is constructed and developed, public service costs are automatically generated which must be largely financed by permanent residents of the mining community. The resulting imbalance in revenues and expenditures can thus create excessive local tax burdens. Under traditional tax arrangements (severance taxes, profits levies) the mining firm itself cannot be taxed until it is finally readied for operation, which may take several years.

A recent federal government interagency report provides a review of this problem and rates four types of mineral taxes—ad valorem, severance, gross production, and net production—for their ability to address this issue. [77] In general, the ad valorem tax (levied on the value of the resource in the ground or growing on the land) ranks highest on the revenue-productivity criteria. In contrast, the pure severance tax and its gross production and net production tax variants (levied only after the unit amount mined is actually produced) fails to address the front-end load issue.

The preference for the ad valorem tax on revenue criteria, however, does not make it superior to the severance tax. This is true for two reasons. First, the ad valorem approach is administratively most cumbersome. Estimating the value of an unmined mineral deposit is difficult even for the most trained assessor. Second, because the tax comes due regardless of the mine's output, it encourages an accelerated depletion of the taxed resource.

Accordingly, in order to maintain their use of the administratively superior and more neutral severance tax,[78] some coal states have recently modified their mineral tax laws to specifically address the front-end financing squeeze. Montana has taken the lead by enacting a measure which under certain conditions requires a new firm or mine to prepay property taxes on the basis of the estimated tax base at time of completion.[79] This prepaid amount is then returned in the form of a tax credit during each of the first five years of actual operation. Utah has taken a similar approach, requiring a prepayment of sales and use taxes on equipment and machinery involved in the development and production of a resource.[80]

Whether such prepayment programs will either produce the necessary revenues and/or survive the criticism that they are excessive and inefficient will no doubt be a topic for research in the next few years once the programs (and the mines) are in operation.

In order to address the future benefits problem, at least two states have established special mineral tax trust funds. North Dakota earmarks 15 percent of its severance tax revenues to a state trust fund to "establish a form of compensation for the cost to future generations of losing a nonrenewable resource."[81] In 1975, Wyoming voters approved a constitutional amendment creating a permanent mineral trust fund. Revenues from an excise tax on minerals are to be deposited in this fund, with the special fund's investment earnings to be deposited annually in the state's general fund.[82]

Notes

1.   Nancy Amon Jianakoplos, "The Growing Link Between the Federal Government and State and Local Financing," *Federal Reserve Bank of St. Louis Review* (May 1977), p. 1320.

2.   At this writing, a major tax limitation has been given voter approval by Californians with the 2-to-1 passage of the Jarvis-Gann amendment to that state's constitution on June 6, 1978. The amendment (a) limits real property taxes to one percent of market value, thus cutting annual property tax revenues from $12 billion to about $5 billion; (b) provides that market value for most property is to be placed at the 1975–76 valuations (new appraised value is used for property which is newly constructed or changes ownership), with upward adjustments of no more than 2 percent per year; and (c) requires a two-thirds vote of the state legislature or a two-thirds vote of all eligible voters to increase other taxes. At present, the California Supreme Court has the amendment under consideration.

3.   For a review of the fiscal condition of small cities (population less than 50,000), see Herrington J. Bryce, ed., *Small Cities in Transition: Dynamics of Growth and Decline* (Cambridge, Mass.: Ballinger, 1977).

4.   A major reason for the rejection of school bond issue proposals by Ohio voters in April 1978 was to protest new school busing plans.

5.   Advisory Commission on Intergovernmental Relations, *Trends in Fiscal Federalism*, Report M-86 (Washington, D.C.: Government Printing Office, 1975), Table V.

6.   David Greytak and Bernard Jump, *The Effects of Inflation on State and Local Government Finances: 1967–74*, Occasional Paper No. 25 (Syracuse, N.Y.: Metropolitan Studies Program, Maxwell School, Syracuse University, 1975). For a brief summary of this outlook, see Advisory Commission on Intergovernmental Relations, *Inflation and Federal and State Income Taxes*, Report A-63 (Washington, D.C.: Government Printing Office, 1976), pp. 58–59.

Emil Sunley disagrees with this pessimism, concluding ". . . overall, the next ten years should not be years of fiscal crisis for the state and local sector as a whole." Emil M. Sunley,

Jr., "State and Local Governments," in *Setting National Priorities: The Next Ten Years* (Washington, D.C.: The Brookings Institution, 1976), pp. 405–409.

7.   Edward M. Gramlich, "State and Local Budgets the Day After It Rained: Why Is the Surplus So High?" *Brookings Paper on Economic Activity*, 1 (1978); and David Levin's article in *Survey of Current Business* (May 1978).

8.   Advisory Commission on Intergovernmental Relations, *City Financial Emergencies*, Report A-42 (Washington, D.C.: Government Printing Office, 1973); and Philip M. Dearborn, *Elements of Municipal Financial Analysis* (New York: First Boston Corporation, 1977).

9.   Elizabeth Dickson, "Fiscal Trends: Local Revenue Bases, Expenditures, and Tax Burdens," Working Paper 09-0251-08, The Urban Institute, Washington, D.C., January 1978.

10.   See Roy W. Bahl and David Greytak, "The Response of City Government Revenues to Changes in Employment Structure," *Land Economics* 52 (November 1976); and David Greytak and Edward M. Cupoli, "Changes in the Structure of Employment and Taxation: Revenue Implications, Washington, D.C.," a report prepared for the District of Columbia Tax Revision Commission (Washington, D.C.: District of Columbia Tax Revision Commission, 1977).

11.   Advisory Commission on Intergovernmental Relations, *Measures of State and Local Fiscal Capacity and Tax Effort*, Report M-16 (Washington, D.C.: Government Printing Office, 1962).

12.   The most recent SREB report is: Kenneth G. Quindry and Niles Schoening, *State and Local Revenue Potential, 1976* (Atlanta: Southern Regional Education Board, 1977).

13.   D. Kent Halstead, *Tax Wealth in Fifty States*, a report of the National Institute of Education (Washington, D.C.: Government Printing Office, 1978).

14.   Advisory Commission on Intergovernmental Relations, *Significant Features of Fiscal Federalism 1976–77*, Report M-110, Vol. II (Washington, D.C.: Government Printing Office, 1977), Table 5.

15.   For discussions of these issues, see Diane Fuchs, "State and Local Tax and Expenditure Limitations," a report prepared for the Tax Reform Research Group, Washington, D.C., June 23, 1978; and John Shannon, "After Jarvis—Hard Questions for State-Local Policymakers," testimony before the Committee on Government Affairs, U.S. Senate, Washington, D.C., June 28, 1978.

16.   Advisory Commission on Intergovernmental Relations, *State Limitations on Local Taxes and Expenditures*, Report A-64 (Washington, D.C.: Government Printing Office, 1977), and Jack Suyderhoud, unpublished Ph.D. dissertation on state tax and expenditure limits, Purdue University, July 1978.

17.   Advisory Commission on Intergovernmental Relations, *Inflation and Federal and State Income Taxes*, Report A-63 (Washington, D.C.: Government Printing Office, 1976), especially Chapter IV. Colorado and California have this year become the first states to index their personal income tax.

18.   For example, see John Shannon, "Property Taxation: Federalism and Federal Policy," in *Property Taxation, Land Use and Public Policy*, Arthur D. Lynn, Jr., ed. (Madison: University of Wisconsin Press, 1976), pp. 215–252.

19.   Henry J. Aaron, *Who Pays the Property Tax: A New View* (Washington, D.C.: The Brookings Institution, 1975), Chapter 3.

20.   David Greytak and Bernard Jump, *The Effects of Inflation on State and Local Government Finances 1967–1974*, Occasional Paper No. 25 (Syracuse, N.Y.: Metropolitan Studies Program, Maxwell School, Syracuse University, 1975).

21.   See discussion by Sunley, "State and Local Governments," pp. 405–409.

22.   In 1974, the Massachusetts Supreme Judicial Court ruled that all cities and towns in the commonwealth must institute the practice of assessment on the full market value of taxable property. At the time, fractional assessment was (and, as a practical matter, still is) used. Two studies of the effects of the switch to full-value assessment have concluded that the result would be that in the aggregate business would pay less and residences more. Lynn E. Browne and William C. Wheaton, "100 Percent Assessment: Higher Taxes or More Inequity?" *New England Economic Review* (September/October 1975), pp. 3–14; and Daniel M. Holland and Oliver Oldman, "Estimating the Impact of Full Value Assessment on Taxes and Value of Real Estate

in Boston," in *Metropolitan Financing and Growth Management Policies: Principles and Practice*, ed. George F. Break (Madison: University of Wisconsin Press, 1978), Chapter 9.

23. However, the evidence indicates that the share of property taxes in local own source revenue is not much affected by tax limits. See ACIR, *State Limitations on Local Taxes and Expenditures*, pp. 22–23.

24. Harold D. Guither, *Tax Choices for Illinois: Effects on Agriculture and the Rural Community*, Department of Agricultural Economics Report AE-4435 (Champaign: University of Illinois, 1977); and Richard R. Almy, "A Study of Real Property Assessment Practices in the United States," a report prepared for the U.S. Department of Housing and Urban Development, Washington, D.C., forthcoming.

25. One should note that the value of open space and outdoor recreational space may well exceed its market value for development purposes. For a discussion of important developments in the area, see John V. Krutilla and Anthony C. Fisher, *The Economics of Natural Environments* (Baltimore: Johns Hopkins University Press, 1975). Also see International Association of Assessing Officers, *Property Tax Incentives for Preservation* (Chicago: International Association of Assessing Officers, 1975).

26. ABT Associates, *Property Tax Relief Programs for the Elderly*, a report prepared for the U.S. Department of Housing and Urban Development (Washington, D.C.: Government Printing Office, 1975), 3 Vols.; Aaron, *Who Pays the Property Tax;* Steven D. Gold, "State Property Tax Relief Measures: A Framework for Analyses," Working Paper, Department of Economics, Drake University, Des Moines, Iowa, June 1977. Gold identifies 10 property tax relief devices, including the use of state aid and preferential assessment. Each of these studies provides a good bibliography on tax relief.

27. Aaron, *Who Pays the Property Tax*, pp. 79–80.

28. For a description, see Advisory Commission on Intergovernmental Relations, *Property Tax Circuit Breakers: Current Status and Policy Issues*, Report M-87 (Washington, D.C.: Government Printing Office, 1975).

29. For an evaluation, see John H. Bowman, "Property Tax Circuit Breakers: Continuing Issues Surrounding a Popular Program," Working Paper in Public Finance, No. 7778-6, School of Public and Environmental Affairs, Indiana University, Bloomington, Ind., March 1978.

30. This section is based on an empirical study of the effects of a classified tax in the District of Columbia. See Jon Sonstelie, "The Classified Property Tax," a report prepared for the District of Columbia Tax Revision Commission, Washington, D.C., 1977.

31. The size of these burden shifts depends on how responsive land rents (prices) are to the tax change. If the demand for commercial real estate is elastic relative to the demand for residential land, landowners will bear the larger burden. However, to the extent that land use plans, zoning regulations, or capital improvements inhibit the conversion of land from commercial to residential uses, the greater the burden is on the consumer. Further, in this latter circumstance, if one shows that the housing rents in a given market are regressively distributed, then it follows that many of the benefits of a reduction in these rental costs due to classification will accrue to low-income residents. Thus, a case is sometimes made for classification as a form of residential property tax relief.

32. For a review of the issue, see the following: ABT Associates, *Property Tax Relief Programs*, Vol. II (Evaluation), pp. 42–63; George F. Break, "Property Taxation: A Reappraisal of Burden Distribution, Incidence and Equity and Their Policy Implications," in *Property Taxation, Land Uses, and Public Policy*, ed. Arthur D. Lynn, Jr. (Madison: University of Wisconsin Press, 1976), pp. 23–38; District of Columbia Tax Revision Commission, *Financing an Urban Government: Final Report of the District of Columbia Tax Revision Commission* (Washington, D.C.: District of Columbia Tax Revision Commission, 1978), Chapter 6; Charles E. McLure, Jr. "The 'New View' of the Property Tax: A Caveat," *National Tax Journal* (March 1977), pp. 69–75; Peter Mieszkowski, "The Property Tax: An Excise or a Profits Tax?" *Journal of Public Economics* (April 1972), pp. 73–96.

33. Aaron, *Who Pays the Property Tax*, p. 55.

34. McLure, "The 'New View' of the Property Tax."

35. Summarized in ABT Associates, *Property Tax Relief Programs*, Vol. II (Evaluation), pp. 52–56.

36. For example, see David E. Black, "Property Tax Incidence: The Excise Tax Effect and Assessment Practices," *National Tax Journal* (December 1977), pp. 429–434.

37. A review of site-value proposals is provided by Richard M. Lindholm, ed., *Property Tax Reform: Foreign and United States Experience with Site Value Taxation*, Monograph 77-11 (Cambridge, Mass.: Lincoln Institute of Land Policy, 1977). For a discussion of the theory coupled with a case study, see George E. Peterson, "Differential Taxation of Land and Improvements Values," a report prepared for the District of Columbia Tax Revision Commission, Washington, D.C., 1978.

38. Tax Foundation of Hawaii, *Legislative Tax Bill Service* (January 31, 1977).

39. Richard L. Pollock and Donald C. Shoup, "The Effect of Shifting the Property Tax Base from Improvement to Land Value: An Empirical Estimate," *Land Economics* (1977).

40. Philip Finkelstein, *Real Property Taxation in New York City* (New York: Praeger, 1975).

41. District of Columbia Tax Revision Commission, *Financing an Urban Government*.

42. Oliver Oldman and Mary Miles Teachout, "Land Valuation Under a Separate Tax on Land?" *Proceedings of the 70th Annual Conference on Taxation*, National Tax Association/ Tax Institute of America (Chicago: National Tax Association, 1977). In their paper, the authors also distinguish between "site" value and "land" value. Also see Arthur D. Lynn, Jr., "Legal and Public Policy Aspects of Implementing Site Value Taxation," in *Property Tax Reform*, ed. Lindholm, pp. 19–27.

43. Committee on Enquiry, "Local Government Finance," a report to Parliament, London, May 1976.

44. For an examination of some of the underlying economic issues see Daryl A. Hellman and Costas Sifniotis, "Distributional Considerations of Property Tax Exemption: Analytical Framework," *Public Finance Quarterly* (January 1977), pp. 127–135; and R. L. Pfister, "A Re-Evaluation of the Justifications for Property Tax Exemptions," *Public Finance Quarterly* (October 1976), pp. 431–452.

45. U.S. House of Representatives, Committee on Interior and Insular Affairs, *Payments-in-Lieu-of-Taxes Act*, H. Report 94-1106, 94th Cong., 2nd sess., May 1976.

46. Payments-in-Lieu-of-Taxes Act, Public Law 94-656 (1976).

47. Advisory Commission on Intergovernmental Relations, *Adequacy of Federal Compensation to Twenty Local Governments for Tax Exempt Federal Lands* (Washington, D.C.: Government Printing Office, forthcoming).

48. Lillian Rymarowicz, "Availability of Data on Assessed Valuations of Exempt Property with Particular Reference to Properties Owned by the Federal Government," Congressional Research Service, Washington, D.C., October 1977.

49. The five are local cost of services provided, in lieu of taxes, net cost of federal presence, comparative tax burden, and fixed percentage formula. See Michael E. Bell, "Alternative Treatments of Governmentally Owned Tax Exempt Properties in Urban Economies," *Proceedings of the Seventy-First Annual Conference on Taxation*, National Tax Association/Tax Institute of America (Chicago: National Tax Association, forthcoming).

50. The multistate tax issue relating to both financial and nonfinancial business is treated extensively in Advisory Commission on Intergovernmental Relations, *State and Local Doing Business Taxes on Out-of-State Financial Depositories*, a report prepared for the Committee on Banking, Housing and Urban Affairs, U.S. Senate, 94th Cong., 1st sess., 1975, Part II, Chapter 3.

51. For a detailed discussion of this issue see Jerome B. Hellerstein, "The Unitary Business Principle and Multicorporate Enterprises: An Examination of the Major Controversies," *The Tax Executive* (July 1975), pp. 313–329; and "Multinational Corporations and Income Allocation Under Section 482 of the Internal Revenue Code," *Harvard Law Review* 89 (1976), pp. 1202–1238.

52. Jerome R. Hellerstein, "State Tax Discrimination Against Out-of-Staters," *National Tax Journal* (June 1977), pp. 113–133.

53. Indiana Department of Revenue, "Results of a Survey on the Uniformity of State Tax Laws," Indianapolis, Ind., 1977.

54. Supreme Court of the United States, *Moorman Manufacturing, Co. v. Bair, Director of Revenue of Iowa*, No. 77-454, argued March 21, 1978, decided June 15, 1978.

55. Ibid., p. II.

56. Economic Policy Council, New Jersey Department of Treasury, *Annual Report* (Trenton: New Jersey Department of Treasury, 1976); and District of Columbia Tax Revision Commission, *Financing an Urban Government,* Chapter 3.

57. For a dissent to this conclusion, see Robert A. Woodford, "Tax Incentives Can Pay Off: A Business View," *Proceedings of the Seventieth Annual Conference on Taxation,* National Tax Association/Tax Institute of America (Chicago: National Tax Association, 1977).

58. For example, see Roger J. Vaughn, *The Urban Impact of Federal Policies,* Vol. 2, "Economic Development" (Santa Monica, Calif.: The Rand Corporation, 1977); George E. Peterson, *Federal Tax Policy and Urban Development* (Washington, D.C.: Urban Institute, 1978); and Gary C. Corina, William A. Testa, and Frederick D. Stocker, *State-Local Fiscal Incentives and Economic Development* (Columbus, Ohio: Academy for Contemporary Problems, 1978).

59. Corina et al., *State-Local Fiscal Incentives;* and Gene F. Summers, Sharon D. Evans, Frank Clemente, E. M. Beck, and Jon Minkoff, *Industrial Invasions of Nonmetropolitan America* (New York: Praeger, 1976).

60. Corina et al., *State-Local Fiscal Incentives.*

61. David Mulkey and B. L. Dillman, "Location Effects of State and Local Industrial Development Subsidies," *Growth and Change* (April 1976), pp. 37–43.

62. Stephen S. Fuller and Joan E. Towles, "Impact of Intraurban Tax Differentials on Business and Residential Location in the Washington Metropolitan Area," a paper prepared for the D.C. Tax Revision Commission, 1978. A shorter version of this is published by Professor Fuller in the *Proceedings of the Seventieth Annual Conference on Taxation,* National Tax Association/Tax Institute of America (Chicago: National Tax Association, 1977).

63. Daryl A. Hellman, Gregory H. Wassall, and Laurence H. Falk, *State Financial Incentives to Industry* (Lexington, Mass.: Lexington Books, 1976). This study was summarized by Gregory Wassall for the *Proceedings of the Seventieth Annual Conference on Taxation,* National Tax Association/Tax Institute of America (Chicago: National Tax Association, 1977).

64. Thomas Vasquez and Charles W. DeSeve, "State/Local Taxes and Jurisdictional Shifts in Corporate Business Activity: The Complications of Measurement," *National Tax Journal* (September 1977), pp. 285–297.

65. Advisory Commission on Intergovernmental Relations, *The Michigan Single Business Tax: A Different Approach to State Business Taxation,* Report M-114 (Washington, D.C.: Government Printing Office, 1978).

66. The taxes replaced by the "Single Business Tax" were the corporate income tax, corporate franchise tax, personal property tax on inventories, business intangible tax, financial institutions tax, insurance company privilege fee, and savings and loan company privilege tax.

67. *United States Steel Corporation et al. v. Multi-state Tax Commission*, U.S. Supreme Court Docket No. 76-635 (38 C.C.H., S. Ct. Bull., p. 732) Affirming 417 F. Supp. (S.C.N.Y. 1976).

68. For further discussion of this issue, see Otto G. Stolz and George A. Purdy, "Tax Simplification and Efficiency through Federal Collection," a special report of Advocates and Analysts, Arlington, Va., June 13, 1977. A longer version of the Stolz and Purdy article appears in the *Duke Law Journal* 1977 (1978).

69. Two solutions to this problem are available, however. The first would be to grant an executive agency emergency power to set income tax rates on an equal yield basis. Nebraska, one of the three full conformity states, uses just such an approach. The second solution might be for the U.S. Government to follow Canada's example and have the federal government work out a guarantee against unexpected revenue losses on a no-strings attached basis. Of course, details would have to be worked out on what an "unexpected" loss is and how the federal grant might be repaid.

70. Fuller and Towles, "Impact of Intraurban Tax Differentials."

71. The most recent data available shows that for 1970 in the metropolitan area, total taxes as a percent of money income was 6.4 percent in D.C.; and 6.0 percent and 4.8 percent in the

Maryland and Virginia suburbs respectively. The burden of Virginia's state income tax is about half that of the D.C. and Maryland burden. Kenneth V. Greene, William B. Neenan, and Claudia D. Scott, *Fiscal Interactions In a Metropolitan Area* (Lexington, Mass.: Lexington Books, 1974), Tables 6-2 and 6-8.

72. Letter from Clara Penniman, April 7, 1978.

73. Rising from 28.8 percent of total in 1968 to 29.9 percent in 1975. These data exclude the Hawaii, Indiana, Washington, and West Virginia gross receipts (income) taxes. Advisory Commission on Intergovernmental Relations, *Significant Features of Fiscal Federalism* Vol. II, 1976–77. Currently, 45 states use the tax.

74. For a detailed discussion of these issues as well as those of administration of the sales tax, see John F. Due, *State and Local Sales Taxation* (Chicago: Public Administration Service, 1971).

75. The primary source for this discussion is Thomas F. Stinson, *State Taxation of Mineral Deposits and Production*, an Interagency Energy-Environment Research and Development Program Report of the USDA and EPA (Washington, D.C.: Office of Research and Development, Environmental Protection Agency, January 1977).

76. For other general discussions, see Jim Wead and Lois R. Koepf, *Coal: State Coal Severance Taxes and Distribution of Revenue* (Lexington, Ky.: Council of State Governments, 1976); and Mason Gaffney, ed., *Extractive Resources and Taxation* (Madison: University of Wisconsin Press, 1967).

77. Stinson, *State Taxation of Mineral Deposits*.

78. In 1976, 31 states utilized some form of severance tax with revenues generating more than $2 billion. While this accounts for only 2 percent of total state collections nationally, the tax is quite important to certain states. Louisiana, New Mexico, Oklahoma, Texas, Montana and Wyoming generate over 10 percent of their severance tax revenues from severance taxation, with Wyoming and Louisiana collecting 21 percent and 33 percent respectively. Source: Advisory Commission on Intergovernmental Relations, "The States in 1977," *Intergovernmental Perspective* (Winter 1978), p. 29.

79. C.H. 571, Montana Laws of 1975.

80. Utah Code Annotated, 63: 51, pp. 5–6.

81. For a description and defense of the North Dakota system, see Byron L. Dorgan, *Taxing Coal* (Bismarck, N.D.: Office of the Tax Commissioner, 1977).

82. Stinson, *State Taxation of Mineral Deposits*, p. 18.

State and Local Government Expenditure

Robert T. Deacon

Public finance, the economic study of public-sector activity, has undergone an important transformation in the last 30 years. As a subdiscipline in economics, it was once largely confined to analysis of the effects of taxation upon resource allocation in the private sector and upon the distribution of income. Government expenditures were generally viewed as being exogenous, outside the realm of economic analysis, and the positive and normative aspects of public-sector decision making received little attention.[1] This situation has changed markedly since the late 1940s, and this essay outlines some of the more significant developments that have taken place in the study of public expenditures.

Casual observation suggests that the rise in research interest in the public sector has been correlated with the growing importance of government spending, especially at the state and local level. If recent trends are any guide, the level of interest appears destined, for better or for worse, to grow still further in years to come. Coincident with growth has come an increasing number of new policies that impinge upon the activity of state and local governments. Much of the effort directed toward developing a positive theory of government spending has resulted directly from a desire to understand and predict the effects of matching or equalization aid to state and local governments, local government consolidation, tax relief legislation, and other policies.

Consideration of these issues has also forced an awareness of the complexity of our "system of government." Economists now generally recognize that it is inaccurate to regard the "government sector" as a single unified entity. Rather, the American fiscal system is a highly decentralized one in which a complex hierarchy of single- and multiple-purpose local governments exist within an overall federal structure. Further, the individual pieces of this puzzle are connected to one another through constitutional service responsibilities, intergovernmental aid policies, and by force of the simple fact that each citizen is served by a variety of governments.

Simultaneous with the development of positive analysis have come a number of contributions to theoretical welfare economics and attempts to apply normative criteria to the government decision-making process. Encouraged by apparent successes in the evaluation of natural resource and defense policy, analysts sought to apply the techniques of benefit-cost and cost-effectiveness analysis, and the general

---

Robert T. Deacon is Professor of Economics at the University of California, Santa Barbara.

"Planning-Programming-Budgeting" approach to other policy areas. Several of the most recent applications have been aimed at evaluation of the multitude of public programs instituted during the last 15 years to deal with unemployment, poverty, crime and other perceived "urban problems."

In the remainder of this essay, the directions of recent research on public expenditures are briefly summarized and interpreted. The first of the following three sections addresses the question of whether or not there is any discernible structure in the varied array of individual government expenditures and, if so, what the sources of this structure might be. The second section analyzes current public expenditure patterns within the overall historical context of public-sector activity. In contrast to the largely positive or descriptive subject matter in the first two sections, the third treats recent attempts to apply normative criteria to public expenditure decisions. In keeping with the general tone of this volume, research pertinent to state-local government is emphasized, though it is often not possible to separate this sector from the overall federal structure.

Determinants of Government Expenditures

Analysis of variations in the expenditures of state and local governments has, at least in terms of volume, been the most important area of empirical research in state and local public finance. In part, the length and variation in this literature is due to the fact that it largely proceeded in the absence of an underlying theory. Successive studies did not always build upon the results of earlier work and, until recently, the literature showed little promise of converging upon any widely accepted paradigm of public expenditure determination. This research has, however, identified some important and interesting empirical relationships and has indirectly suggested directions for a more unified approach.[2]

In a typical "expenditure determinants" study, multiple-regression analysis is used to relate a measure of state or local government expenditure on a service to various socioeconomic or demographic characteristics of the resident population. Since long time series are generally not available for individual spending units, cross-section analysis has generally been used. Individual studies are primarily differentiated by the level at which data are aggregated and by the range of functional spending categories studied. In studies of a given service, it is not uncommon to find that expenditures have been aggregated across all governments (state and local) in an area. At first glance, this appears objectionable since analysis of aggregates may not accurately describe the behavior of any particular spending unit.[3] Yet such aggregation is one approach to the state-by-state variation which one often finds in the allocation of service provision responsibilities among different levels of government. An alternative approach is to confine local public expenditure analysis to governmental units within a particular state.[4] Presumably, this imposes a common constitutional delegation of service responsibilities for all spending units studied. In general, such analysis has documented significant "state specific" effects in the spending patterns of local governments.

The modern literature on the determinants of public expenditures begins with Fabricant, who used income, population density and urbanization (percent of population living in urban areas) to statistically explain variations in aggregated *state and local expenditures*.[5] These three variables, listed in order of significance, were capable of explaining as much as 70 percent of interstate variations in per capita spending. Subsequent studies of the same type have also found that intergovernmental revenue is positively associated with expenditure levels, and that income distribution measures (e.g., the percent of the population with family income below $3,000) exert an influence in addition to the effect of mean or median income.

Empirical analysis of *city government expenditures* has largely corroborated the positive influences of income and intergovernmental aid upon general expenditure levels. Income elasticities (the percentage expenditure difference associated with a one-percent difference in income) are almost always positive, but generally less than unity.

Although intergovernmental aid generally bears a significant and positive relationship to spending, the magnitudes of estimates obtained show little consistency across studies. This is probably due, in large measure, to the diversity in provisions of actual grant programs, and to the way in which these provisions are incorporated in econometric models. Interestingly, it has been observed that per capita expenditures in central cities are positively related to the population of the urban fringe (the metropolitan population living outside the central city). Plausible explanations for this phenomenon are that suburbanites make use of several central-city services, or that central cities surrounded by large urban areas tend to be industrialized and, as a consequence, are obliged to provide rather specialized (and expensive) packages of service. The latter explanation is partially corroborated by evidence that residential cities generally exhibit lower propensities to spend, and allocate outlays to different services, than do industrialized cities.

In addition to these more or less general effects, a variety of service-specific influences have been identified. Per capita expenditures on police and fire protection usually increase with size of the area served, the percent of low-income families in the population, measures of ethnicity, and the relative importance of commercial-industrial activity in the local economy. Spending on highways tends to be inversely related to population density. Not unexpectedly, it is possible to relate the number of persons receiving public welfare to factors such as urbanization, unemployment, measures of poverty and intergovernmental aid. However, it has been noted that average payments to recipients are generally lower in low-income areas.

Due to the importance of public education, a great deal of research attention has been devoted to spending on this particular service.[6] It has generally been found that statistical relationships are sharper and more plausible when the variable chosen for analysis is school spending per student (or per pupil school outlay less expenditures on busing) rather than a per capita measure. As with other services, school expenditures are positively associated with income levels; elasticity estimates generally lie between .25 and .60.

Federal aid payments are generally found to exert a positive and significant influence on local school spending. State aid payments, on the other hand, typically display a smaller and less significant association with educational outlays, a finding that is plausible considering the differences in provisions of most state versus federal school-aid formulas. Questions of scale economies in public education have been pursued both at the level of the school district and of the individual school, primarily by analyzing the effect of student population upon per pupil expenditures. At both levels, some evidence for scale economies has been found in very small districts, but no consistent scale effects have been documented for the majority of units that are average or above average in size.

A fundamental problem with the line of research summarized above is exhibited in discussions of scale economies and the influence of intergovernmental revenue upon local spending. The notion of scale economies is drawn directly from the theory of production and cost functions and refers to the relationship between cost per unit of output and the level of output produced. Correspondingly, attempts to infer the existence of scale economies from expenditure determinant studies are implicitly interpreting the estimated equations as average cost (cost per person) relationships, i.e., supply phenomena.[7]

On the other hand, those who study the effect of intergovernmental revenue upon local public spending generally point out that the effect of such aid depends upon the nature of the aid policy. For example, matching grants, in which a higher level of government effectively pays some fraction of the cost incurred by the local jurisdiction, lower the locally borne price of the aided service. Correspondingly, this price effect is expected to induce the local agency to spend more on the aided service, a demand response. Occasionally, both effects (scale and intergovernmental aid) are discussed in a single study, a practice which must lead the reader to question what exactly is being estimated, a cost function, a demand function, or a confused mixture of the two.

Recently, attempts have been made to sort out these issues and to settle on a single paradigm to guide the formulation of empirical models and to aid the interpretation of results. Although this process is far from complete, the recent vintage of studies is characterized by increasing attention to the nature of the public choice process and by a demand theoretic orientation. Considering individual demands for public services, it is expected that each person's desired level of public consumption will fall as the individual's implicit cost per unit of service rises. Of course, in the public sector these implicit costs or prices are paid through taxation and other financing instruments. Thus, the pattern of implicit prices paid is dependent both upon costs of public service production and upon the distribution of tax liabilities in the population. In addition to price effects, one would generally expect desired consumption levels to be positively related to income and other socioeconomic attributes.[8]

In this area of research, a great deal of interest has centered around the nature of public service price effects and their implications for public expenditure levels. If the locally borne cost per unit of service is reduced, for example by lower prices for public service inputs, then all citizens will revise their desired public consumption levels upward. As a consequence, one would naturally expect the collectively chosen level of public service to rise, and empirical research has generally found this to be the case. Thus, cost enters the expenditure equation, but the nature of the effect is essentially a demand response.

A more interesting and difficult set of questions regards the effect of a change in the distribution of tax burdens, e.g., a policy that raises tax liabilities for some citizens and reduces them for others. To address such issues requires a view of the political process and how it reaches an equilibrium. In most studies, a simple characterization based upon political competition and majority-rule decision making has been adopted. Within this framework, equilibrium occurs where the actual spending level coincides with the median of individually desired expenditure levels in the voting population.

Given certain assumptions on the general form of demand functions, it is possible to estimate public service income elasticities and price elasticities (the percentage change in quantity consumed resulting from a one-percent change in price). As in previous studies, most estimated income elasticities are positive though less than unity (typically between .4 and 1.0). Estimated price responses are almost always found to be less than unity and are typically smaller, in absolute value, than income elasticities. An implication of inelastic price effects is that a simple policy of matching aid will actually reduce the local government's support of the aided service, though total spending (including aid funds) will increase.

Of more interest than actual estimates are some of the relationships underlying observed price effects. In cases where local services are financed by property taxes, it is often found that per capita public spending is positively related to the relative size of the commercial-industrial (as opposed to residential) tax base. If taxes on such nonresidential property are largely borne by persons outside the local jurisdiction, the tax yield on commercial-industrial property reduces the tax liability per unit of service for local citizen-voters and increases their desired spending levels. Similarly, renters may (correctly or incorrectly) believe that they do not bear the full burden of property taxes on housing units they occupy. If this is true, the existence of a large proportion of renters in the voting population would be expected to increase per capita public outlays. This general hypothesis has also been confirmed in empirical analysis.

An interesting application of this general line of reasoning concerns the expenditure effects of property tax relief policies, particularly "circuit breaker" measures in which a higher level of government reimburses individuals for a portion of their local property tax payments. In essence, such relief lowers the locally borne costs of services financed by the property tax. Hence, it would be expected to increase both per capita spending on such services and local government reliance on the property tax. Although this conjecture has not been corroborated empirically, it would be an important subject for future study.

The study of public spending patterns has not yielded final answers to a variety of important policy questions. It would, for example, be interesting to know how expenditure levels on particular services vary with the level of government at which responsibility for provision lies. This would be of direct relevance to the question of whether public school expenditures would increase or decrease if provision were moved from the local to the state level. Future study may also shed light on how (and if) spending patterns are related to the method of collective decision making, e.g., direct versus representative democracy, simple majority versus two-thirds majority rule, etc. Finally, further effort is needed in the area of identifying and measuring the quality and quantity dimensions of public services. This matter is of obvious importance to the investigation of economies of scale in public service provision and, ultimately, to the issue of local government consolidation.

Trends in State and Local Government Spending

Although most of the empirical analysis of nonfederal outlays has looked across spending units at a given point in time, it is the rapid growth in state and local government that has captured the attention of the popular press. In 1975, spending by nonfederal governments in the U.S. amounted to over $265 billion, or about 17.5 percent of Gross National Product (GNP), as opposed to less than eight percent of GNP in 1950.[9] However, lest one think this apparently explosive trend is unprecedented, it should be pointed out that in 1932 state and local outlays accounted for over 14 percent of GNP. Thus, the historical record is not one of simple monotonic growth, and cannot be understood without identification of the factors underlying fluctuations in the size of the public sector.

To provide a context for the following discussion, trends in public spending since 1900 are briefly described below. To ease interpretation and to reduce confusion from such factors as population growth and inflation, it is useful to state expenditure figures as percentages of GNP. Total public spending in the U.S. rose from about seven percent of GNP in 1902 to over 34 percent in 1970. Most of this increase occurred at the federal level, where the share of GNP rose by almost 800 percent (from 2.4 percent to 21.3 percent) during the period. Very rapid growth in federal expenditures was, of course, experienced during the 1940s. Nonfederal spending, on the other hand, has not grown as dramatically, and its growth has not been monotonic. State and local outlays accounted for about 4.4 percent of GNP in 1902, and the broad changes in magnitude since that time were noted above. The state and local sector accounted for 37 to 45 percent of all public spending in 1970, depending upon whether intergovernmental transfers are allocated to the donor or recipient government, compared to about 66 percent in 1902. Thus, the currently large federal share of public expenditures represents a dramatic increase of the centralization of public activity, most of which took place prior to 1950.

It is interesting to compare rates of government growth during the 1960s to overall trends experienced since the turn of the century. (The following annual rates of increase are all expressed in constant dollars.) In the sixties, the annual growth rate for all government spending (federal and nonfederal) fell slightly in absolute terms and dropped markedly relative to the rate of growth in GNP. The largest declines were in the federal sector, primarily in defense spending where the annual rate of increase was less than four percent per year in the 1960s as compared to an overall growth rate of 6.6 percent since 1902. The rate of growth in state and local spending rose significantly during the 1960s, particularly in the provision of public education. Much of the increase in this service is, no doubt, attributable to shifts in the age distribution of the population experienced during the last 30 years. The other major area of increase in state and local spending is in welfare, where the annual growth rate was over 11 percent in 1960–1970, as compared to 6.4 percent for the 70-year period since 1900.[10]

Empirical analysis of the intertemporal pattern of state and local spending is severely limited by lack of appropriate time-series data, particularly on social and economic attributes of individual spending units. There have been two general responses to this deficiency. The first is time series analysis of *aggregate* state and local spending (expenditures of all nonfederal governments in the economy). An obvious shortcoming with this approach is that significant "micro" relationships may be masked in a study of aggregate trends. The second approach has been to infer intertemporal relationships from cross-sectional analysis. That such inferences can be risky, however, follows from evidence that estimated cross-section relationships often display a marked and significant degree of variation over time.[11]

Aggregate time-series studies of government expenditure have generally adopted a demand theoretic approach in which expenditure patterns are modeled as a function of income, "price" terms, intergovernmental aid, and socioeconomic variables intended to reflect the demand for specific services. The importance of income in explaining public expenditure trends has consistently been documented.[12] Further, experiments with lagged responses have shown long-run income responses to be significantly larger than short-run effects. Long-run income elasticities generally appear to be close to unity, both for total public spending and for state-local outlays, in contrast to the relatively low income elasticities usually obtained in cross-section analysis. Not surprisingly, the relative number of school-age children in the population has been found to exert a significant positive influence on spending levels, particularly at the state and local level. Construction outlays generally exhibit a positive association with income and intergovernmental revenue, and a negative relationship to interest rates, as theory would predict. Further, significant lags in the response to changed incomes and interest rates have generally been observed. This is consistent with the hypothesis that the desired capital stock is related to long-term expected levels of these variables, and that over time the capital stock is gradually adjusted toward the desired level.

Considerable attention has been devoted to the influence of intergovernmental transfers upon the spending patterns of state and local governments. One consistent and rather surprising finding is that block grants (lump-sum transfers that are not tied to a specific service or program) appear to stimulate spending considerably more than do similar increases in local private income.[13] Analysis to date indicates that an extra dollar of such aid raises local spending by about 40 cents; evidently, the balance is indirectly channelled to the private sector through tax reductions. Categorical aid (earmarked for provision of specific services or programs) is even more stimulative, increasing local spending by approximately twice as much as nonspecific aid. The third major type of transfer, the matching grant, encourages spending by lowering the effective price of the aided service. Analysis of specific services has corroborated such price effects, although the spending response tends to be rather inelastic (a finding which agrees with cross-section studies). Thus, matching aid appears to lower locally financed expenditure on the aided service, although total spending (including grant funds) is expanded.

At the "micro level" there have been a few attempts to study relatively short time series for groups of disaggregated spending units. In one such study, the expenditure trends of a group of large cities was analyzed to discern the price and income effects of various aid policies.[14] Here, the results obtained were highly similar to those found in the aggregate analysis described above. Elsewhere, the finances of individual state governments have been examined to identify the effect of a state's current financial position upon short-run changes in expenditures.[15] It has been found that a large state deficit (relative to total outlay) in a particular year significantly reduces the growth rate of state expenditures in the next period. Capital outlays, on the other hand, appear to be influenced more by the state's long-term financial position. Short-run swings in population are generally followed by corresponding changes in current outlays, but are not significantly related to capital spending. Interestingly, the timing of capital outlays appears to be closely related to the timing of major elections.

From a very broad policy perspective, it would be useful to have time-series models that would permit one to attribute overall historic increases in public outlays, by service category, to various independent influences. Those who subscribe to "Wagner's Law" would attribute observed growth largely to rising real incomes.[16] Yet, the rather consistent finding that income elasticities do not exceed unity implies that other factors must be considered in order to explain the rising share of real income allocated through the public sector. Evidence from time-series analysis is in general agreement with a theory of governmental growth put forth by William J. Baumol.[17] The hypothesis is that, because the governmental sector is highly labor intensive, its rate of productivity growth is small relative to the more capital-intensive private sector. This implies that production costs will increase in the public economy relative to prices of private-consumption items. If the demand for (state and local) public services is price inelastic, the total share of resources devoted to public production will rise over time. Available estimates do indicate that public service demands are price inelastic, and indirect evidence indicates that the relative costs of public consumption items have been rising.[18] To decide whether or not these factors can explain a major portion of observed spending increases, however, will require better estimates, particularly on costs.[19]

At the local decision-making level, the uses of time-series analysis are more practical. In this context, the need is for econometric models to forecast various revenue and expenditure items for use in the fiscal planning process. From the local agencies' viewpoint, structural models which estimate a relationship between expenditures and various influencing factors (e.g., income, unemployment, population, the price level, etc.) are generally more useful than pure time-series models that simply forecast the future course of a variable from its own historic movements. This is so because structural models seek to identify the underlying factors that shape trends, thus permitting policy analysis.

For example, one might be interested in how public recreation or fire protection expenditure will respond to a change in the size or distribution of population or a change in the composition of the housing stock, particularly since the latter variables are coming under increasing control by the local public sector. Similarly, a local government may use a forecasting model to estimate the time at which mandated expenditure limits or tax rate ceilings will become binding, or when new capital facilities will be needed. By making the forecast conditional upon a set of explicit values for the "exogenous" variables (rather than simply extrapolating historic trends), such models allow the analyst to consider a range of alternative outcomes. This in itself is somewhat problematic, since it is often difficult to identify which variables are really "exogenous," and the task of estimating plausible future values for these variables remains. However, by working within the context of an explicit model, the decision maker is forced to view policy in terms of the future configuration of the local economy, and the notion of developing contingency plans arises naturally.

In a sense, it may seem rather incongruous for a local government to forecast its own future expenditure decisions. Yet, to the extent that social and economic parameters in a jurisdiction can be systematically related to public spending levels, the observed relationships are indicative of the political and economic pressures that bear on the decision-making activity.

Expenditure Evaluation

In contrast to the largely positive or predictive subject matter of the preceding two sections, the term "evaluation" in the present heading implies a shift in direction toward normative or prescriptive analysis. Among the tools of program or public expenditure evaluation, benefit-cost analysis (and its less ambitious counterpart, cost-effectiveness analysis) has obtained the highest degree of methodological refinement.[20] First applied almost exclusively in the areas of water resource development (e.g., navigational improvement, flood control, irrigation), the technique was extended to national defense programs in the 1960s. In the last decade, the range of policy areas in which benefit-cost analysis is applied has grown rapidly, and now includes public health, recreation, human development, and general transportation programs.

Benefit-cost analysis is probably best thought of as a systematic method for reporting the measurable economic factors that should be taken into account when considering a social resource allocation decision. Used in this fashion it is a valuable tool, in that it provides a logical framework for organizing information relevant to the decision.

Most of the criticism that has been leveled at benefit-cost analysis appears to stem from two sources: improper application of accepted theoretical concepts, and the use of a benefit-cost ratio (or net benefit estimate) as the *only* criterion for evaluating a public program. It is difficult to generalize about the first of these two shortcomings. Deficiencies in methodology and systematic biases in results have been well documented both in public agency evaluations (e.g., regarding interest rates, project lifetimes, secondary benefits, etc.) and in studies by private organizations.[21] Though the notion of comparing benefits and costs appears deceptively simple and straightforward, accurate quantification requires all the tools and subtleties of microeconomics. In an economy characterized by taxes, price supports, minimum wages, noncompetitive elements, and other impediments, the requisite information can seldom be *directly* inferred from market data. In a real sense, it is the treatment of these problems that makes benefit-cost analysis an art or science unto itself.

The second criticism appears to arise inevitably from a conflict between the extremely ambitious goal of policy evaluation—comparison of long-term social welfare under different resource-allocation programs—and the desire for quantification and scientific decision making. In practice it is rarely, if ever, possible to account fully for and measure all of the impacts associated with a policy change. A simple listing of "intangibles" alongside dollar values for tangible factors may bias the final decision, since the two are expressed in different dimensions and the latter appears more concrete. In truth, cost and benefit estimates are always probabilistic or risky in nature, though they are seldom reported in this fashion. Even if these difficulties could be overcome, the distributional implications of simply adding up the benefits and costs of different individuals, "to whomsoever they may accrue," remain.

It is easy, though not terribly productive, to recite the deficiencies in benefit-cost analysis and other program evaluation techniques. In fact, progress is being made in several areas. The estimation of costs and benefits associated with items that are not transferred through markets, typically the most difficult problem in benefit-cost analysis, has been the subject of considerable research effort. A few of the more significant developments in this general area are discussed below.

Until recently, recreational benefits yielded by public projects were commonly considered intangible, despite the fact that a framework for valuing them, the so-called travel-cost approach, was first suggested three decades ago.[22] Publicly provided recreation is generally a nonmarket item in that access to a recreational area is seldom explicitly priced. However, the individual visitor often bears a significant cost (or implicit price) for the recreational experience in the form of travel expense and time required to visit the site. The travel-cost approach seeks to estimate demand relationships, and hence willingness to pay, by comparing individual visitation rates to cost per visit, as well as other demand variables. *Ex ante* analysis requires estimates of demand prior to development of the facility, before actual cost and visitation data can be observed, and the approach generally suggested is to estimate demand functions from existing sites that offer a similar recreational experience. These estimates are then used, together with economic and demographic data on the local population, to forecast use patterns and benefits for the new area. A topic of current concern is the valuation of time spent in transit to the site, an obviously important factor in the resulting benefit estimate.

Closely related to the travel-cost technique are recent attempts to use property-market data to estimate benefits from public programs which yield localized or spatially limited services. Current applications have focused primarily on benefits from air quality improvements and from the provision of local services.[23] As with the travel-cost technique, the property-market approach examines the outlays that individuals make in order to gain access to a particular service. In the property-market literature, these outlays are observed in housing price differentials that are associated with varying levels of nonmarket amenities and disamenities such as air pollution, congestion, airport noise, etc. In this fashion, implicit prices for such items can be inferred, and demand relationships estimated. To date, empirical analysis has yielded plausible and encouraging results. However, at its current state of development the technique is by no means foolproof, and analysts generally advise caution in interpreting results.[24]

The enormous volume and variety of benefit-cost applications prohibits any systematic review of the empirical methodology or nature of results in individual studies.[25] However, an indication of the diverse range of issues to which this technique is presently being applied may be gained from a brief description of evaluations of two services commonly provided in the local public sector.

The first of these concerns a common municipal function, urban traffic patrol, and addresses the problem of determining an efficient allocation of manpower to patrol areas.[26] The setting for the study was an experiment in which actual patrol levels were altered for a period of nine months. It was postulated that benefits from increased patrols would be realized in the form of reduced accident rates, and possibly lower crime rates due to increased police visibility. Costs were primarily attributed to the extra manpower involved, though it was also recognized that average speeds may be reduced (travel times increased) and that some traffic might be diverted to alternate routes. Estimates of the losses incurred in a typical traffic accident were used to value improvements in safety. In the area studied, increased patrols invariably produced benefits via accident reductions, though the magnitudes of benefits were not sufficient to offset added costs incurred when patrols were expanded beyond traditional levels. No significant changes in traffic speed or volume were observed, though it was noted that even slight reductions in travel times would have yielded substantial benefits.

The second study analyzed provision of higher education in two-year colleges, a function often carried out at the county or special-district level.[27] Such educational programs appear to provide benefits to two sorts of students: those who seek initial training for eventual entry into four-year institutions, and those desiring immediately applicable employment skills. Estimation of benefits requires the measurement of earnings differentials (with and without the educational program provided) for both types of students. The value of these differentials will, of course, vary by individual according to age (time until retirement), labor force participation, initial skill or education level, and future labor-market conditions. The latter factors may, in turn, be statistically related to such individual characteristics as sex, age, ethnicity, etc. Costs include not only direct outlays required to operate the system, but also expenditures by students on books and supplies. The major cost item in such studies is invariably the opportunity cost of the student's time, measured in terms of foregone earnings, while in the educational process.

Many of the more recent applications of benefit-cost techniques have relied heavily on theories of "human captial" and the allocation of time. In the area of health care, analysis has been conducted on medical research, disease prevention programs, and large-scale disease detection efforts. In the field of transportation, navigational improvements, urban mass transit systems, and airport siting have been important areas of application. Even policy issues in law enforcement, such as prison reform, rehabilitation programs, and drug suppression, have come under the scrutiny of program analysis. While these efforts to carry systematic evaluation methods into important new policy areas are encouraging, it is apparent that the profession is still learning how to do policy analysis. This is evident in a certain unevenness in the quality of individual studies. Although debate continues over some fundamental conceptual issues (e.g., the treatment of risk, unemployment, and discount rates), important theoretical refinements have been realized in the last 30 years. In the opinion of several observers, the most important area for advance at present is in the application of existing principles and concepts.

Concluding Comments

If there is a single feature that connects the multitude of issues introduced in this paper, it is an integration of previously separate disciplines. Economics is making important inroads in the analysis of government spending and public-sector phenomena in general, areas that were once almost the exclusive domain of students of politics and public administration. With this has come a certain change in the way we view the state, as an organization populated by individuals who respond to incentives and constraints in essentially the same way that people do elsewhere, rather than as an organic entity. At the same time, economists are coming to realize the importance of political institutions and collective decision making in understanding the overall allocation of resources in the economy. In the same vein, the rapid rise of efficiency-oriented policy evaluation techniques has fostered a general belief that economic concepts can be used to guide policy formulation. On the other hand, economists are becoming aware that policy analysis never really takes place in a political vacuum, and that the inertia and resistance encountered when attempting to implement economic evaluation methods can often be traced to the vested interests of the public organizations involved. On balance, our current understanding of governmental processes may appear rudimentary, but recent trends in development of new ideas and integration of old ones, give some reason for optimism.

Notes

1.   For further discussion, see Robert H. Haveman, "Public Expenditures and Policy Analysis: An Overview," in *Public Expenditures and Policy Analysis*, ed. R. H. Haveman and J. Margolis (Chicago: Markham Publishing Co., 1970).

2.   The literature on expenditure determinants analysis is surveyed, in considerable detail, by Roy W. Bahl, "Studies on Determinants of Public Expenditure: A Review," in *Sharing Federal Funds for State and Local Needs*, ed. Selma J. Mushkin and Joseph F. Cotton (New York: Praeger, 1969).

3.   One often finds that expenditure data are summed *across functional spending categories*, e. g., by examining total city spending on all services. There appears to be little justification for this sort of aggregation, particularly since it may unnecessarily hide significant relationships for specific services.

4.   See, for example, William J. Scanlon and Robert P. Strauss, "The Geographic Heterogeneity of Public Expenditure Functions," *Review of Economic Statistics* 54 (1972).

5.   Much of the discussion in this section is drawn from Bahl, "Studies on Determinants."

6.   Arthur T. Denzau, "An Empirical Survey of Studies on Public School Financing," *National Tax Journal* 28 (June 1975), pp. 241–250. Surveys much of the literature on school spending and compares the empirical content of alternative expenditure equations by estimating them on a single set of jurisdictions.

7.   The absence of quantifiable output or service quality measures precludes the study of scale economies in a formal "cost function" sense. Probably, the only services for which natural

output measures are readily available are public enterprise activities such as water and power supply, waste treatment, etc.

8. This literature is surveyed in more detail in Robert T. Deacon, "Review of the Literature on the Demand for Public Services," in *National Conference on Nonmetropolitan Community Services Research*, Committee on Agriculture, Nutrition and Forestry, 95th Congress, 1977 (Washington, D. C.: Government Printing Office, 1977), pp. 207–230; and Robert T. Deacon, "Private Choice and Collective Outcomes: Evidence from Public Sector Demand Analysis," *National Tax Journal* 30 (December 1977), pp. 371–386.

9. The data presented in this section are drawn from three major sources: Thomas E. Borcherding, ed., *Budgets and Bureaucrats: The Sources of Government Growth* (Durham: Duke University Press, 1977); U. S. Bureau of the Census, *Historical Statistics of the United States, Colonial Times to 1970* (Washington, D. C.: Government Printing Office, 1975); and U. S. Bureau of the Census, *Statistical Abstract of the United States, 1976* (Washington, D. C.: Government Printing Office, 1978).

10. Several students of public finance have offered broad generalizations regarding public expenditure trends. Probably the most famous of these is "Wagner's Law" which states that public spending rises relative to national output, at least in growing, industrialized economies. Peacock and Wiseman have postulated the so-called "displacement hypothesis." According to this view, citizens who have become accustomed to a particular level of taxation will resist further increases, unless a crisis situation (e. g., war) develops. Faced with a crisis, the citizenry will generally allow increased tax burdens. However, when the crisis passes, tax rates and expenditures do not decline to former levels, because the populace has become accustomed to a new tax threshold. A third hypothesis, offered by Hansen and Perloff, claims that state and local public spending is procyclical, i.e., that it falls (relative to other sectors) in periods of recession and rises in recovery, thus accentuating swings in the business cycle. The details of these hypotheses and analysis of their empirical content will not be reviewed here, but for a more thorough discussion, see John A. Henning and A. Dale Tussing, "Income Elasticity of the Demand for Public Expenditures in the United States," *Public Finance* 29 (1974), pp. 325–341, and Thomas E. Borcherding, *Budgets and Bureaucrats*, Chapter 2.

11. Richard Tresch, "Estimating State Expenditure Functions: An Empirical Test of the Time Series Informational Content of Cross Section Estimates," *Public Finance* 29 (1974), pp. 370–385.

12. Edward M. Gramlich, "State and Local Governments and Their Budget Constraint," *International Economic Review* 10 (June 1969), pp. 163–181; and Walter W. McMahon, "Cyclical Growth of Public Expenditures," *Public Finance* 26 (1971), pp. 75–105.

13. Edward M. Gramlich and Harvey Galper, "State and Local Fiscal Behavior and Federal Grant Policy," *Brookings Papers on Economic Activity* 1 (1973), pp. 15–58.

14. Ibid.

15. Elliot R. Morss, J. Eric Friedland, and Saul H. Hymans, "Fluctuations in State Expenditures: An Econometric Analysis," *Southern Economic Journal* 34 (April 1976), pp. 496–517.

16. See Henning and Tussing, "Income Elasticity."

17. William J. Baumol, "Macroeconomics of Unbalanced Growth: The Anatomy of the Urban Crisis," *American Economic Review* 57 (June 1967), pp. 415–426.

18. On the latter point, see David F. Bradford, R. A. Malt, and Wallace E. Oates, "The Rising Cost of Local Public Services: Some Evidence and Reflections," *National Tax Journal* 22 (June 1969), pp. 185–202.

19. According to Borcherding, *Budgets and Bureaucrats* (Chapter 3), relative cost increases account for only about one-eighth of expenditure increases. His estimates indicate that growth in income and population are the major identifiable factors explaining the rise in spending though, in total, the factors measured fall short of accounting for observed spending increases.

20. The methodology of benefit-cost analysis will not be surveyed here; see E. J. Mishan, *Economics for Social Decisions: Elements of Cost Benefit Analysis* (New York: Praeger, 1973).

21. It is still fairly common to see future costs and benefits summed without discounting [Jack Hirshleifer and David L. Shapiro, "The Treatment of Risk and Uncertainty," Joint Economic Committee, 91st Congress (Washington, D. C.: Government Printing Office, 1968)] and to find benefits equated to various measures of gross receipts, e. g., recreation benefits and total

expenditures by tourists [Dennis Tihansky, "A Survey of Empirical Benefit Studies," in *Cost Benefit Analysis and Water Pollution Policy*, ed. H. M. Peskin and E. P. Seskin (Washington, D. C.: The Urban Institute, 1975), pp. 127–174.]

22. Further discussion on this topic appears in A. M. Freeman, "A Survey of the Techniques for Measuring the Benefits of Water Quality Improvement," in *Cost Benefit Analysis of Water Pollution Policy*, ed. H. M. Peskin and E. P. Seskin, pp. 67–104.

23. For an interpretive discussion, see D. L. Rubinfeld, "Market Approaches to the Measurement of the Benefits of Air Pollution Abatement" (Ann Arbor, Michigan: Institute of Public Policy Studies, University of Michigan, 1976).

24. One practical problem is to separate the effect of, say, air pollution from other factors that influence property values. Another is that the amenity or disamenity studied may be only partially localized; some of the associated cost benefits may spill over to outlying areas and be missed in a study of local property prices.

25. A very useful source of theoretical and empirical contributions is A. C. Harberger et al., eds., *Benefit Cost and Policy Analysis: An Aldine Annual* (Chicago: Aldine Atherton, 1971–1974).

26. Donald C. Shoup, "Cost Effectiveness of Urban Traffic Law Enforcement," *Journal of Transport Economics and Policy* 7 (January 1973).

27. Harry N. Heineman and Edward Sussna, "Criteria for Public Investment in the Two-Year College: A Program Budgeting Approach," *Journal of Human Resources* 6 (Spring 1971), pp. 171–184.

Public Budgeting

Edward A. Lehan

The Budget Idea

American experience with public budgeting now spans three quarters of a century. In the beginning, the "budget idea," as it was called, was part and parcel of the reform ideal of "responsible government." To turn-of-the-century reformers, budgeting procedures enhanced the popular control of government in two ways: (1) by concentrating financial authority in the chief executive, and (2) by providing formal, open procedures for the exercise of that authority. As a consequence, budgeting was justified primarily on politico-administrative grounds. About four decades were to pass before this original emphasis on the coordination and control features of budgeting was seriously questioned, and the broader, policy making and economic potentials of the budget idea debated and explored.

It all started when New York City embraced the budgeting idea in 1907. Thence, riding on the reform tide, the idea spread rapidly to other local governments, and to the states. The crest of this remarkable movement came 14 years later with the passage of the Federal Budget and Accounting Act of 1921, which one commentator, C.F. Willoughby, said "made the President the working head of the administration in fact as well as in name."[1] Willoughby's remark may be regarded as quintessential, as it reflected the reformer's faith in the coordinating and control values of budgeting.

The phenomenal spread of the budget idea during the early decades of the twentieth century was due far more to its intimate connection with the dominant "responsibility ethos" of the reform movement than to any widespread appreciation of its possible utility in the determination of public policy.[2]

To be sure, the coordination and control features of budgeting were defined in economic as well as political terms by many of the early advocates of public budgeting, particularly by the business allies of the reform movement, who saw budgeting as cost cutting, pure and simple. Naturally, all this emphasis on budgeting as a negative force meant that the positive, or goal-fulfilling, potential of the budget idea as a device for rational decision making was pretty much dormant during the first four decades of the twentieth century. As a result, the commodity, or line-item, form of budgeting (LIB) became entrenched throughout the American governmental system. It was not until 1940, when V.O. Key published his trailblazing critique, "The Lack of a Budgetary Theory," that the latent potential of the budget idea became the principal focus of interest.[3]

Edward A. Lehan is Director of Finance for the City of Rochester, New York. The author wishes to thank John E. Petersen for his assistance in the preparation of this essay.

The Format Issue

What might be called the "format issue" was also largely dormant during the first four decades of American experience with budgeting, despite two significant efforts to call attention to the advantages of a "functional" approach to expenditure classification.

In 1912, the Taft Commission on Economy and Efficiency submitted its famous report recommending that the national government adopt budget procedures. The commission counseled against adopting an itemized commodity approach, suggesting instead that expenditures be classified by type of work, organizational unit, source of funding, and the character, rather than the item, of expense.[4]

In 1917, the New York Bureau of Municipal Research also attacked the utility of the itemized commodity format in the New York City budget. Instead of a detailed itemization of commodities, the Bureau recommended that the city's budget be designed to facilitate policy planning and decision making, a concept which would command much attention from budgeteers 50 years later, in the 1960s.[5] In addition to foreshadowing the planning/programming/budgeting system (PPBS) approach of the 1960s, the Bureau report is also noteworthy as the first systematic inquiry into the operational consequences of budgeting procedures. One might say that this report marked the beginning of the critical literature on budgeting, as the Bureau's researchers tried empirically to assess the impact of budget format and procedures on city decisions and operations.

Although neither the Taft Commission nor the Bureau of Municipal Research effort had any noticeable effect on the spreading use of commodity formats, both reports reflect a lively appreciation for the power of procedures. The authors of these reports frankly acknowledge that procedures are not neutral, that the *means* of budgeting somehow affect the *ends* of budgeting. This powerful and complex idea was well stated by Jesse Burkhead in the preface to his classic, *Government Budgeting:* ". . . the way in which revenues and expenditures are grouped for decision-making is the most important aspect of budgeting."[6]

The possibility that different formats and/or procedures might produce different budgetary outcomes also fascinated other distinguished students of budgeting—Wildavsky, Mosher and Barber, to name but three who have competently explored the impact of formats and procedures on decision making.[7] Aaron Wildavsky, for example, placed great emphasis on the format issue in *The Politics of the Budgetary Process.* This influential work provided a defense of commodity budgeting, suggesting that factions found it easier to compromise differences by bargaining over items of expense, rather than by open struggling over the underlying policy issues. He pointed out that programmatic formats, and the accompanying tendency toward comprehensive annual reviews of all programs, would simultaneously threaten many interests, burdening the budget process with unmanageable political tension and conflict.

Formats are important. People tend to think about what is put in front of them. Budget classifications, as F.C. Mosher pointed out, define reality for budget makers and reviewers, and thus channel their attention and thought. As a case in point, study the following exhibit, which shows a code enforcement budget in a commodity format:

Exhibit One

CODE ENFORCEMENT	BUDGET
Personal Services	$60,238
Contractual Services	7,863
Supplies	1,376
Outlay	235
	$69,712

35

There is little question that this commodity format invites (almost compels) discussion about things to be bought, rather than stimulating concern with policy and procedural issues. Furthermore, a display of commodities often tempts reviewing officials to alter the expenditure pattern in ways which are unrelated to policy issues and/or service levels. Often, such changes (usually reductions) are not accompanied by explanations or expressions of legislative intent. Now, study Exhibit Two. It reclassifies the code enforcement budget of Exhibit One along programmatic lines.

Exhibit Two

CODE ENFORCEMENT	BUDGET
Leadership	$15,526
Plan Examination	12,331
Inspection	40,339
Innovation	850
Education	666
	$69,712

The expenditure titles of Exhibit Two invite questions about work routines, and focus the attention of budget makers and reviewers on such important issues as code revision, improved inspection procedures, and the effort put into the "education" of personnel, the regulated interests and the general public, as a code compliance technique.

As already indicated, the format issue was raised by the Taft Commission and by the New York Municipal Research Bureau, without success. The issue lay dormant until 1949, when another Presidential commission, appointed by President Truman and chaired by former President Hoover, again turned a spotlight on format reform. This time, the message sank in. The commission recommended that

 . . . the whole budgetary concept of the federal government should be refashioned by the adoption of a budget based upon functions, activities, and projects; this we designate a performance budget.[8]

This call for "performance" budgeting excited and inspired a whole generation of budgeteers, and initiated the contemporary era of experimentation in format and procedure.

On the whole, however, despite the enthusiasm engendered by the Hoover Report, the performance budgeting idea found only partial lodgment in American budgetary practice. Today, a quarter century after its introduction, one can find only selected use of unit costs, the key technique of performance budgeting, in many jurisdictions. See Exhibit Three for an example of a budget display using unit costs to relate expenditures to work load. Budgeteers found the performance budgeting concept of practical use in only those activities for which measurable work units, such as inspections, were easily available. It must also be noted that performance budgeting requires sophisticated accounting support, a grave deficiency in almost every American jurisdiction.

Exhibit Three

FIRE PREVENTION	LAST YEAR	THIS YEAR	NEXT YEAR
Expenditures	$24,085	$27,875	$29,295
Inspections	9,634	10,100	10,500
Unit Costs	$ 2.50	$ 2.76	$ 2.79

Goal-Oriented Approaches

Performance budgeting, using unit-cost calculations and comparisons, is the best way to relate expenditures to work loads. Relating expenditures to work loads may help in rationalizing expenditures in a jurisdiction, but the performance budget approach does not, in itself, help budget makers and reviewers solve *the* fundamental problem of budgeting, which is: determining the relative worth of the various purposes supported by budget allocations.

It was V. O. Key who first went to the heart of the budgetary problem in his 1940 essay. Key noted that much energy had been absorbed in the tasks of establishing the mechanical foundations of budgeting, but little attention had been given to the basic budgeting problem on the expenditure side—deciding on what basis funds should be allocated to one activity as opposed to another.[9]

Curiously, Key was pessimistic about the practical value of applied economics in budget making, particularly the application of the doctrine of marginal utility, even though his article defined budgeting as a problem of economic theory. Despite this pessimistic appraisal, his idea that budget making should be examined from the perspective of economic theory proved seminal.

Verne Lewis, for example, carefully examined the potential use of the theory of marginal utility in an influential article in 1952. Lewis proposed the idea of alternative budgets: a basic budget accompanied by alternatives which might be set at 80, 90, 110 and 120 percent of the basic amount.[10] According to Lewis, this structure of incremental alternatives would assist budgeteers in exploring the marginal benefits of different spending plans. This idea was popularized in 1973 under the rather misleading rubric, "zero-base budgeting" (ZBB).[11]

Serious criticism of budgetary practices mounted during the 1950s, with economists in the van. This stream of criticism stimulated widespread experimentation with program budgeting (ProB) and its evolutionary successors, PPBS and ZBB. Each of these approaches involves budgeting formats and procedures organized around goals to be achieved with public funds, rather than things to be bought (the line-item approach), or things to be done (the performance approach). These goal-oriented approaches represent attempts to work allocation criteria into the budget process by asking budgeteers to weigh the costs and benefits of alternative ways of achieving public ends. A noble vision, but what is the contemporary reality? Have budgeteers found an answer to Key's fundamental question? Recent studies reveal that the concepts of desirable practice have outrun the apparent capacity for application.

Budgetary Behavior

Allen Schick, in a comprehensive study of state budget innovations, found techniques of performance budgeting (PerB) and PPBS only partially incorporated in the budgetary practice of the states by the late 1960s.[12] He blamed the weight of the control and management tradition and bureaucratic inertia for the failure of the states to swing more completely to the goal-oriented approaches, but remained hopeful for the future. Aaron Wildavsky, already noted as a critic of programmatic approaches, was not as optimistic, concluding in his latest work on budgeting that the goal-oriented approaches have failed, and will continue to fail, because no one knows how to do them.[13]

In 1975, Lewis Friedman reported on the results of an 88-city survey, noting that only 10 cities of this sample seemed to be heavily engaged with the techniques of goal-oriented budgeting, such as benefit/cost studies, multiyear forecasting, etc.[14] Friedman's report also shed some light on the validity of Allen Schick's hypothesis that budget reform is an evolutionary process involving stages of control, management and planning, each providing the foundation for the next. He found some evidence to support Schick's thesis that governments probably must build up their capability in budgeting generally before they are ripe for tackling the new techniques.

Cities without a heavy commitment to control forms of budgeting were not heavily engaged in performance budgeting, for example. Further, cities without a commitment to performance budgeting were not found to be heavily engaged with goal-oriented budgeting.

In a widely noted 1973 article reviewing the state of the art as revealed in the literature, Don Axelrod reflected the exasperation of many practitioners and students of budgeting. Axelrod warned against "new acronyms" and the "packaged panacea," pointing out that budgeting techniques were not mutually exclusive procedures or stages, and that governments were using—and would continue to use—a variety of techniques to solve allocation and efficiency problems.[15]

Since Don Axelrod's review in 1973, things have gotten worse. A new acronym, ZBB, has invaded the field. This newest "packaged panacea" (fervently endorsed by President Jimmy Carter) requires that budget proposals be presented in priority order at each level of decision making, thus focusing attention on the criteria of allocation. At the time of this writing, a large number of jurisdictions appear to be experimenting with this latest attempt to find answers for V. O. Key's fundamental question: "On what basis shall it be decided to allocate x dollars to activity A instead of activity B?"

The jury is still out on the practical results of the ZBB approach. However, its onset has underscored the schizophrenia of the budgetary world, a world already marked by a wide rift between the realities of budget preparation and control (firmly anchored in itemized, incremental decision making) and the ideal, goal-oriented models (PerB, ProB and PPBS) featured in the literature and classroom.

Empirical Studies of Budgetary Behavior

Much research has been devoted to explaining how—budget formats and official pronouncements aside—decisions are, in fact, made among the competing sources and uses of funds. The analyst must be forever wary in this respect, because how public officials act in allocating may vary greatly from what they report they are doing, perhaps even from what some believe they are doing.

An important example of this divergence is found in the reporting of uses of funds, such as is required under various federal grant programs. In the use of general revenue sharing, for example, researchers kept coming up with the results that actual fiscal impacts varied from those reported by the recipients.[16] The problem, of course, is embedded in the fungibility of dollars: a dollar received from a particular source becomes submerged in the flood of other dollars and may be put to any of a great number of uses. A variety of effects can be generated by the added dollar, including its substitution for other funds in the budget (that once freed are spent on other items), a reduction in other revenues (substituting among revenue sources), building up assets (increasing revenues but not expenditures), or even stimulating more than a dollar of expenditures and revenues (because of matching requirements or expenditure complementarity).

Tracing how marginal changes in funds affect the budget thus becomes a complex analysis of patterns of behavior, capturing "fiscal effects," as funds are added to or, conversely, taken away from the budget. The thrust here is a positive analysis of how governments behave in their budgetary outcomes. Perhaps the most active area of surveillance has been that of the designs of various intergovernmental assistance programs. Results of empirical studies indicate that governmental budgetary reactions will vary depending on program design (such as the matching nature of the formula).[17] Responses will also be conditioned by the degree of fiscal pressure that recipients are under and the presence that local budgeteers ascribe to the assistance program.[18]

Another branch of research that has blossomed to assist in the "what is" analysis of budgetary behavior relies on the approach of organization theory. In this discipline, public budgeting is viewed as a large, complex process. In carrying out the process, officials operate with limited information and analytical skills and under sundry constraints. To conquer the maze, they adopt problem-solving routines—a series of "rules-of-thumb"—by which they bring the budget into balance.[19]

Computer simulations of government budgetary behavior incorporating such decision rules have been created and tested. While handicapped by lack of data and inherent simplicity of their rendering of the process, they nonetheless present some hope of sorting out the maze of decision relationships. Their policy implications are clear: behavioral models that have some explanatory and predictive power will be useful in projecting the consequences of additions or subtractions of dollars into municipal budgets.[20] A word of caution: the mathematical relationships hold only so long as the behavior repeats itself. In the real world, that is likely to be the very short run.

Budgetary Literature

Is it far from the mark to say that most practitioners regard the budgetary literature as a lush growth of description and prescription without firm roots in the procedural reality of government? Able students of budgeting, including Aaron Wildavsky, point out that goal-oriented approaches to public budgeting confront, and go beyond, the limits of politics. Surely these rationalistic approaches require intellectual capabilities which the actors in the budgetary drama most likely do not possess.

What is "good" budgeting? This is a normative question, which even experienced budgeteers have trouble answering. The field is marked by semantic and procedural confusion, torn by conflicts of professional perspective and political interest, and lacks accepted criteria for judging "good" from "bad". For example:
- To an economist, a "good" budget produces equivalent benefits at the margin of expenditure; that is, the last dollar spent on public safety, let us say, yields a benefit equal to that produced by the last dollar spent on other functions.
- To a student of politics, a "good" budget promotes civic morale by incorporating the interests of "interests" within the expenditure and revenue scheme.
- To an elected chief executive, a "good" budget redeems the promises of the last campaign and consolidates support for the next.
- To a finance director, a "good" budget reflects accurate, balanced estimates, useful in financial planning and control.

In addition to coping with the variations in criteria that flow naturally from such differences in perspective and/or interest, a conception of "good" budgeting must cut through the semantic and procedural confusion introduced into the field by the four alternatives to LIB, that is, PerB, ProB, PPBS and ZBB.

Empirical research on the subject of optimal budgeting should be directed toward two objectives: (1) the reconciliation of a voluminous and growing theoretical literature with actual practice, and (2) the establishment of an authoritative factual and normative basis for improvement of public budgeting.

It is hypothesized that the practice of public budgeting has not been significantly affected by the literature advocating the so-called "output" or "goal-oriented" approaches.[21] This hypothesis, and a number of derivative researchable issues,[22] could form the core of a research agenda designed to probe the basic reification and relationship problems of public budgeting, such as:
- Ambiguous terminology;
- Impact of different formats and procedures on budgetary outcomes;
- Relative costs (in time, talent, accuracy, money, etc.) of different approaches;
- Impact of different procedures on informational needs of user groups; and
- Accounting, data base and other institutional and pedagogical requirements of different approaches.

Education of Budgeteers

One important point remains. It concerns the educational foundations of budget work. Apparently, most budgeteers are trained on-the-job and thus are dependent on the quality of supervision found in their budget units—a most unsatisfactory state of affairs from a pedagogical point of view. Further, the literature of budgeting is silent on the pedagogy of budgeting. Given the strategic placement of budgeteers in the decision-making process, and the profusion of budgeting models which provoke broad and deep thinking about society and its problems, this "pedagogic deficit" should alarm the academic and training community—and stir it into action.

Notes

1.   C. F. Willoughby, "The Budget," *Encyclopedia of the Social Sciences,* Vol. III (New York: Macmillan Co., 1930), p. 40.

2.   For a sample of the literature on the "budget idea" at the high tide of the reform movement, see an excellent collection of essays on budgeting in *The Annals of the American Academy of Political and Social Science* (November 1915).

3.   V. O. Key, "The Lack of a Budgetary Theory," *American Political Science Review* 34 (December 1940), p. 1138.

4.   U.S. President's Commission on Economy and Efficiency, "The Need for a National Budget," H. Doc. 854, 62nd Cong., 2nd sess., 1912.

5.   New York Bureau of Municipal Research, "Some Results and Limitations of Central Financial Control in New York City," *Municipal Research* 81 (1917).

6.   Jesse Burkhead, *Government Budgeting* (New York: John Wiley and Sons, 1956), p. viii.

7.   Aaron Wildavsky, *The Politics of the Budgetary Process* (Boston: Little, Brown and Company, 1964); F. C. Mosher, *Program Budgeting* (Chicago: Public Administration Service, 1954); and J. D. Barber, "The Intellectual Work of the Board of Finance" (Storrs, Connecticut: Institute of Public Service, University of Connecticut, 1973).

8.   U.S. Commission on Organization of the Executive Branch of Government, "Budgeting and Accounting" (Washington, D.C.: Government Printing Office, 1949), p. 8.

9.   Key, "The Lack of a Budgetary Theory."

10.   Verne B. Lewis, "Toward a Theory of Budgeting," *Public Administration Review* 12 (1952), pp. 42–54.

11.   Peter A. Pyhrr, *Zero-Base Budgeting: A Practical Management Tool for Evaluating Expenses* (New York: John Wiley and Sons, 1973).

12.   Allen Schick, *Budget Innovation in the States* (Washington, D.C.: Brookings Institution, 1971).

13.   Aaron Wildavsky, *Budgeting* (Boston: Little, Brown and Company, 1975).

14.   Lewis C. Friedman, "Control, Management and Planning: An Empirical Examination," *Public Administration Review* (November/December 1975), pp. 625–628.

15.   Donald Axelrod, "Post Burkhead—The State of the Art or Science of Budgeting," *Public Administration Review* 33 (November/December 1973), pp. 576–584.

16.   See Richard Nathan, Allen Manvel, and Susannah Calkins, *Monitoring Revenue Sharing* (Washington, D.C.: Brookings Institution, 1975).

17.   See, for example, Edward M. Gramlich and Harvey Galper, "State and Local Fiscal Behavior and Federal Grant Policy," *Brookings Papers on Economic Activity* (1973).

18.   General revenue sharing research provided a wealth of information on the differential impacts of a widespread, broad-scale block program of assistance. See F. Thomas Juster, ed., *The Economic and Political Impact of General Revenue Sharing* (Ann Arbor: Institute of Social Science Research, University of Michigan, 1976).

19.   The field was pioneered by John P. Crecine. *Governmental Problem Solving: A Computer Simulation of Municipal Budgeting* (Chicago: Rand McNally, 1969).

20.   Thomas Anton, ''Understanding the Fiscal Impact of General Revenue Sharing,'' *General Revenue Sharing,* Vol. 2: Summaries of Impact and Process Research (Washington, D.C.: National Science Foundation, 1975).

21.   For an illuminating insight into the state of the art, see Municipal Finance Officers Association, ''Budget Committee Questionnaire'' (Chicago: Municipal Finance Officers Association, 1977). In response to this poll, over 1100 local finance officers identified the most pressing information and training needs of local government budgeteers as 1) revenue forecasting, 2) budget planning and priority selection, and 3) budget execution and control.

22.   For an example of an empirical evaluation of budget hypotheses along the lines here suggested, see Lewis Friedman, *Budgeting Municipal Expenditures* (New York: Praeger Publishers, 1975).

Capital Budgeting

Michael J. White

Recent literature on local government capital programming continues to be sparse. This review of that literature notes some promising developments toward greater volume, stronger emphasis on comparative and empirical research, and greater awareness of political reality. After a review of the prescriptive and descriptive literature on capital programming in local governments, research needs relevant to federal policy making are proposed. Before presenting the overview, some definitional matters must first be considered.

Government researchers and public administration scholars have neglected capital budgeting in recent years. This elusive subject lacks clear definitions, organized traditions of inquiry, conceptual boundaries, standard questions, and reliable data sets. However, its importance to federal as well as local decision makers has increased as the portion of municipal capital budgets supported by federal monies has increased. As the federal government's role expands, the subject of capital improvements also becomes more complicated.

Complication begins with basic definition. Precise characterization of the field of capital budgeting founders on the multiple and overlapping sets of phenomena to which the term "capital budgeting" refers. Some municipal capital budgets are documents which reflect careful planning and analysis; some are merely superficial documents produced for public show. Not all capital improvements will be contained in a capital budget, and not all that is in the capital budget is a capital improvement.[1] A municipality may share responsibility for capital improvements within its geographic boundaries with other general government units, special districts, state and regional agencies, and the private sector. Therefore, the capital improvements for a defined territory or population may not be congruent with the capital budget of that territory. Furthermore, federal funding for certain types of capital investment may provide operating funds, resulting in the inclusion of items other than capital improvements in the capital budget.

There is also ambiguity about the size of a project that can legitimately be called a capital improvement, and that size varies with the size of the jurisdiction. Packaging of projects together may allow one jurisdiction to finance with debt what another jurisdiction includes as an operating budget item. State law may also affect what can be classified as a capital budget item. All of this definitional confusion impedes the recognition of capital improvement programs as an important public matter and diverts research attention as well.[2]

Michael J. White is Professor of Public Administration of the University of Southern California. The author wishes to thank Philip Rosenberg and Catherine Lavigne Spain for their assistance in the preparation of this essay.

Analysis of capital budgeting is hindered by the lack of reliable data. Data are fragmented according to the functional concerns of professional groups and government agencies. There may be a wealth of data on school construction or sewer projects, but it is unlikely that the data are recorded on a unit-record basis, that they can be combined easily for common geographic areas from general and special purpose districts, or that they can be aggregated by municipality across functional areas.

Not surprisingly, the literature on capital budgeting remains fragmented and anecdotal. Much of what is written about capital budgets is instructional. Manuals, handbooks and guides for the preparation of capital improvement programs have been produced by state governments, associations, institutes, and municipalities. A substantial untapped anecdotal literature exists in the professional magazines concerned with specific types of projects.[3] Another untapped source of anecdotal prescriptions is the political science case-study literature. Many urban politics studies focus on site selection, facilities location, or major development decisions (e.g. school location or highway planning). This literature has not been systematically reviewed for its relevance to capital budgeting. Ignoring these two large bodies of literature, one can still infer that the literature on capital budgeting is growing steadily.[4]

The recent literature on capital budgeting breaks down into the following categories: manuals, studies of government programs, capital budgeting and planning, capital budgeting and financial analysis, determinants of capital budgets, and behavioral studies of capital budgeting. This review will discuss each of these topics and suggest research areas requiring further study.

Recent Literature

Manuals

The largest number of items classified under any of the above topical headings are manuals. They represent the state-of-the-art, or at least what is thought to be the state-of-the-art, by those concerned enough to write. About a dozen manuals prepared since 1975 have been identified in the literature search which resulted in the publication of this volume by the Government Finance Research Center of the Municipal Finance Officers Association (MFOA).[5] These documents usually build around a "steps-in-the-process" approach, and are prescriptive in nature. They may include some basic concepts, such as:

○ Discounting;
○ Recommended capital budget calendars;
○ Discussions of what a capital improvement is and what kinds of expenditure items should be included in the capital budget;
○ Discussions of the functions different institutions of the government serve and how documentation should pass through these units;
○ Finance law;
○ Guidelines for cost estimation;
○ Forms and reports; and
○ Perhaps some contemporary planning theory.

Given the number of such manuals prepared recently, it would appear the public interest presently is in dissemination rather than sponsorship of further efforts along this line. Recent manuals seem to present more economic analysis than older manuals such as that of Moak and Killian.[6] Increasing emphasis seems to be placed on planning and coordination and on participation, and decreasing emphasis on administrative procedures.[7]

With the exception of the MFOA's work for small cities, the manuals typically lack any realistic consideration of the political dynamics of the capital programming process, any serious discussion of the bewildering variety of financing sources, and any discussion of the uncertainties inherent in projecting action several years ahead. In this sense, the newer manuals retain the formalistic character of the older ones. While the newer manuals show more analytic consciousness among those who write for practitioners, they do not give evidence of field examination of the actual operations of capital improvements programming. The field remains substantially nonempirical.

Recent survey work of the MFOA identified and documented capital budgeting policies and practices useful in the variable small local government (population less than 50,000) environments.[8] These policies and practices have been adopted and formated to the needs of small units of government and are presented in a financial-management policy guide and capital budgeting manual.

Studies of Federal Programs

The most striking advance in the past few years has been in studies of federal programs. These programs are the source of a rapidly growing proportion of local capital improvements financing. For instance, the Community Development Block Grant Program (CDBG) provides nearly 10 percent of total local spending for capital improvements.

Richard P. Nathan is largely associated with the advance of this type of inquiry.[9] His studies of general revenue sharing and community development block grants will likely influence others to undertake similar studies of federal programs.

Along with an increased regional awareness in American politics,[10] these changes in the source of funds for capital improvements make a compelling argument for annual attention to distributional impacts. Major shifts in the regional and intrametropolitan distribution of this amount of money should be recognized and made evident to federal policy makers. When Nathan and his colleagues examined community development block grants in 62 jurisdictions while hold-harmless provisions were still in effect, they found substantial changes in the regional distribution of federal assistance.

Nathan and his associates have also been interested in how individual jurisdictions spend their CDBG money. They have found that CDBG funds are not exclusively used to replace local sources of revenue. They explain this as a consequence of CDBG being a replacement for an existing set of federal programs rather than a whole new source of funds, as was the case with general revenue sharing. It should be noted that the CDBG provisions call for a local maintenance of effort wherein CDBG monies may not replace local funds for ongoing activities.

In addition, the Nathan study was concerned with project characteristics. Individual projects tended to be short term in time horizon, dispersed throughout the jurisdiction rather than concentrated (as was the case in the terminated urban renewal and model cities programs), and directed toward conservation and rehabilitation rather than major new construction. Park improvements, street lighting, sidewalk repairs and the like are the homely stuff of community development block grants. What makes this especially notable is that such projects have always comprised a major portion of municipal capital programs in all but the most rapidly growing jurisdictions.

Another reason for remarking on these findings is that they reveal something about the behavior of local government decision makers. Local governments may be reluctant to become committed to major capital projects due to the uncertainty of federal funding.[11] If this is so, then it is evidence of a shift in the risk preferences, or perhaps the risk perceptions, of local officials compared to a decade ago. As federal programs grow in importance for local capital improvements, it will be increasingly important that federal policy makers understand the shifting risk preferences and perceptions of local officials. For, as Nathan and his associates argue, local officials will adapt the federal purposes as expressed in legislative language to their own ends.[12]

Research attention has recently focused on an important aspect of federal programs for capital improvements—financing the state and local shares of programs partially funded by the federal government. The federal government is beginning to question the capability of local governments in particular to meet their share of the costs of capital facilities. Although the local governments may be required to raise only a small portion of the total cost of the project, this can place a substantial burden on the local government.

A recent study for the Environmental Protection Agency (EPA) examined the potential problems and burdens associated with heavy reliance upon borrowing by local governments to finance their share of the Federal Water Pollution Control Program.[13] Grants covering 75 percent of the total costs of plans and construction of local wastewater treatment facilities are provided under this program. Local governments are required to pay from 0 to 25 percent of the costs, depending on the state's contribution in meeting the program's goals. The analytical methods devised and demonstrated in this study were used in assessing local government credit capacity as it relates to sewer bond financing. However, the methodologies are transferable to analyzing the fiscal capacity of units to support their share of federal capital programs in general. The study contains a "working guide" for EPA personnel to use in identifying potential problem borrowers.

Other studies of federal programs have defined a set of research questions of growing importance.

o What are the distributive consequences of federal funding for capital improvements?
o Are federal funds substituted for local funds, or are new projects undertaken?
o Upon what time horizon are these projects predicated?
o What do we know about the risk preferences and perceptions of local officials?
o To what extent are local officials able to bend federal purposes to their own goals?

Through the answers to these questions a window will be opened on the larger issues of interregional conflict, the implementation of federal policy objectives through local government, and distributional equity in the public sector. Hopefully, there will be more studies, similar to those of Nathan and his associates, of other federal programs sponsoring local capital improvements such as plants and energy conservation projects.

Capital Budgeting and Planning

The integration of capital programming with planning for the purposes of growth management has been the subject of a recent research effort directed by the American Society of Planning Officials (ASPO) in cooperation with others.[14] This project has considered capital programming as an instrument of growth management and subsidiary to the planning process. A review of the draft background papers for this project makes it clear that at present capital programs are only occasionally integrated with growth management planning.[15]

The focus of the ASPO study was very broad. It examined the use of capital improvements to achieve development objectives, which were defined to include renewal, rehabilitation and stabilization, in addition to new growth. The important distinctions between capital budgeting needs of mature cities (particularly in the Northeast) and younger municipalities are recognized, since many of the largest central cities are experiencing declines in population and public revenues. At the same time, these areas find their costs of providing services increasing due to an aging physical plant.

Capital programs too often represent passing political compromises and formal compliance with legal publication deadlines, rather than well-thought-out plans for community improvement. However, capital programs are more than a community's master plan. In a single document, they incorporate a statement of the community's current financial needs and opportunities with a plan for the maintenance of service levels and the replacement of facilities in an orderly manner, and they integrate locally financed, federally sponsored, and extrajurisdictional projects. Clearly, the growth management focus directs attention to a small part of what should be incorporated into a capital program.

The ASPO project attempts to analyze the functional possibilities of capital improvements programming. It also endeavors to develop a more coherent rationale for capital programming, since it integrates theory with field investigation. Interestingly, the theory that capital improvements programming and budgeting is a long-range planning device emerges from the data somewhat shaken. The study suggests that the purposes of capital programming are still quite open to debate. Therefore, any simple instrumental view of the capital program seems at variance with reality. The flow of the action from plan to capital program appears simplistic and wishful. Among the reasons for this, one might speculate, is the likelihood of critical growth management decisions being made in community forums too broadly based for consideration of other issues important to the completion of a capital program, such as the mundane projects of replacement and maintenance. The capital program, then, may include growth management decisions and policies in its pages. But the capital programming process may be unable to implement growth management policies in any more profound sense than that. Nevertheless, it is clear from project reports that the planners recognize the need for other growth management instruments in addition to the capital program.[16]

Like the Nathan studies of federal programs, the ASPO research on capital programming and growth management represents a move toward empirical study of capital programming. The study, even in its inconclusiveness, sharpens conceptualizations of capital budgeting and exposes some hollow rhetoric. The multiple functions of capital programming become clearer, as do the tensions and contradictions among them. This should further the understanding of capital budgeting as organizational decision making of a particularly ambiguous kind. The private sector has become more involved in the provision of capital improvements recently. The private land developer is increasingly required to construct capital improvements at his own expense. Whether these requirements are often excessive, as has been alleged, is a question to be answered by future investigations. Information will be required about what communities require and the costs and benefits of the private investments in streets, utilities and other components of the infrastructure.

There have been a number of recent works, such as the study done by George Sternlieb, which offer a model for measuring the impact of various types of development—housing, for example—on the capital infrastructure of a neighborhood, city or region.[17] These models allow local officials to weigh the various costs and benefits of private and/or public-sector developments.

Capital Budgeting and Financial Analysis

The process by which projections of revenues and expenditures are made relative to the capital budgeting process is extremely important. Local governments may go about the analytical task using perhaps three approaches:

1. Judgmental Analysis—forecasts based on historical data, assumptions about changes in various sources of revenue. This approach has the objective of arriving at reasonable estimates. Although the possibility of error is increased, this approach does not require extensive facilities or expertise.
2. Statistical Analysis—more precise than judgmental analysis. Regression analysis can be used to examine, for example, the trend of property tax over time and effects of population increases on expenditures in various categories. It may also be used to determine operating costs. This may require computer capability, expertise and time.
3. Econometric Analysis—revenues and expenditures are a function of the economic activity within a community. Econometric models can be constructed which recognize the economic forces that affect city finances. They require expertise, computer capability, time and accurate data.

Likewise, the effect of capital budgeting on operating and maintenance costs must be taken into account by the analyst. The need for good analytical work in accurately costing capital items becomes acute in light of pressures to limit local government expenditures.

One researcher suggests that the failure to have adequate tools for analysis may

46

have an impact on units' ability to market debt and pay for capital items.[18] He points out that the budget process and format may influence bond ratings.

Determinants of Capital Budgets

The subject of determinants of capital budgets is particularly fraught with definitional problems. Data development requires clear definitions and an ability to cope with, or ignore, the inadequacies of the available capital budgeting documents. Wallace E. Oates questions the common presumption that budgets are the exclusive means of regulating the supply of government services. He suggests that zoning is an alternative instrument that acts through shaping population characteristics.[19] This converges with the thrust of the ASPO study of growth management. Douglass, collecting data on capital programs of 40 cities, attempted to discover the determinants of capital budget levels in a manner similar to the more familiar operating budget determinants of expenditure studies. He found intergovernmental aid of critical importance.[20]

Behavioral Studies

Aside from the field work undertaken in conjunction with the Nathan and the ASPO projects, there have been few recent behavioral studies of capital budget decision making. White and Douglass studied four upstate New York municipalities and found little evidence that the prescriptive literature had any relevance.[21] They suggested that the prescriptions were not adapted to the reality of municipal governments. City officials managed the capital programming process through managing participation, not through the application of analytical methods or administrative formalities. Decision making was open-ended due to the numerous trade-offs that can be made between capital and operating expenditures, between alternative financing sources, between this year and next, and between one jurisdiction and another. Municipal officials, at least in declining or steady-state jurisdictions, will often seek to shift responsibility for a function rather than meet it from their beleaguered revenue resources.

Major capital projects require drawn-out negotiations on financing, legal arrangements, and political beneficiaries. The success of such negotiations may be contingent on swift recognition of chance opportunities. Accordingly, these types of projects are not comfortably encompassed and scheduled in the annual capital program update. This paper takes as its starting point the ambiguities, uncertainties, and risks of capital programming and then describes how the participants deal with these factors by restricting the players, shifting the risks, and negotiating the uncertainties. The paper is largely descriptive, but suggests the possibility of applying the theories of Cyert and March, and March and Olson, to capital programming.[22] Another descriptive piece which finds a discrepancy between planning ideals and capital programming reality is by Krumholz and Cogger. This is a case study of Cleveland, and is summarized in the background papers prepared for the ASPO study.[23]

Several trends emerge from this review of the recent literature. The past three years have seen important advances in the study of capital programming in municipalities. Major efforts have been empirical and comparative in nature, involving field work in as few as four (White and Douglass) and as many as 60 (Nathan et al.) municipalities. Federal impacts have come under scrutiny, questions of distribution, substitution, instrumentality, purpose, and rationality have been raised. Even the manuals evidence a change in direction toward analytical method rather than administrative procedure. The divergence between planning "myth" and political "reality" is being documented and, hopefully, understood.

Research Needs

Of course, further study is required in most areas this paper has reviewed. However, there are other major research needs that must be met if informed policy making is to prevail.

Most basically, there is a need for studies of the sources and applications of funds for local government capital improvements. An input-output table would help clarify and track aggregate changes in the financing of capital improvements, and in the functions to which these improvements are dedicated. The latter can be obtained, to some extent, from a review of the *Census of Government Finances*,[24] but an annual source would be preferable.

On the financing side, major changes may be taking place. Renshaw estimates that federal grants as a percentage of new state and local construction activity will more than double, from 26 to 63 percent between fiscal year 1975 and fiscal year 1979.[25] This is shocking in its implications for both the funding stability and autonomy of local governments, and for the stability of expenditure allocations across functional areas. One specific implication is that the description offered by White and Douglass would become more accurate, and the standard manual prescriptions less feasible, in this event.

On the outside, some shifts among functions should be evident: relative increases in the shares devoted to mass transit and pollution abatement, and decreases in the share allocated to school construction. However, more exact monitoring would be useful.

The transfer of government functions among jurisdictions is another area in need of investigation. In older, declining cities, one means of coping with replacement needs for sewers, stadiums, roads, libraries, and other facilities and utilities has been the transfer of functional responsibility. An important analysis of this subject has been presented by Joseph Zimmerman to the Advisory Commission on Intergovernmental Relations.[26] An attempt to link these changes to federal policies regarding capital improvements subsidies might lead to policies favoring counties and special districts over central cities. Further empirical work in this area would be aided by improved sources and applications of funds data regarding capital improvements.

Given the growing role of the federal government, researchers should determine the effects of federal budget procedures on local capital programming efforts. The Congressional Budget Office (CBO) has devoted some attention to the issue of advance budgeting, but the lead time between initial budget estimates and final enactment already is very long. The emphasis in the CBO work has been on program operations rather than capital improvements.[27] The need seems more for acceleration of federal procedures, and for stability and continuity in federal programs, rather than for advance budgets.

The development of useful classification schemes for capital expenditures is another effort which should be undertaken. The Community Development Block Grant Program uses a scheme particularly well suited to community development objectives as stated in its legislative authorization. However, it is unknown whether other programs classify their data using this scheme.[28]

The extensive system of categorical grants-in-aid should be reviewed for its impact on local government capital programming. Some of those grants are offered as incentives for local governments to undertake projects considered to meet national priorities. Others are mandated by the federal government, with capital costs partially or wholly financed by it. Airport facilities standards and municipal waste treatment programs are in this category. Of course, there are also federal activities which may have substantial consequences for local capital budgets, yet have little grants-in-aid money directly connected to them, as in the area of air pollution.

Among the relevant research questions here are:

o What proportion of local government capital expenditures is devoted to meeting federal priorities?

o Of this share, how much is federally financed and how much involves locally raised "matching" funds?

o What are the constraints placed down the road on the operating budget and the unit's ability to handle debt service requirements?

o To what extent are local priorities distorted by federal mandates and incentives for capital projects serving federal policy priorities?
o What differential impacts on municipalities do these federal programs have?
o What further capital project needs are caused by categorical programs, and can expenditures for these additional requirements fulfill cost-sharing responsibilities?
o How is the availability of federal funding included as a factor in project-ranking decisions?
o How is the timing of capital programming decisions affected by federal grant programs?
o Do federal grant programs disrupt the orderly progress of projects through a multiyear capital program?

The answers to questions like these would clarify the extent to which the local capital programming processes can be a vehicle for local government priority setting. Some jurisdictions have sought to involve citizens in capital programming procedures in order to involve citizens in local priority setting.[29]

The role of capital programming in service-level planning is only beginning to be explored.[30] The treatment of capital improvements as part of service-production functions offers much fruitful research work on substitutions between capital and operating expenditures.

Another subject for inquiry is the flow of federal funds from congressional appropriation to local spending. As local governments become chosen instruments for countercyclical stabilization by the federal government (countercyclical revenue sharing), there will be an increasing need for the federal government to understand better the incentive structures and decision-making processes of local governments.

Research on capital needs and, more specifically, replacement needs is overdue. George Peterson has a study under way, but more regular monitoring of replacement needs should be undertaken.[31] White and Douglass found municipal officials delaying maintenance and replacement projects in the hope that state or federal programs would relieve them of the financial burden.[32] Operating budgets acquire attention because of their more immediate political returns for public officials. Replacement needs studies, one hopes, will not be dominated by professional evangelism with respect to service and facility standards. Yet, it will be hard to find indicators of need independent of professional judgments and association standards. Objectivity is a myth in such matters. Research on needs should be subject to constant skeptical review.

Another area requiring research has come to the fore in the wake of the recently passed Jarvis-Gann amendment to the California state constitution. As John E. Petersen notes, this is "clearly the most important happening in public finance since the New York City fiscal crisis."[33] Certain local debt instruments used in California to fund the acquisition of capital needs are under a cloud of doubt relative to their ability to repay under the new property tax regime. How governments meet capital needs when placed under such fiscal restrictions merits investigation.

A final area for research and one closely related to capping of revenues and expenditures is the impact of capital expenditures on operating costs. Clearly, tax limitation actions such as Jarvis-Gann will facilitate a growing awareness of the impact that operating and maintenance costs associated with capital improvements projects can have on future operating budgets. The federal government is beginning to show interest in this area and is raising questions which are attempting to determine whether federally mandated design standards impose unnecessary operating and maintenance costs on local governments.

Summary and Conclusion

This paper reviews a scanty literature, but draws from it the impression that research on municipal capital programming has taken a notable leap forward in conceptualization, if not in volume. The literature has become more empirical, more questioning, more realistic, and more analytical. Yet, as the federal involvement in local capital programming grows, a host of new questions emerges.

Some are questions more for federal action than for new research. But there are needs for basic data-set development and for further conceptual clarification. Specific studies of federal capital subsidy programs, of municipal decision making, or of the histories and activities in specific functional areas have not been called for, because they have been implied in other parts of the paper. The pioneering work of Douglass on determinants of capital expenditures needs to be extended. Along with the work of White and Douglass, it offers some prospect of organizational decision theories developed from capital budgeting decisions. Such a theoretical base would help federal officials project local reaction to federal initiatives.

Some research is not urgent. There are enough manuals, and more formal business models of capital budgeting than the local-government sector will absorb in many years. There is a self-sustaining literature in political science and sociology on community decision making, and another self-sustaining literature from the practitioners on specific project experiences. These two areas also need no encouragement. But, as mentioned earlier, synthesis of these bodies of writing could prove useful.

Notes

1.   New York City's debt financing of operating expenses needs only to be mentioned in passing.

2.   For example, a recent report on county budget processes by Price, Waterhouse & Co., *Report Number Two: County Budgetary Processes* (Los Angeles: 1976–77 Grand Jury of Los Angeles County, 1977) did not include mention of the capital budget. Yet the 1972 *U.S. Census of Governments* showed that local governments in the U.S. spent $19 billion on capital outlays in 1971–72 and paid an additional $4.8 billion in interest on local debt—representing over 20 percent of total local outlays.

3.   Articles with titles like "City of Fairview Cuts Cost of Trash Compactor Through Low Bidding Procedures" and "Fire Station Location Improved in East Meadow" fall into this category.

4.   Reviewing the literature several years ago, Scott Douglass and the author could find only two field studies of capital programming in the previous 15 years: Brown and Gilbert's *Planning Municipal Investment: A Case Study of Philadelphia* (1961) and Richard Chakerian's study of a Florida local parks department, "Organization Function and Participation in Policy Making," a paper presented at the 1970 Annual Meeting of the American Political Science Association.

5.   The following is a list drawn from the MFOA literature search and from American Society of Planning Officials, "Local Capital Improvements and Development Management Literature Synthesis" (Washington, D.C.: U.S. Department of Housing and Urban Development and National Science Foundation, July 1977). Vogt, Fujardo and Steiss were reviewed in depth, others on the basis of abstracts or outlines.

Eugene Burr, "Preparation of a Capital Improvement Program," MTAS Technical Report (Knoxville: Municipal Technical Advisory Service, Institute for Public Service, University of Tennessee Municipal League, November 1975); *Capital Improvements Programming for Local Governments* (Denver: Denver Regional Council of Governments, 1975); Richard D. Evans, *Guidelines for Municipal Capital Programming* (Boston: Massachusetts Department of Community Affairs, 1975); Richard P. Fujardo, *Capital Budgeting: Guidelines and Procedures,* Research Reports in Public Policy, No. 9 (Santa Barbara: Urban Economics Program, University of California at Santa Barbara, July 1976); *Capital Programming* (Indianapolis: Indianapolis-Marion County Department of Metropolitan Development, 1976); *A Guide to Capital Improvements Programming and Budgeting in Kansas Cities* (Topeka: League of Kansas Municipalities, August 1976); *Procedures Manual for the City of Memphis Capital Improvement Budget and Program* (Memphis: City of Memphis, September 1975); *A Guide for Develop-*

ing a Capital Budget (Montgomery: South Central Alabama Development Commission, June 1975); Capital Improvement Review System (Tucson: City of Tucson Department of Planning, October 1975); Instructional Manual for Use in Preparation of CIP (Winston-Salem: City of Winston-Salem, 1976); A. John Vogt, Capital Improvements Programming: A Handbook for Local Officials (Chapel Hill: Institute of Government, University of North Carolina, 1977); Roger D. Lee, Capital Improvements Budgeting: A Manual for Local Governments in Utah (Salt Lake City: Utah Department of Community Affairs, March 1975); and Alan Walter Steiss, Local Government Finance: Capital Facilities Planning and Debt Administration (Lexington, Massachusetts: D.C. Heath & Co., 1975).

6.   Lennox L. Moak and Kathryn W. Killian, A Manual of Suggested Practice for the Preparation and Adoption of Capital Programs and Capital Budgets by Local Governments (Chicago: Municipal Finance Officers Association, 1964).

7.   See Morris C. Matson, "Capital Budgeting: Fiscal and Physical Planning," Governmental Finance 5 (August 1976), pp. 42–50, 58.

8.   Municipal Finance Officers Association, A Guidebook to Improved Financial Management in Smaller Municipalities (Chicago: Municipal Finance Officers Association, August 1978); and A Capital Improvement Programming Handbook for Smaller Municipalities (Chicago: Municipal Finance Officers Association, August 1978).

9.   Richard P. Nathan et al., Block Grants for Community Development (Washington, D.C.: U.S. Department of Housing and Urban Development, January 1977). See also Nathan et al., Monitoring Revenue Sharing (Washington, D.C.: The Brookings Institution, 1975) and Revenue Sharing: The Second Round (Washington, D.C.: The Brookings Institution, 1977). These latter two works are less immediately relevant to capital budgeting.

10.   See, for example, Daniel P. Moynihan, "The Politics and Economics of Regional Growth," The Public Interest 51 (Spring 1978), pp. 3–21.

11.   Nathan et al., Block Grants, Chapter 7. See also the comments reported by Edward F. Renshaw in "Urban Development Banking: An Overview and Summary of a Roundtable Discussion Which Was Held at the Brookings Institution, March 21, 1977," Journal of Urban Analysis 5 (1978), pp. 71–86.

12.   Nathan et al., Block Grants, p. 245.

13.   John E. Petersen, "Debt Financing of the State and Local Share of Constructing Municipal Wastewater Treatment Facilities," a report to the Environmental Protection Agency, Government Finance Research Center, Municipal Finance Officers Association, Washington, D.C., 1978. This report was prepared in conjunction with Peat, Marwick, Mitchell & Co. and the Municipal Finance Study Group, State University of New York at Albany under EPA Contract 68-01-4343.

14.   American Society of Planning Officials, "Local Capital Improvement and Development Management Project," a research project funded jointly by the Office of Policy Development of the Department of Housing and Urban Development and Research Applied to National Needs Program of the National Science Foundation (HUD Contract H-2496) and prepared in conjunction with the Municipal Finance Officers Association; Peat, Marwick, Mitchell & Co.; Ross, Hardies, O'Keefe, Babcock & Parsons; and Dr. Carl Patton.

15.   Philip Rosenberg, "Background Paper for Task 3.1," paper prepared for the American Society of Planning Officials for Local Capital Improvements and Development Management research project, Municipal Finance Officers Association, Washington, D.C., November 1976.

16.   Rosenberg, "Background Paper;" American Society of Planning Officials, "Local Capital Improvements;" and Peat, Marwick, Mitchell & Co., "The Effects of Capital Improvements on Land Development Patterns," draft background paper prepared for ASPO Local Capital Improvements and Development Management research project, Washington, D.C., October 1976.

17.   George Sternlieb, Housing Development and Municipal Costs (New Brunswick, New Jersey: The Rutgers Center for Urban Policy Research, 1974).

18.   Lewis Friedman, "City Budgets," Municipal Performance Report (New York: Council on Municipal Performance, August 1974).

19.   Wallace E. Oates, "The Use of Local Zoning Ordinances to Regulate Population Flows and the Quality of Local Services," Essays in Labor Market Analysis, ed. Orly Ashenfelter and Wallace E. Oates (New York: John Wiley and Sons, 1977).

20.   Scott Douglass, "Determinants of Capital Budgets," paper presented at the 1977 National Meeting of the American Society for Public Administration, Atlanta, Georgia.

21.   Michael J. White and Scott Douglass, "An Interpretation of Capital Programming as a Political Process in No-Growth Municipalities," paper presented at the 1975 Annual Meeting of the American Political Science Association, San Francisco, California.

22.   Richard Cyert and James G. March, *The Behavioral Theory of the Firm* (Englewood Cliffs, New Jersey: Prentice Hall, 1963); and James G. March and Johann Olsen, *Ambiguity and Choice in Organizations* (Oslo: Universitatsforlag, 1976).

23.   Norman Krumholz and Janice Cogger, "The Capital Improvements Programming Process in Cleveland: Myth and Reality," paper presented at the 1975 Annual Conference of the American Society of Planning Officials, Chicago, Illinois.

24.   U.S. Bureau of the Census, *Governmental Finances in 1975–76* (Washington, D.C.: Government Printing Office, 1977).

25.   Edward F. Renshaw, "Capital Improvement and Energy Conservation Fund Held a Vital Need," *The Daily Bond Buyer, MFOA Supplement,* May 15, 1978, p. 24.

26.   Joseph F. Zimmerman, *Pragmatic Federalism: The Reassignment of Functional Responsibility* (Washington, D.C.: Advisory Commission on Intergovernmental Relations, July 1976).

27.   Congressional Budget Office, *Advance Budgeting: A Report to Congress* (Washington, D.C.: Government Printing Office, March 1977).

28.   For the classification scheme, see the U.S. Department of Housing and Urban Development's *Community Development Block Grant Program: Second Annual Report* (Washington, D.C.: Government Printing Office, December 1976).

29.   Matson, "Capital Budgeting."

30.   Steiss, *Local Government Finance*. See also the efforts of John Dever, City Manager of Long Beach, California.

31.   George E. Peterson, "Urban Capital Investment Needs and Financing," a current research project of the Urban Institute, Wash., D.C., funded by the U.S. Department of Housing and Urban Development.

32.   White and Douglass, "An Interpretation of Capital Programming."

33.   John E. Petersen, "Jarvis-Gann: What It Is and What It Means," speech given at the 1978 Annual Meeting of the U.S. Conference of Mayors, Atlanta, Georgia, June 1978.

State and Local Government Cash Management Practices

Ronald W. Forbes

Effective and efficient cash management has been a focus of research and application in the public sector for many years. The importance of the cash management function has become increasingly evident as rapid increases in both the levels and volatility of interest rates have highlighted the opportunities for governments to earn income on their investible funds.

The attention placed on economical cash management is based in large part on the fact that cash balances, which may be defined as holdings of currency and demand deposits, are nonearning assets. Some inventories of cash are necessary to meet the needs of nonsynchronous transactions and for precautionary balances. But, cash balances in excess of such transactions and precautionary needs represent nonproductive resources. Higher than necessary holdings of idle cash balances may add to taxpayer burdens in two ways: (1) directly, by requiring added tax revenues to maintain cash inventories; and (2) indirectly, through the foregone earnings from the investment of temporary cash surpluses.

Not infrequently, state and local governments have been criticized for experiencing substantial opportunity costs because of their accumulation of idle balances.[1] With approximately $300 billion in cash flowing through the state and local sector each year and well over $100 billion in operating-fund assets being held at any point in time, the stakes are obviously large.

The day-to-day practice of cash management encompasses four interrelated functions:

- Cash forecasting, or the methods by which future inflows and outflows of cash are estimated;
- Cash mobilization, or the technical arrangements and managerial actions developed to improve the availability or "usability" of cash flows;
- Banking relationships, which include the methods and procedures used to select and compensate financial institutions; and
- Investment strategies, including the selection of instruments used and the portfolio practices followed to achieve returns on surplus cash balances.

These functional operations in cash management are common to all governments and have been subject to discussion and review in a variety of manuals intended for

Ronald W. Forbes is Professor of Finance at the State University of New York at Albany. The author wishes to thank John E. Petersen for his assistance in the preparation of this essay.

users.[2] However, public-sector cash management has certain peculiar characteristics that give its practice a distinctive quality and often hinder the use of the most efficient management practices. The most important distinction is provided by the complex set of regulatory and statutory constraints on how monies may be accounted for, stored, and invested. Because these laws differ among jurisdictions—as do other questions of tradition, policy, size, and sophistication—each state (and often classes of local jurisdictions within states) will exhibit its own cash management problems and solutions.[3]

Most laws that circumscribe public treasury managers can be understood as responses to improper or unethical practices that stimulate attention-getting headlines and public reaction. Typically, the fundamental emphasis in reconciling these perceived problems has been to ensure the safety of taxpayer resources. Not surprisingly, the types of controls legislated to promote safety can create conflicts with standards of economy and efficiency. Thus, research efforts need to be directed to measuring this trade-off and identifying mechanisms by which the safety of public funds can be realized without overly sacrificing efficiency.

Beyond the constraints of safety, cash management is also conditioned by aspects of the political environment that surround governmental jurisdictions. In some instances, governmental cash management can be a stepchild to budgetary practices designed to meet political or programmatic goals. In other instances, cash management is viewed as a technique to apply leverage for social change. Finally, cash management practices can have important direct linkages to debt management and the quality of municipal credit. The timely repayment of municipal debt obligations depends upon the availability of adequate cash resources when needed. Clearly, the conflicting needs of these goals raise problems for public treasury managers, and research in these areas is just beginning.

Cash Forecasting

Cash forecasting is virtually identical in scope, purpose and method to revenue and expenditure estimation, and the techniques applied are similar. An important distinction between cash forecasting and budget estimation is the need to identify, with more precision, the specific timing—by month, week or day—of cash receipts and expenditures. The degree of accuracy in forecasting cash position relates directly to the desired cash inventory. Precise forecasts reduce the need for nonearning buffer stocks, while highly uncertain estimates generally are associated with larger desired cash inventories.

Early models of transactions demand for cash were derived under the implicit assumptions that the information costs required to specify, in detail and with accuracy, the timing of itemized receipts and expenditures were too onerous to be of practical utility. Instead, these models were constructed with a more limited set of assumptions about the processes that generated cash flows.[4] Stated simply, the key assumptions hold that:

o Past patterns (seasonal, etc.) of cash flows are good estimates of future activity levels; and

o Cash flows are stochastic, but the basic parameters—upper and lower bounds—are subject to managerial control. Under the so-called control limit models, then, the need to forecast becomes somewhat less important than the need to identify (1) the upper limits on cash stocks, at which point the opportunity costs from holding additional cash become excessive, and (2) the lower bound beyond which the risks and costs of cash shortages become excessive.

The early models emphasized the goal of minimizing nonearning cash balances, and are useful techniques when transactions costs are high. But, much of the rationale for these approaches has been superseded by technological and other innovations in payments processing. In today's environment, with computerized bookkeeping and electronic funds transfer, and with the availability of instruments such as savings accounts and repurchase agreements, larger governmental units have the mechanisms at hand to achieve zero-balance daily cash management. As a result, the focus for cash forecasting has shifted to the development of longer-term forecasts of cash flows so that more refined investment strategies can be developed to maximize investment earnings.

Cash Mobilization

A good deal of progress has been made in the development of techniques to improve the availability or usability of cash flows. These techniques are rooted in the information and transactions networks under which cash flows are processed and recorded. The application of lock-box systems, concentration accounts, zero-balance disbursement accounts, and wire transfers of funds acts on these networks to speed up the collection and reduce the transaction time for cash managers. An important result is to facilitate the concentration of available cash balances to achieve economies of size. Many transactions costs are "fixed." That is, the costs of processing are the same regardless of the dollar amount of the transaction. Total costs, therefore, depend on the number of transactions. One example is the well-known observation that yields on certificates of deposit and other money market instruments are often scaled upwards for larger denominations.

Mobilizing cash balances to achieve the benefits of more economical size does require a comprehensive and coordinated internal cash management system that may be beyond the needs and capabilities of small governments. Also, outdated practices or statutes can inhibit efficient management practices.

Many state or local laws require localities to marry the bank account system to the fund accounting system and this often leads to a proliferation of bank accounts, each with its own pattern of cash flow over the fiscal year. Dispersal and decentralization of balances often extends to the selection of depository institutions as well and results in a large number of accounts with individually small balances. Fractionalizing overall cash flows in this manner inhibits pooling of cash for investment purposes and restricts the range of investment possibilities to the individual characteristics of the separate funds and accounts.

One recent survey of cash management provides evidence of the widespread practice of decentralized account management. On the average, the more than 200 local governments responding to this survey maintained 21 different demand deposit accounts in more than seven different banking institutions. Average account balances, as a consequence, were relatively small—$121,000, even though aggregate demand deposit balances exceeded $2 million.[5]

Managing Bank Relationships

An important and sometimes central focus for effective cash management is the unit's relationships with the financial system, which include the accounts and all financial services available from commercial banks and other financial institutions.

Bank relationships have often been conditioned by long-standing traditions, sometimes based on political considerations or nonprice-based allocation schemes. Statutes in many states require deposits to be prorated among all eligible intermediaries regardless of cost or service, with laws that prescribe the eligibility of institutions by geographic location and size. In some instances, prices (e.g., interest rates on time deposits) are even legislated outside the marketplace.[6]

With standard economic analysis, it is easy to point out that the effects of these statutes and practices are to inhibit competition among depositories and to raise the costs of treasury management. However, devising empirical measures of the foregone earnings opportunities is difficult, and the topic remains a fruitful area for future research.

There are case studies of the remarkable improvements in cash management that can follow from restructuring of municipal banking relationships, and many state and local governments have coupled the revision of accounts systems with new practices in the selection of bank depositories. Perhaps the leading development is the increasing use of formal competitive bids to select financial institutions for "one stop" financial services.[7]

Competitive bidding is often required by state law in the sale of general-obligation debt issues and in the purchase of other goods and services. The advantages are well-known. Inviting or soliciting tenders for banking services can, in a competitive marketplace, result in objective criteria for selecting institutions with the lowest price. There are, however, unresolved issues in the practice of competitive bidding.

Banks can offer, and municipalities request, "packages" of financial services. These packages are sometimes difficult to "unbundle" and price on an individual basis. The result is that nominal price quotations for bank services can span a very wide range. In fact, the price dispersion may be misleading—it can stem from the fact that banks are offering quite different packages of services. Therefore, governmental units must provide a very precise specification of the financial services desired in order to be sure that quoted costs cover essentially similar products.

Review of practice also suggests other problem areas in implementing competitive bids. Most governmental units are simultaneously lenders of funds to banks, consumers of financial services and, sometimes, borrowers. The costs of transactions services, such as deposit or check processing, can be measured and quoted on a unit basis; fixed-price bids for these services present no more difficulties in evaluation than bids for other types of goods or services. However, municipalities also borrow from and lend (e.g., deposit) funds to banks, and the level of these loan and deposit balances will vary over the contract length. The value or cost to the bank also can be expected to vary daily as interest rates change. Because of volatility in borrowing and lending rates, it is not practical to achieve a "fixed cost" contract for all future financial services. Instead, "benchmarks" are used whereby quoted time deposit rates will be linked in advance to specific money market rates such as the 90-day treasury bill rate or the federal funds rate. Since different banks may peg borrowing or lending rates to different market rates, the municipal finance officer is forced to become a student of interest rates and yield spreads on different instruments. Moreover, integrating loan and deposit quotes with transaction services to measure the lowest net cost is an exceedingly difficult task.

Because of the complexity and the need to design standard specifications for bids, more research needs to be carried out on effective methods for implementing proposals for competitive bids on bank services.

Pooling Idle Funds

A leading innovation in the investment practices of local governments has been the creation of statewide investment pools that centrally collect the idle funds of local units into large aggregations of investible funds. These pools, acting as intermediaries in the public sector, then invest funds with greater efficiency and sophistication than would be possible at the local level. Also, they may provide ancillary services, such as overcoming local investment restrictions and assisting in cash management and accounting systems.[8]

Local government investment pools are very recent additions to the arsenal of tools and instruments available for the municipal treasurer. The first states to implement the pool concept were Connecticut and Montana in 1973. Oregon, Illinois and Wisconsin followed suit in 1974 and 1975; in 1977, pools began operating in California, Florida, and Massachusetts; and New Jersey is about to implement its Local Government Pool.

The specific modes of operation of these investment pools differ somewhat among states, but all pools share a common objective and that is to provide local govern-

56

ments with the opportunity to commingle their cash balances for investment purposes on a voluntary basis and to realize certain economies of scale.

The concepts that underlie the success of government investment pools are not new, and certain attributes are shared with other existing institutions. All pools allow participants a wide degree of latitude in selecting the amounts and the length of time that funds will be placed in the pool. Pools also offer potential economies of scale in investment management by combining individually small sums into a larger common pool of available cash. And the resources of the pool also permit funds to be diversified over a wider range of investments than may be possible for individual participants.

These attributes—ready divisibility, optional investment maturities, economies of scale, and diversification—describe the services performed by other institutions commonly referred to as financial intermediaries, and local government pools are appropriately viewed as a form of state financial intermediation.

Local government investment pools do represent viable alternatives for the very small municipality that is constrained by small size, inexperienced management, and unfortunate regulations (Regulation Q) that discriminate against the earning power of its funds. For larger municipalities, however, the long-run attractiveness of an investment pool depends upon the ability of the pool to achieve consistently higher returns than other investments.

There are some important policy issues raised by local government investment pools, and two of these issues will be discussed. The first relates to the technical operation of a pool—specifically its asset maturity structure, holding periods of participants and valuation methods. The second issue relates to investment policy and the impact on local credit markets, a matter to which we will return shortly.

For many governmental units, pool participations are likely to be substitutes for time or savings deposits or repurchase agreements with local banking institutions. There are some important differences between an investment in a pool and the purchase of a bank certificate of deposit (CD) or time deposit. The CD rate is stated at the time of purchase, and the return is sure as long as the CD is held to maturity. On the other hand, the effective earnings rate on a pool is not known in advance and cannot be determined prior to the withdrawal of funds by a participant. This uncertainty may preclude governmental units from participating, at least in the initial stages of a pool's operations. On the other hand, pools that continue to achieve a consistent pattern of investment returns higher than local bank rates will very likely experience continued growth in local unit participations.

One key to the investment performance record is the relationship between pool asset maturities and cyclical interest rate patterns. In periods of low market rates, the need to demonstrate favorable returns may encourage investment managers to reach out on the yield curve for longer maturities and higher returns. But, during periods of very rapidly rising interest rates, these long maturities will suffer the greatest decline in value and thereby retard the return on pool participations relative to short-term market rates. It is conceivable that monthly pool returns could fall below quoted CD rates, and this adds another element of uncertainty—namely, that local units could withdraw funds in such volume that the pool would be forced to liquidate investments at a loss.

This risk further points up the close analogy between pools and other financial intermediaries. Banks, for example, experience withdrawals when the market rate exceeds the deposit rate, a phenomenon labeled "disintermediation." Because pools offer withdrawal privileges on demand, the possibility of disintermediation requires investment managers to adopt conservative policies regarding the maturity profile of assets. This, in turn, suggests that pools may not always achieve the returns otherwise available on alternative assets for those governmental units that desire to invest in instruments with longer maturities.

An important consideration in developing appropriate strategies for investment maturities is the stability of the overall level of participations. As noted earlier, participations in pools are basically similar to interest-bearing demand deposits and can be withdrawn at any time. Therefore, investment maturities have to be developed in the context of potential liquidity demands. Important in analyzing these demands is the seasonal pattern of cash flows for local governments. In most states, major inflows of cash receipts, such as property taxes, are very lumpy—these revenues are collected within a short period and most units of the same class (e.g. towns, cities) receive collections over the same period. If the cash-flow patterns of different governmental units are highly intercorrelated with each other, then the volume of participations is likely to be volatile over the fiscal year with major inflows in some months and major outflows in other months. Under these circumstances, investment maturities have to be scheduled according to the general cash-flow patterns of local participants. Since state aid is a major revenue source for many units, it may make sense to consider merging state cash flows with local cash flows in a common investment pool. This may promote a more stable investment base and, concomitantly, reduce potential liquidity demands on the pool's operations.[9]

In view of the expanding use of investment pools and the need to maximize returns at all levels of government, empirical research into the operations of pools is an important and promising field.

Socioeconomic Returns Versus Yields

The growth of local government investment pools has also raised anew the debate over the supposed advantages of "keeping the money at home" versus investing for the highest direct yield. Investment yields represent the conventional guides to treasury managers to measure objectively the dollars contributed to governmental revenues from cash management.

But there is an alternative view which holds that the use of cash balances has secondary effects that indirectly influence the returns to the local economy and government. As this line of reasoning goes, government funds placed in investments that finance local projects contribute directly to the growth in incomes of residents. This growth in income thereby contributes to the tax base. Other investments in the national money market instruments, say U.S. Treasury bills, take funds out of the state, and thereby reduce the amount of credit available for state residents and retard overall economic growth within the state. This ultimately reduces spending, incomes and the tax base. Accordingly, this view holds that the appropriate measure for treasury managers is total return, defined as the stated yield from an investment *plus* the incremental change in government revenues induced by these investments.[10]

Studies have attempted to measure the relationship between permanent injections of public deposits, the deposit expansion multiplier, and the income and tax revenue effects that finally flow from the incremental deposits.[11] However, review of these studies suggests that the requirements necessary to track this process are beyond the capacities and resources of existing data.

Income and other resources in a state are the result of demands for goods and services produced for state residents and out-of-state residents. Incomes and spending patterns of state residents also generate demands for in-state and out-of-state goods and services. Government revenues and expenditures similarly place demands on and supply resources for local and out-of-state goods and services. Each of the countless individual transactions generates flows of funds through local and non-local financial institutions.

The overall concern of the policy debate is with one significant but nevertheless small proportion of these total transactions and that is the *temporary* cash balances created by government spending patterns. Even if one accepts that public deposits can add to local credit availability, particular forms of that credit have a tremendous variety of influences on aggregate income.[12]

Establishing a precise and direct link between specific deposit accounts and the uses of the funds from those accounts is difficult. Indeed, most bankers do not themselves operate on such a basis. At best, research can indicate general patterns of response and these will, presumably, depend upon the manner in which innovations such as investment pools alter the size and timing of public deposits in individual institutions.

Assuming, for the moment, that some institutions experience declines in their deposit base, there are a number of possible asset reallocations that could be hypothesized. Under one view, for example, banks may respond to losses of volatile public deposits by reducing short-term investment securities, say U.S. Treasury bills. In this event, there is little impact on local credit availability. As an opposing hypothesis, the loss of public funds may occasion less lending in all loan categories. It is necessary to determine whether either of these (or other) responses have been experienced in order to evaluate the impact of pooling on local credit availability.

The substantial variability in public-unit cash balances is believed by many to force commercial banks and other depository institutions to match relatively short-lived deposits with equally short-term, highly liquid assets.[13] This view is based on observations of the uneven time patterns and the lack of synchronization of government revenues and expenditures. Many government units have large inflows of revenues concentrated in relatively short periods of time, such as around tax payment dates. These large inflows generate temporary surplus funds that are drawn down over subsequent months. Depository institutions plan their asset holdings to meet these probable outflows.

It is important to recognize that the variability of cash balances for any individual governmental unit may *not* translate into equally variable balances for depository institutions. Individual financial institutions may have a number of different public deposits, and the high point in one public unit's accounts may be the low point for another public unit. Individual accounts may fluctuate greatly, but overall, total public deposits may be reasonably stable. Moreover, public receipts and expenditures do generate offsetting transactions in private accounts. Tax payments, for example, can be viewed as a transfer of funds from a private account to a public deposit.

As another dimension to the "keep the money home" debate, it is sometimes alleged that banks provide many "free" services to local governments and these services will be reduced or become more costly if public units withdraw funds and seek higher returns elsewhere.[14]

Services provided by banks are not "free." Indeed, these so-called "free" services are in fact paid for with deposit balances which enable banks to generate loan and investment revenues. The use of deposits as a form of compensation for services does disguise the cost of these services and does inhibit cost comparisons between banks. If deposit balances were just at the level necessary to compensate banks for the services provided, then the withdrawal of these balances would indeed raise the cost or reduce the availability of services to local governments. However, governmental units will assess the potential added revenues from outside investments and weigh these benefits against the added costs of banking services. As a result, such investment alternatives may promote more explicit pricing for banking services and banks may even offer more services.

Borrowing and Cash Management

Borrowing capacity and cash management have become even more closely linked in the 1970s. The aggressive management of public funds for investment returns stimulated some public units to trade on borrowing capacity for arbitrage opportunities in the early 1970s. Borrowing at a low tax-exempt rate and relending the proceeds at a higher "taxable" interest rate does offer the allure of "free" resources for public treasurers. However, the added supply of new debt for such purposes, left unchecked, can escalate all borrowing costs, and recent research on these supply factors has demonstrated that this impact can be significant.[15] Nevertheless, the continuing revised and updated arbitrage regulations by the Internal Revenue Service illustrate the incentives that profitable arbitrage opportunities can present.

There has been a growing recognition that liquidity management and long-term credit capacity are closely associated. For many governmental units in some periods of the fiscal year, shortfalls in cash inflows relative to expenditure needs due to tax cycle or grant payments require access to the credit market for liquidity or "bridge" financing. These working capital loans are generally designed to be retired within the fiscal year from normal operating revenues.

For some governmental units, however, these bridge loans bulk large relative to total revenues and this raises the risk that future revenues may fall short of expectations, thereby endangering all contractual obligations. In New York State, this problem is compounded. The state has to borrow a large fraction (approximately 40 percent) of its revenues early in its fiscal year. These borrowings are used primarily for state aid payments to localities. But the timing of these payments is late in the local fiscal year, and therefore, localities are required to bridge finance these expected aid payments to meet their cash needs. The result is that local government credit quality has become closely linked with the riskiness of the state's spring borrowings.[16]

Continued research on cash management in government can promote further gains in efficiency, but equally important, this research can continue to explore the interrelationships of cash management with other governmental decision processes.

Notes

1. For studies of state and local idle funds that noted the sector's large balances, see: Advisory Commission on Intergovernmental Relations, *Investment of Idle Cash Balances by State and Local Governments* (Washington, D.C.: Government Printing Office, January 1961), and *Supplement* (January 1965); J. Richard Aronson, "The Idle Balances of State and Local Governments: An Economic Analysis of National Concern," *Journal of Finance* (June 1968); and Rita Moldonado and Lawrence Ritter, "Optimal Municipal Cash Management: A Case Study," *The Review of Economics and Statistics* (November 1971).

2. There are several recent publications that provide guidance to state and local officials in day-to-day cash management techniques, including: John Jones and Kenneth Howard, *Investment of Idle Funds by Local Governments: A Primer* (Chicago: Municipal Finance Officers Association, 1973); and Frank Patitucci and Michael Lichtenstein, *Improving Cash Management in Local Government: A Comprehensive Approach* (Chicago: Municipal Finance Officers Association, 1977).

3. For an overview, see Advisory Commission on Intergovernmental Relations, *Understanding State and Local Cash Management*, Report M-112 (Washington, D.C.: Government Printing Office, May 1977).
    The variety of state and local cash management practices can be observed in such recent studies as: Eileen Anderson, "Study and Evaluation of the Cash Management Programs of the State of Hawaii," mimeographed, State of Hawaii, Department of Budget and Finance, May 1977; Merlin Hackbart and Robert Johnson, *State Cash Management Policy* (Lexington, Kentucky: Council of State Governments, 1975); John Laezza, "Investing Municipal Funds in New Jersey, Final Report," (Trenton: Office of Public Information, New Jersey Department of Community Affairs, February 1976); and John P. Hamilton, "Short-Term Surplus Funds Management for the State of Texas, Final Report," (Austin, Texas: LBJ School, January 1977).

4. For examples of the type and range of transaction models for cash management see: William J. Baumol, "The Transactions Demand for Cash: An Inventory Theoretic Approach," *Quarterly Journal of Economics* 65 (November 1952), pp. 545–56; Robert F. Calman, *Linear Programming and Cash Management/CASH ALPHA* (Cambridge, Massachusetts: The M.I.T. Press, 1968); Daniel Orr, *Cash Management and the Demand for Money* (New York: Frederick A. Praeger, Inc., 1970); and Bernall K. Stone, "Allocating Credit Lines, Planned Borrowing,

and Tangible Services Over a Company's Banking System,'' *Financial Management* 2 (Summer 1975), pp. 65–78.

5.   ACIR, *Understanding State and Local Cash Management,* Chapter 5.

6.   Ibid., Chapter 3.

7.   Ronald W. Forbes, ''Selecting Banking Services and Banks: A Guide for Municipal Finance Officers,'' mimeographed, Government Finance Research Center, Municipal Finance Officers Association, Washington, D.C., May 1978.

8.   See ACIR *Understanding State and Local Cash Management,* Chapter 4; Council of State Governments, *Investing State Funds: The Wisconsin Investment Board* (Lexington, Kentucky: Council of State Governments, May 1976); and Ronald W. Forbes, ''A Review of Local Government Investment Pools,'' mimeographed, Government Finance Research Center, Municipal Finance Officers Association, Washington, D.C., May 1978.

9.   Wisconsin, for example, offers to hold its local governments' assistance payments in that state's investment pool until they wish to take down the cash. All investments are managed by a common agency, and state and local unit short-term funds are kept in a common fund. See Council of State Governments, *Investing State Funds.*

10.   For a description of and an attempt to reconcile these two objectives of investment return, see Donald G. Simonson, ''Funds Management by State Treasurers: Direct v. Socio-Economic Returns,'' mimeographed, Albuquerque, New Mexico, October 1977.

11.   L. Wayne Dobson, ''A Note on the Alternative Uses and Yields of Idle Public Funds,'' *National Tax Journal* (September 1968); Jerry Hollenhurst, ''Alternative Uses and Yields of Public Funds, Comment,'' *National Tax Journal* (December 1969); and R. J. Monsen and Garth Mangrum, ''Alternative Investment Outlets for Idle State Operating Funds,'' *State Government* (Summer 1963).

12.   A new car loan, for example, does provide the borrower with one means for obtaining transportation services and may lead to better income opportunities. It also generates a car sale, but here most of the proceeds will accrue to an out-of-state (or foreign) car manufacturer. The net income in this first round is only the dealer's markup. These effects are undoubtedly less significant than a business loan to a small new enterprise or a mortgage loan to finance a new housing start. And these latter examples of credit flows are probably more ''productive'' in generating new incomes, jobs, and spending than loans for the exchange of existing facilities.

13.   For a discussion of the volatility of public funds and its impact on bank behavior, see Advisory Commission on Intergovernmental Relations, *The Impact of Increased Insurance on Public Deposits,* a study prepared for the United States Senate, Committee on Banking, Housing and Urban Affairs (Washington, D.C.: Government Printing Office, 1977).

14.   Ibid.

15.   See, relative to estimates of the interest rate effects of the increased supply of municipal bonds due to arbitrage, Patric Hendershott and David S. Kidwell, ''The Impact of Advanced Refunding Bond Issues on State and Local Borrowing Costs,'' *National Tax Journal* (March 1978).

16.   Ronald W. Forbes, Louise Flynn, and Todd Whitestone, ''Annual Rites of Spring: Short-Term Borrowing by New York State,'' *The Daily Bond Buyer* (October 1977).

State and Local Government Debt Policy and Management

John E. Petersen

Recent research in state and local government debt policy and management has been heavily influenced by the New York fiscal crisis and its impact on the municipal securities market.[1] Many concerns transcending debt policy and practices were at hand in the crisis, such as the burdens of government in declining economies, the use of dubious fiscal management procedures, and the impenetrability of municipal financial reporting practices. But it was in the securities market that the drama was played out most vividly and the worries about the fiscal condition of cities, states and regions found sharpest definition through the prices placed on their securities.

New York City's difficulty in the securities market and the splash effects that engulfed other governmental borrowers at the time underscored the importance of the market to the formulation of debt policy by state and local governments. The municipal securities market has always received a large amount of attention from researchers because of its size and complexity and the fact that mountains of dollars and cents data lend themselves to the tools of economic analysis. In practice, much capital investment planning and most debt policy formulation are necessarily tethered to the realities of the municipal bond market. Expenditures may be greatly desired and genuinely innovative, but the ultimate question frequently controlling their realization is: "Can we borrow this much for this purpose?" Although the market has its limitations, it functions daily as a price allocative mechanism in the classical sense. And while issuers may, from time-to-time, be able to view it as a virtually inexhaustible source of low-cost, long-term capital, there are limits that act as a check on the amount of borrowing a unit can do.

The New York fiscal crisis and the related wide spread concerns over state and local government fiscal condition reinforced some familiar strains in debt analysis— the limits of debt capacity, the determination of risk premiums, and the probity of credit analysis. It also introduced some new areas of research: investor information needs, disclosure methods, and fiscal condition indicators. Meanwhile, certain other topics, such as those dealing with the structure of investor demand, the efficiency of tax exemption, various technical innovations in the design and marketing of debt instruments and new types and uses of borrowing continue to be the subject of research.

John E. Petersen is the Director of the Government Finance Research Center of the Municipal Finance Officers Association.

Overall and in keeping with the moods of recent times, debt policy analysis took on a practical bent: It focused primarily on improving the efficiency of existing machinery used in the marketing of debt, rather than projecting future capital needs and spinning out theories of the optimum amount or use of debt. Events and changes had occurred so rapidly that practitioners and researchers alike were more concerned in finding out where they were rather than speculating on where they might be heading. Therefore, analysis has tended to be policy- and user-oriented and to manifest growing awareness of the increasing budget constraints placed upon state and local borrowers.

In this essay, there will be an explicit recognition of the centrality of the municipal bond market and its behavior to the research now underway in state and local debt policy and management. Initially, use will be made of the familiar components of demand and supply analysis, with a review of that research dealing primarily with the structure and operation of the municipal bond market. Next, there will be a review of certain types of borrowers that have received special attention and then a discussion of research aimed essentially at determining credit quality and debt capacity. Clearly allied to these concerns are the new questions involving investor needs for information and disclosure.

After a brief review of work regarding various restrictions and controls in the municipal bond market, new types of instruments and innovations in the techniques of designing and issuing securities will be considered.

Finally, this review will include a section dealing with overall efficiency and equity considerations in the tax-exempt municipal bond market and various proposals for its restructuring and reform. The essay will conclude with some observations on major trends in debt policy and practices and suggest areas where further study is needed.

Structure and Operation of the Market

The structure and operation of the municipal bond market are different from those of other financial markets not only because of the special nature of the borrowers, but also because of the exemption of the interest income received by investors from the federal income tax. Because of tax exemption, state and local governments borrow at lower rates of interest and the market structure takes on a peculiar configuration of individual and institutional investors seeking shelter for their income. Much research has been devoted to explaining how the municipal market behaves under these circumstances and the consequences of such behavior in terms of the cost and availability of capital to governmental borrowers. Overviews of the market structure and its behavior have sometimes led to extensive policy recommendations designed to broaden the market and improve its efficiency.[2] Frequently, such analysis has been the basis of specific proposals to supplement (and, sometimes, to replace) the conventional tax-exempt market with alternative sources of borrowed funds, a point to which we shall return later.

Whatever the particular policy conclusions of the study, there have been numerous attempts to model the behavior of the municipal securities market, usually combining both the demand for credit and supply of funds to determine the rate and amount of borrowing. Models, of course, vary in detail, but more sophisticated versions take into consideration the interrelationship between the municipal bond market and other financial markets. A common finding has been that municipal bond rates of interest exhibit great volatility—rising faster than rates rise in other financial markets and, correspondingly, dropping more rapidly. In part, these responses are caused by the tax treatment afforded capital gains. These fluctuations have also been associated with changes in the composition of investors in municipal securities.[3]

Demand for municipal securities is dominated by three major sets of investors: commercial banks, fire and casualty insurance companies, and the household sector. The major institutional investors in tax-exempt securities through the 1960's into the early 1970's were commercial banks. While strong bank demand led to lower interest

63

rates in the municipal market (in relationship to those found in the taxable securities market), fluctuations in tax-exempt interest rates were closely associated with the changing investment demand of commercial banks. In the early 1970's, bank demand for municipal securities waivered and researchers worried about a secular decline in bank support as these institutional investors, particularly the larger ones, found other tax shelters and began to place more emphasis on liquidity in their portfolios.[4]

A common assumption, given the evident insensitivity of bank demand to rates of return on tax-exempts versus other investments, was that bank investment was largely determined by the residual availability of funds after loan demands had been met and liquidity kept at a desirable level through other investments. This amounted to saying that demand in the municipal bond market was segmented and that banks did not act continuously as arbitrageurs between the tax-exempt and taxable market. This explanation of bank investment behavior has been challenged by attempts to apply profit-maximizing models, but research to date gives no clear decision on which model of behavior is most appropriate.[5] What is obvious is that bank demand for municipal securities has undergone change and become less overwhelming as a market factor.

Other major investor groups—fire and casualty companies and the household sector—have attracted much less study. It would appear that fire and casualty insurance company investment depends largely upon their profit positions. Research into the behavior of the household sector, which contains both individual investors and certain institutional investors, has been thwarted because of the lack of data. However, it does appear that the recent creation of the municipal bond funds has helped to broaden the market and has mobilized individual investors in municipal securities.[6] A question of major research interest is what will be the behavior of mutual funds when market prices begin to deteriorate as rates rise: If individual investors choose to redeem their fund shares, and new buyers are not found, it could have a depressing effect on the market.

The supply of municipal bonds is usually seen as being determined primarily by the real capital needs of state and local governments. New borrowing can be, of course, influenced by the level of interest rates, the availability of alternative sources of funds, and the activities of state and local governments as financial intermediaries. In particular, it has been well established that state and local borrowing and capital outlays are sensitive to changes in interest rates, particularly in the timing of their bond sales.[7] But it has been observed that the relationship between capital outlays and the supply of municipal bonds has weakened over the recent past as state and local governments have found alternative sources of funds, especially federal grants.[8] Furthermore, state and local governments have become active as financial intermediaries so that much of their borrowing is done for purposes other than supporting their own outlays.[9]

Another complicating—and complicated—factor is the opportunity of issuers to refinance outstanding debt when rates of interest decline or original financing arrangements must be redesigned. This may be done through call provisions but one particular approach—advanced refunding—has been the subject of considerable controversy and study. Inducements to refinance are also enhanced by the possibility that governments and others may arbitrage by borrowing at tax-exempt rates while investing in taxable returns.[10]

The composition of state and local capital outlays and, accordingly, borrowing has changed dramatically. Bonds sold to finance the construction and acquisition of traditional governmental facilities are now less important in the market. This change is attributable to slower population growth (and its lessening mobility), the changing demographics of the population, and the transfer of certain capital spending responsibilities to the private sector.[11] As we discuss below in greater detail, new uses for tax exemption have diminished the relative importance of borrowing that is done for purposes of financing capital outlays by the governments themselves, as opposed to borrowing as financial intermediaries on behalf of others.

Problem Borrowers

The financial crisis of New York City and the consequent disruptions in the municipal bond market in 1975 and early 1976 were dramatic evidence of a long-standing concern, that of the continued access of certain types of borrowers to the market. Until recently, many state and local governments might have been faced with fiscal stresses, but they had not had any great difficulty in capital financing. This observation is borne out by the convergence of interest rates among different grades and types of borrowers—a shrinking of risk premiums. [12]

However, the market disturbances of 1975 drastically changed the situation. It became readily evident that the market place, responding to new fears regarding state and local financial condition and its consequences for the repayment of debt, was inclined to charge much higher risk premiums and in some cases not lend at all. [13] These impacts were particularly great in the case of the older cities and those regions in the Northeast part of the country, where debt burdens had been increasing and bond ratings had been falling, in contrast with the younger cities and sunnier climes. [14] Recent research has shown that cities found their market acceptance to be highly correlated to their location, level of unemployment, and unfunded pension liabilities. As bond market conditions improved through 1975 and 1976 and the financial circumstances of cities and states proved to be less perilous than earlier perceived, these jurisdictions typically found it easier to borrow, although there remained large differences in borrowing costs among individual units. [15]

Of continuing interest has been the access of small, local government borrowers to the municipal bond market. Analysis has shown that smaller units pay higher costs per dollar borrowed both in terms of interest rates and the costs of marketing expenses. In part, the higher costs are associated with diseconomies of scale. Other factors contributing to the higher costs include lower (or no) credit ratings and a lesser degree of competition among underwriters, resulting ultimately in less investor interest. [16]

Numerous aids for the small issuer problem have been suggested—ranging from technical assistance to state credit programs. The more popular concepts appear to be those of a state bond bank and the use of insurance programs, both public and private. [17] Akin to the small borrower problem has been the analysis of market structure and the existence of regional markets for local issuers. Research indicates that small issuers tend to have markets primarily in their own backyard with local institutions and individuals. The geographic limits of the small-issue market tends to make it more sensitive to the relative supply of securities in the immediate region. [18]

Types of Instruments and Purposes for Borrowing

In recent years, the municipal bond market has shown an important change in the types of securities offered, with the expansion of the limited obligation and revenue bond securities. Several factors account for the growth of these nonguaranteed securities, as they are often known, including the existence of restrictions on the issuance of the general obligation (tax-supported) security, expansion of the concept of public purpose, and changing definitions of securities recognized as being those of "governmental" entitites. Of particular note has been the rapid growth in new forms of industrial revenue bonds, the proceeds of which are used to finance facilities that are used by private parties. Research has focused on the pollution control bond and its effects on the market and effectiveness as a subsidy. The additional pressures on the market generated by the sale of these bonds increase interest rates for other state and local borrowers. Furthermore, the benefits of such financing must be shared between the intended beneficiary, the firm, and unintended beneficiaries, namely, all investors in tax-exempt securities. [19]

The same arguments regarding pressure on the market hold for other nontraditional uses of tax-exempt borrowing, such as the financing of power facilities, hospitals, and stadiums. One area that has become particularly dependent upon the use of tax-exempt borrowing is housing construction—either directly through housing projects or by purchases of mortgages originated by private lenders. In this area, in particular, tax-exempt instruments have been designed to supplement various federal assistance and guarantee programs. State housing agencies tend to be very highly leveraged, with practically all bond sale proceeds going to the support of programs and with little or no equity capital supplied. To reduce the risk to investors while steering clear of various restrictions and requirements on the use of general credit, several ingenious types of securities have been employed. The most notable of these was the moral obligation bond, the distinguishing feature of which was a government's backing of debt with a "moral obligation," but not a legally binding promise, to make up any deficiencies in debt service.[20]

In the wake of the default of the Urban Development Corporation, New York State and other states moved rapidly to reconsider the advisability of such contingent liabilities and to tighten the degree of public control over the indebtedness being incurred by various special purpose authorities. Research into the growth of these entities and their consequences for the debt markets led to a series of reforms to better control the debt-creating capacities of these special authorities. Several states undertook general assessments of their debt capacity and policies in hopes of avoiding the catastrophe that befell New York State, and almost several others, in the crisis conditions of 1975.[21]

Another casualty of the New York fiscal crisis was the rapid growth of short-term borrowing that occurred in the late 1960's and early 1970's. In fact, it was New York City's inability to refinance a large floating debt that had accumulated over the years that set off the near panic in the financial markets. Short-term borrowing (debt of original maturity of less than a year) had been most heavily used by New York State and its jurisdictions. But other state and local borrowers also contributed to the rapid increase in volume of short-term debt.

Research has been aimed at analyzing the varieties of short-term borrowing that had grown up and, in particular, the relationship between the use of short-term borrowing and irregularities in cash flows caused by tax cycles and the receipt of state and federal aid payments. Clearly, a heavy reliance on short-term borrowing can lead governments to a dangerous illiquidity.[22] This phenomenon of amassing large amounts of floating, short-term debt was not new; it had occurred in the 1930's and was a leading cause of default in that earlier period.[23] As a result of the strains of 1975, state and local governments rushed (and were pushed) to convert their short-term debt into longer-term obligations. As a result, the volume of short-term borrowing has dropped sharply.

Debt Restrictions and Controls

There has been a renewal of interest in the various techniques of controlling borrowing and a reexamination of the effectiveness of restrictions placed on debt creation. Ironically, much of the "uncontrolled" debt expansion that had occurred in the post-World War II period had been fomented by the existence of restrictions that had made traditional borrowing either impractical or politically distasteful. The flowering of new uses of borrowing and the wide assortment of new instruments to accomplish the expanded notions of public purpose took place outside of the traditional restrictions on the amount of debt outstanding and public referendum requirements. As a result, local governments have encountered a market that has become increasingly complex and makes heavier professional demands upon the would-be borrower.

Correspondingly, interest has grown in how states can better monitor the financial conditions and affairs of their local jurisdications and provide meaningful assistance to, if not direct regulation of, the local government borrowing process. Research indicates that where such activities are pursued with vigor and professionalism, there appear to be substantial benefits to be reaped in terms of savings for local jurisdictions.[24] Despite the obvious interest, there remains to be seen substantial progress on this front and research is needed dealing with those techniques that are most successful under the variety of political conditions and relationships found among the states and their progeny.

Credit Analysis

The events of 1975 awakened municipal credit analysis from a long slumber. For years, the analysis of municipal securities (and governmental financial condition) had been dominated by the two rating agencies—Moody's and Standard and Poor's. Techniques of analysis were slow to change because of a lack of measurable default risk, the subdued and systematic volatility in municipal bond prices (which lessen the economic inducement to analysis), and the paucity of readily comparable and up-to-date information concerning the finances and economies of borrowers. As a result, analysis tended to focus on a few straight-forward traditional measures of debt burden and eschew more sophisticated techniques of financial analysis and forecasting.[25]

As a result of the disruptions of 1975 and the looming possibility of defaults or major losses in market value, interest in municipal credit analysis accelerated. There was increased emphasis on discovering the financial condition of borrowers, especially their cash flows, short-term debt, and pension liabilities. Taking a longer view, interest was also stimulated in exploring the relationships between the basic economic setting and the financial results and conditions of units. Analytical models have been devised in an attempt to better integrate immediate financial results with the longer-term trends in local economies.[26] But institutional factors, such as the quality of financial management and the political environment, while difficult to quantify, also need to receive increasing emphasis.[27] The position of the bond rating agencies remains dominant, but it is clear that more investors seek to perform their own analysis of credit quality. Unfortunately, the task is becoming increasingly difficult because of the complexity of many debt issues.

Credit Information and Disclosure

Assessment of credit quality is only possible if reliable, timely, and complete information is provided to investors. The veracity of this observation has been reinforced by the belated recognition that there are legal requirements under the antifraud provisions of the federal securities laws.[28] These suddenly became important in 1975. Amid great uncertainty as to credit quality and alarms for federal regulation, research set out on some uncharted paths involving disclosure needs and responsibilities. The initial effort was part of the Municipal Finance Officers Association (MFOA) Credit Information and Quality Project and led to the MFOA *Disclosure Guidelines*, a guide to recommended information practices to be followed by issuers in conjunction with the sale of their securities.[29] A large volume of analytical and interpretive studies have followed, seeking to measure the level of disclosure, to affix disclosure responsibilities among municipal bond market participants, and to design procedures appropriate to that particular market.[30]

Another important aspect of the disclosure question has been investigation of exactly what information investors use in making their decisions. Surveys indicate that investors may have a limited capacity to absorb such information given existing analytical techniques. Information pertaining directly to debt and debt burden, the traditional measures, and to financial operating performance tend to be the most important items to investors.[31] Progress in the field of credit analysis will depend on the ready availability of the right information. Furthermore, such analysis constitutes only one use of information that may be gathered under the general heading of economic and financial indicators, an area of research that has seen explosive growth in recent years.[32]

Some Technical Innovations

A peculiarity of the municipal bond market has been the method by which bonds are awarded at competitive sale on the basis of a simple interest concept (net interest cost). Such a procedure can lead to distortions in the pricing of securities and market inefficiencies that mean higher interest costs for issuers when calculations are correctly performed using discounted values. Building on pioneering but largely unheeded efforts of others, the Center for Capital Market Research at the University of Oregon has carried on research and waged an increasingly successful campaign to convert issuers to improved bidding practices that incorporate present value concepts.[33]

Other innovative work has dealt with ways to "immobilize" municipal securities, which typically are bearer form, have the physical dimensions of a bedspread, and are expensive to print, house, and ship. However, because of the large number of bonds outstanding and the technical and legal difficulties, actual implementation of centralized storage and book-entry trading techniques appears to be in the distant future.[34]

Ways of Broadening the Market

Much of the research in municipal debt has involved studies of how the market might be changed to improve the efficiency of tax exemption as an implicit subsidy to state and local borrowers or to meet the needs in high priority program areas.[35] Aside from generating a large body of literature dealing with the structure and operations of the market, such efforts have also been the source of much controversy. The general drift of the argument is that tax exemption represents an inefficient form of subsidy because part of the federal tax revenues forgone must be shared with investors and are not captured in their entirety by state and local borrowers in the form of lower interest rates. This feature is also seen as contributing to tax inequities by some since its erodes the comprehensiveness of the federal income tax and dilutes the progressivity of the personal income tax in particular. Last, the present dependency of the market upon certain investor groups and certain peculiarities arising from the tax treatment of capital gains and losses on the tax-exempt security are seen as causing excessive volatility in tax-exempt interest rates and flows of credit in that market. Generally, cures to these problems would be found, it is argued, if the total supply of tax-exempt securities could be reduced, easing the pressure on that market and increasing the scarcity value of the tax shelter it embodies.

Over the years, several proposals have been made to meet these criticisms of tax exemption.[36] The most important two concepts that have been advanced are the taxable bond option (TBO), which would subsidize state and local governments that elected to sell their securities on a taxable basis, and the creation of a federal financial intermediary (URBANK) that would make loans to governments. In both cases, the desired outcome would be to lessen reliance of state and local borrowers on the tax-exempt market, thereby reducing the supply of tax-exempt securities and increasing the efficiency of tax exemption. The essential difference between the TBO and URBANK approaches is that the former, in theory, would work through the existing private market mechanism with individual issuers selling their bonds directly to the market, whereas a financing bank would mean a new institution that would supplant individual issues with its own agency's securities.

Both the federal bank concept and the TBO have been attacked on grounds of potential political interference and practical difficulties in administration. By and large, the TBO, because of its greater operational simplicity and reliance on existing market channels, has found greater favor, but not enough to secure its passage into law.[37] Recently, several of the arguments made on behalf of the TBO's contribution to both market efficiency and tax equity have been challenged.[38] There continues to be a preference to leave the tax-exempt bond market alone and to provide what special help might be needed through tax preferences and special-purpose guarantee programs.

Another characteristic of the municipal bond market has been the exclusion of commercial banks from the underwriting of state and local revenue bonds under the existing banking laws, a situation that banks and their supporters contend limits competition for municipal bonds. As in the case of other research aimed at defending or overturning existing practices, research on this issue has made several important contributions, particularly in the understanding of the determinants of borrowing costs and the structure and operation of the market.

An important outgrowth of the studies has been the examination of the degree of competition in the underwriting for municipal securities and its impact on both reoffering yields and the cost of borrowing.[39] Generally, the findings are that not permitting banks to underwrite revenue bonds lessens the efficiency of that market because of the loss of marketing and capital strength that would otherwise be available and because it constrains competition by reducing the number of bidders on individual issues. A companion concern is found in assessing the relative costs of offering bonds through competitive bidding versus negotiation with one firm. Because of complicated financing arrangements (often attributable to their ramifications for tax treatment under the Internal Revenue Code), the number and volume of negotiated sales has grown rapidly. Recent studies indicate that negotiated bond sales are more costly for issuers than those sold at competitive auction, but there are great difficulties in making valid comparisons between securities sold by the two methods.[40]

Conclusion

Thanks to the drama of the New York debacle and a widespread concern over the condition of many major state and local borrowers, the study of debt policy and management received a considerable boost of attention in the mid-1970's. Several areas of research effort—financial disclosure needs; the measurement of financial condition; the determinants of tax-exempt interest rates, generally; and of risk premiums, in particular—found ready audiences at both the practitioner and policy levels. However, in the absence of any prolonged difficulty in the bond market and because of its demonstrated resiliency, a major restructuring did not take place. Changes were by and large enhancements of existing methods of doing things. The tax-exempt market has been broadened more by incremental changes in the existing tax code and by the growth of demand by investors finding themselves in higher tax brackets and in need of tax shelter.

Questions of the overall capacity of the market and its future growth have for the time being taken a backseat to considerations of the composition of borrowing and the new purposes to which it is being put. Total borrowing needs of the state and local sector are large and growing, but those needs are found in areas that are not traditional government functions, often involve assistance to privately owned and operated entities, and frequently are beyond the control of the public. Meanwhile, capital needs for traditional uses and debt to be repaid from tax receipts have declined. The full ramifications of these shifts have yet to be explored, but surely they constitute a closer linkage between state and local government debt policy and the economic fortunes of individual undertakings in their communities. While the local self-help aspect may be commendable, the fact is that the incentive is provided by the national tax code and the costs are borne by the national taxpayers. Because of the power involved in granting tax preferences, it is always sound policy that there be continued accounting of the costs and benefits.

Another aspect of the expanding purposes of state and local borrowing relates to the greater complexity of government and the fragmentation of power. Much of the proliferation of special districts has been caused by the need to finance improvements outside of historic debt limits and to seek alternative revenue sources. Whatever the practical benefits, the ability of the elected official to exercise control and the public at large to determine accountability has been weakened. The implications of this diffusion of power and confusion of responsibility may encourage development and debt commitments that are excessive and will constitute a future burden on the community, but over which it has no effective control.

Notes

1. "Municipal" is a generic term that applies to both state and local government obligations. The securities may either be "bonds" (original maturity of more than one year) or "notes" (one year or less in original maturity).

2. Roland Robinson, *Postwar Market for State and Local Government Securities* (Princeton, N.J.: Princeton University Press, 1960).

George Hempel, *The Postwar Quality of State and Local Debt* (New York: National Bureau of Economic Research, 1970).

U.S. Congress, Joint Economic Committee, *Changing Conditions in the Market for State and Local Government Debt*, by John E. Petersen, Joint Committee Print (Washington, D.C.: Government Printing Office, 1976).

Ronald W. Forbes and John E. Petersen, *Building a Broader Market*, Report of the Twentieth Century Fund Task Force on the Municipal Bond Market (New York: McGraw-Hill, 1976).

U.S. Advisory Commission on Intergovernmental Relations, *Understanding the Market for State and Local Debt*, Report M-104 (Washington, D.C.: Government Printing Office, 1976).

3. David J. Ott and Allen Meltzer, *Federal Tax Treatment of State and Local Securities* (Washington, D.C.: The Brookings Institution, 1963).

Harvey Galper and John E. Petersen, "An Analysis of Subsidy Plans to Support State and Local Borrowers," *National Tax Journal* (June 1971).

Robert Huefner, *Taxable Alternatives to Municipal Bonds*, Research Report No. 53 (Boston: Federal Reserve Bank of Boston, 1972).

Patric H. Hendershott and Timothy W. Koch, "An Empirical Analysis of the Market for Tax-Exempt Securities: Estimates and Forecasts," Monograph 1977-4 (New York: Graduate School of Business Administration, New York University, 1977).

4. Donald J. Mullineaux, "The Taxman Rebuffed: Income Taxes at Commercial Banks," *The Business Review* (May 1974).

Ralph C. Kimball, "Commercial Banks, Tax Avoidance and the Market for State and Local Debt Since 1970," *New England Economic Review* (January 1977).

5. Ralph C. Kimball, "Commercial Bank Demand and Municipal Bond Yields," Research Report No. 63 (Boston: Federal Reserve Bank of Boston, 1977).

Patric Hendershott and Timothy W. Koch, "The Demand for Tax-Exempt Securities by Financial Institutions," mimeographed, West Lafayette, Ind., 1978.

6. John E. Petersen, "New Directions in the Municipal Bond Market," in *Fiscal Choices of State and Local Governments*, ed. George E. Peterson (Washington, D.C.: The Urban Institute, 1978).

7. Paul McGouldrick and John E. Petersen, "Monetary Restraint, Borrowing and Capital Spending by Small Local Governments in 1966," *Federal Reserve Bulletin* (December 1968).

John E. Petersen, "Response of State and Local Governments to Varying Credit Conditions," *Federal Reserve Bulletin* (March 1971).

8. Paul Schneiderman, "State and Local Government Gross Fixed Capital Formation: 1958–73," *Survey of Current Business* (October 1975).

9. Ralph C. Kimball, "States as Financial Intermediaries," *New England Economic Review* (January 1976).

10. Thomas F. Mitchell, "Advanced Refunding: Concepts and Issues," *Governmental Finance* (May 1976).

David S. Kidwell, "Call Provisions and Their Effect on Municipal Bond Issues," *Governmental Finance* (August 1975).

Manly Mumford, "Arbitrage and Advanced Refunding," *Duke Law Journal* (1976).

11. George E. Peterson, "An Examination of State and Local Governments' Capital Demand, Alternative Means of Financing 'Public' Capital Outlays and the Impact on Tax-Exempt Credit Markets," in *Fiscal Choices of State and Local Governments*, ed. George Peterson (Washington, D.C.: Urban Institute, 1978).

12. Thomas Schneeweis, "An Analysis of Municipal Bond Ratings and Market Determined Risk Measures" (Ph.D. dissertation, University of Massachusetts, 1977).

Gary Pollack and Edward Renshaw, "Risk Premiums in the Municipal Bond Market," *The Daily Bond Buyer*, PSA Conference Supplement (October 5, 1977).

13. Ronald W. Forbes and John E. Petersen, *Cost of Credit Erosion in the Municipal Bond Market* (Chicago: Municipal Finance Officers Association, 1975).

14. Ronald Forbes et al., "Public Debt in the Northeast: The Limits of Growth," in *Managing a Way Out* (Boston: Council for Northeast Economic Action, 1977).

15. Lynn Browne and Richard Syron, "Big City Bonds After New York," *New England Economic Review* (July 1977).

16. John E. Petersen, "Small Borrowers in the Municipal Bond Market: Does Size Matter?" in *National Conference on Nonmetropolitan Community Services Research*, U.S. Congress, Senate Committee on Agriculture, Nutrition, and Forestry (Washington, D.C.: Government Printing Office, 1977).

17. David Minge, "Guaranteeing Municipal Bonds," *Wisconsin Law Review* 89 (1974).

Martin T. Katzman, "Measuring the Services of Municipal Bond Banks" (Cambridge: Harvard University, 1976).

Council of State Governments, *Maine's Municipal Bond Bank* (Lexington, Ky.: Council of State Governments, 1977).

18. George C. Kaufman, "State and Regional Effects on the Interest Cost of Municipal Bonds," *Local Finance* (June 1976).

Patric Hendershott and David S. Kidwell, "The Impact of Relative Security Supplies: A Test with Data from a Regional Tax-Exempt Bond Market," *Journal of Money, Credit, and Banking* (August 1978).

19. Peter Fortune, "The Financial Impact of the Federal Water Pollution Control Act: The Case for Municipal Bond Reform" (Cambridge, Mass.: Harvard Institute for Economic Research, 1975).

George Peterson and Harvey Galper, "Tax Exempt Financing of Private Industry's Pollution Control Investment," *Public Policy* (Spring 1975).

John E. Petersen, "The Tax Exempt Pollution Control Bond" (Chicago: Municipal Finance Officers Association, 1975).

20. See Forbes and Petersen, *Building a Broader Market*; and Kimball, "States as Financial Intermediaries."

21. New York State Moreland Act Commission, *Restoring Credit and Confidence*, Report to the Governor by the Moreland Act Commission on the Urban Development Corporation and Other State Financing Agencies (New York: New York State Moreland Act Commission, 1976).

John E. Petersen, *State Financial Planning* (Washington, D.C.: Council of State Planning Agencies, 1978).

22. Comptroller General of the U.S., *Assessments of New York City's Performance and Prospects Under Its Three-Year Emergency Financial Plan*, Report to the Congress (Washington, D.C.: U.S. General Accounting Office, 1977).

23. Advisory Commission on Intergovernmental Relations, *City Financial Emergencies: The Intergovernmental Dimension* (Washington, D.C.: Government Printing Office, 1973).

24. John E. Petersen, Lisa A. Cole and Maria L. Petrillo, *Watching and Counting: A Survey of State Assistance to and Supervision of Local Government Debt and Financial Administration* (Chicago: Municipal Finance Officers Association and National Conference of State Legislatures, 1977).

25. John E. Petersen, *The Rating Game* (New York: Twentieth Century Fund, 1974).

26. Roy Bahl and Bernard Jump, *The Measurement and Evaluation of Municipal Credit Strength* (Syracuse: Metropolitan Studies Program, Maxwell School, Syracuse University, 1976).

27. Jan M. Lodal, "Improving Local Government Information Systems," *Duke Law Journal* 1976 (January 1977).

Donald D. Kummerfeld, "Improving the Process for Local Spending Decisions: The New York City Experience," *National Tax Journal* 29 (September 1976).

28. Robert W. Doty and John E. Petersen, "The Federal Securities Laws and Transactions in Municipal Securities," *Northwestern University Law Review* 71 (July-August 1976).

29. Municipal Finance Officers Association, *Disclosure Guidelines for Offerings of Securities by State and Local Governments* (Chicago: Municipal Finance Officers Association, 1976).

30. John E. Petersen, Robert W. Doty, Ronald W. Forbes, and Donald D. Bourque, "Searching for Standards: Disclosure in the Municipal Securities Market," *Duke Law Journal* 1976 (January 1977).

Council on Municipal Performance, *Municipal Securities Regulation: A Public Perspective* (New York: Council on Municipal Performance, 1978).

Securities and Exchange Commission, *Staff Report on Transactions in Securities of the City of New York* (Washington, D.C.: Securities and Exchange Commission, 1977).

Robert W. Doty, "The Positive View—What the SEC Missed in Its Report on New York City," mimeographed, Washington, D.C., 1978.

31. For example, see Arthur S. Boyett and Gary A. Giroux, "The Relevance of Municipal Finance Statements for Investor Decisions: An Empirical Study," *Governmental Finance* (April, 1978).

32. Terry Nichols Clark, *Project on Urban Fiscal Strain*, series of reports on urban fiscal strain (Chicago: University of Chicago, 1977).

John E. Petersen, "Simplification and Standardization of State and Local Government Fiscal Indicators," *National Tax Journal* (September 1977).

Series of unpublished papers from the Urban Economic and Fiscal Indicators Project (Washington, D.C.: The Urban Institute, 1978).

33. Lennox Moak, *Local Government Debt Administration* (Chicago: Municipal Finance Officers Association, 1971).

Center for Capital Market Research, *Cost Savings to State and Local Governments in the Selling of New Bonds,* Final Report to the Research Applied to National Needs Program of the National Science Foundation (Oregon: Center for Capital Market Research, University of Oregon, 1975).

George Kaufman and Michael Hopewell, *Improving Bidding Rules to Reduce Interest Costs in the Competitive Sale of Municipal Bonds: A Handbook for Municipal Finance Officers* (Eugene: Center for Capital Market Research, University of Oregon, in cooperation with Municipal Finance Officers Association, 1977).

34. Barnes and Crow, *Designs for Immobilization of Texas State and Local Government Bonds* (Austin, Texas: Texas Advisory Commission on Intergovernmental Relations, January 1976).

35. Peter Fortune, "Tax-Exemption of State and Local Interest Payments: An Economic Analysis of the Issues and Alternatives," *New England Economic Review* (May 1973). Also see Galper and Petersen, "An Analysis of Subsidy Plans," and Huefner, "Taxable Alternatives."

36. See Forbes and Petersen, *Building a Broader Market*.

37. Marnie Shaul, *The Taxable Bond Option for Municipal Bonds*, Urban and Regional Development Series No. 2 (Columbus, Ohio: Academy for Contemporary Problems, 1977).

38. Michael Mussa and Roger Kormendi, "Taxation of Municipal Bonds: An Economic Appraisal," mimeographed (Chicago: University of Chicago, 1978).

39. Reuben Kessel, "A Study of the Effects of Competition in the Tax-Exempt Bond Market," *Journal of Political Economy* (July/August, 1971).

Michael Hopewell and George Kaufman, "Commercial Bank Underwriting of Municipal

Revenue Bonds: New Evidence,'' *The Daily Bond Buyer*, SIA Conference Supplement (November 1, 1976).

Phillip Cagan, *The Interest Saving to States and Municipalities from Bank Eligibility to Underwrite All Non-Industrial Municipal Bonds* (Washington, D.C.: Dealer Bank Association, 1978).

40. Eric Sorenson, ''Negotiated Municipal Bond Underwritings: Implications for Efficiency,'' *The Daily Bond Buyer*, PSA Conference Supplement (October 5, 1977).

Public Employment, Collective Bargaining, and Employee Wages and Pensions

Bernard Jump, Jr.

One of the ironies of state and local public finance and financial management research is that public employment, which accounts for the single largest operating expenditure in most general-purpose governments, has until recently been given so little attention by public finance specialists. As a consequence, policy makers are often required (or allowed) to make decisions concerning the public work force which carry important fiscal implications without having a sound theoretical or empirical basis for their actions.[1]

Not that all policy makers necessarily recognize or feel burdened by this handicap. In the absence of convincing supporting evidence, there is considerable conventional wisdom regarding public employment matters which can be drawn upon as a guide to decisions. As an example, there is the matter of the impact of public employee unionism and collective bargaining on government expenditures and operations.[2] Notwithstanding the paucity of evidence that unions and collective bargaining are on the whole damaging to the public interest, much public policy appears to be based on such a premise. Another example is the widespread use of the prevailing-wage principle whereby a government is required to pay employees at rates comparable to those received by their private-sector counterparts. The standard view is that this practice is necessary because there is usually no direct market test of the "worth" of public jobs (i.e., most public output is not sold in the conventional sense). The prevailing-wage principle is also seen as sufficient to insure that public employees are paid the correct amount (i.e., neither lower than needed to get at least average employees nor higher than required to compete effectively for employees). Yet there is an abundance of evidence that the prevailing-wage principle does not produce the intended results.[3]

In any case, public employment issues are comparatively new subjects for those whose primary interest is with government finance and financial management. Doubtless such issues would not even have been thought appropriate for inclusion had a general survey of research in state and local government finance and financial management been conducted as recently as a decade ago. Indeed, it would have been

---

Bernard Jump, Jr., is Professor, Senior Research Associate, and Director of the Master of Public Administration Program, Metropolitan Studies Program, the Maxwell School, Syracuse University.

a struggle a decade ago to identify even a small handful of true research efforts. Not so now. The 1970s have witnessed a surprising volume of research concerning public employment and allied matters, much of which has at least an indirect bearing on the fiscal fortunes of state and local governments.[4] This research is so vast, so diverse, and in some aspects, so rich that it is impossible here to do more than sample a few of the pickings and sketch some of the lines of inquiry which have been taken.

The next section will explore the state of knowledge about state and local government employee wage and compensation levels and trends. Of particular concern here is whether there is enough information to determine if state and local government employees are better compensated on the average than their private sector counterparts and if one or the other group is gaining ground over time.

However wage and compensation levels and trends compare between the public and private sectors, the central focus in this essay is on research involving the determinants of the cost of state and local government employees. Special attention will be given to that research which has examined the impact of public employee unions and collective bargaining on the pay received by state and local government employees. The dramatic growth during the last 15 to 20 years in unionization of state and local government employees makes questions about the effect of this phenomenon especially important. Also, the research conducted in this area is the best of the lot in a methodological sense and in terms of the consistency of the findings.[5]

Next, this review will turn to what have been described as the "financial time bombs" of the public sector—public employee pensions. Whether such a description is more hyperbole than accurate labeling is itself an unresolved issue. In any event, it is clear that pension commitments can be the source of long-term fiscal problems in ways that few other government obligations can be. It is equally clear from the bits and pieces of emerging evidence that too many state and local government policy makers have carelessly made pension commitments with little attention to or concern for their full financial implications.

Finally, the essay will conclude by identifying some important next steps for public employment research.

State and Local Government Employee Compensation Levels and Trends

Among the most vexing issues in public employment research are those that involve state and local public employee wages and fringe-benefit costs. Deficiencies in the available data have made it especially difficult for researchers to resolve questions such as: How does public employee compensation compare with private industry employee compensation? Despite strong arguments from state and local government employee representatives that their members consistently earn less than their counterparts in private industry in wages, fringe benefits and pensions,[6] the view that public employee compensation exceeds that received by private industry employees has many supporters.[7] Nevertheless, it is by no means certain that generalizations about which of the two employee groups is ahead and which is gaining ground over the other can be justified on the basis of available data.

Those who argue that public employees are in front sometimes rely on Commerce Department aggregate wage and compensation (i.e., wages plus fringe benefits or supplements) data reported on an industry-by-industry, or Standard Industrial Classification (SIC), basis which are a product of the annual national income and product account estimating process. The Commerce data show that average wages and average compensation are higher for state and local government employees, although the value of wage supplements favors private industry employees.[8] But the differences are not large ($82 for wages and $30 for total compensation in 1976), and private industry employees have been gaining ground steadily in recent years. Furthermore, when average wages are computed for state and local government employees other than those in education they fall below average private industry wages.

On the basis of data compiled by the Bureau of Labor Statistics (BLS) in periodic surveys of municipal and private-sector wages for selected occupational groups in large metropolitan areas,[9] a better case can be made that *some* state and local government employees receive higher pay than private industry employees in similar occupations. But even though the BLS survey data generally indicated that municipal pay levels are above private-sector pay levels for the occupations and metropolitan areas included, they are still weak bases for strong and sweeping conclusions about comparative pay levels and trends. For example, the BLS data are compiled on an infrequent basis; they reflect only the situation in selected large metropolitan areas; and they usually contain little or no information about pay levels for state government employees.

Another major shortcoming of BLS and most other data pertaining to the cost of public employees is that they seldom take account of the costs of fringe benefits. Yet these costs can be so substantial that failure to include them in estimates of employee costs and comparisons of public and private compensation could lead to severe underestimates of actual costs and distortions of comparative costs. The best research involving actual fringe benefit costs per employee (in municipalities) has been a series of three biennial surveys conducted by Edward H. Friend & Company for the United States Conference of Mayors.[10] The 1977 version of the Friend survey report is based on 777 municipalities, and its data are refined enough to provide a variety of details about fringe benefit and total compensation costs for police, firefighters, sanitation workers, and all other general personnel. (But none of this information is presented for individual municipalities.)

Principal findings reported in the latest Friend survey include the following:
○ Municipal employees in the West are paid more than municipal employees elsewhere;
○ Municipal employees in larger cities earn more than employees in smaller cities;
○ Police and firefighters receive higher annual pay and more costly fringes than private industry employees;
○ Sanitation workers fare better than other nonuniformed municipal employees; and
○ Both of these latter two groups are well behind private industry employees on wages and fringes—though the authors believe the municipal pension component of fringe costs to be underestimated.

To summarize the situation, deficiencies in the available state and local government employee wage, fringe benefit, and total compensation data are severe. These deficiencies greatly limit both the kinds of wage-related research that can be carried out and the reliability of that which is attempted. As the Council on Wage and Price Stability concluded after examining federally produced data on state and local government compensation, "It is possible to make some comparisons between jurisdictions and to measure some trends over time, but with just a few exceptions there are significant limitations on the scope, detail, and appropriateness of such comparisons."[11]

The Impact of Public Employee Unions on Compensation Levels

The principal catalysts for the first generation of public employment research have been the rapid expansion of state and local government employment and employee compensation which occurred throughout the 1960s and early 1970s and the extraordinary growth in public employee unionism and collective bargaining. Clearly, the fact that unions have come to represent such a large percentage of public employees gives rise to questions concerning the role unions play in driving up the compensation of public employees.[12]

Some observers of expanding public employee unionism and collective bargaining at the state and local government level have assumed that a zero-sum game was involved, with unions holding the bulk of the chips and the better cards.[13] More precisely, some have hypothesized that the demand for most public services is highly inelastic (i.e., unresponsive) to price; hence the demand by state and local governments for employees is also likely to be highly inelastic—certainly more so than the demand for private industry employees.[14] Another characteristic that is commonly associated with most government service production and which is thought to support the notion of inelastic demand for public employees is the difficulty of substituting capital for labor. As Baumol argued in a now-classic article, government is one sector of the economy which is essentially "nonprogressive" in the sense that it cannot achieve significant productivity gains.[15]

If Baumol's diagnosis is correct, and if it is equally correct that public-sector employee compensation is closely tied to private-sector wage gains[16] (which are influenced by productivity increases), it would seem logical that the entry of public employee unions would exacerbate an already difficult situation.[17] Further, the effects of public employee unions on their members' compensation might be more substantial than the effects of private-sector unions on private-sector wages because unions in the public sector are likely to have greater strength in the political dimension which leads to "a tendency for lawmakers and other elected officials to support the wage preference of government employees."[18]

Wage Impact of Unions

As already noted, so far the most impressive research in the impact of public-sector collective bargaining has involved attempts to estimate quantitatively the effects of unions on wages. At least 15 econometric studies of public employee union impact on wages have been conducted since 1970.[19] Most of the studies have dealt with a single employee group—usually police, firefighters, or teachers—and all have confined their attention to the local government level. In general, these studies have focused on whether public employee unions are able to obtain better wages for their membership than the members would receive in the absence of union representation.[20] While it may come as a surprise to those who think that public employee unions are endowed with substantial power relative to the power of private industry unions, the findings of most of the studies indicate that public employee unions affect wages on the average by about five percent, which is a smaller effect than private industry unions are thought to produce. Education unions appear to have the smallest effect, the range being between zero and five percent; for firefighters the range is two (or smaller) to 18 percent with the gains spread about equally between salary increases and reductions in hours worked; and for police the effect is probably less than 10 percent and maybe nil.

Two other conclusions are worthy of note. First, the existence of a unionized work force, per se, is not particularly important vis-a-vis wages unless collective bargaining takes place. Second, there is some evidence that nonuniformed employees may gain more from unionization and collective bargaining than will police and firefighters.

Some authors argue that the wage impact studies underestimate public employee union effects.[21] None of the wage impact analyses take into account the effect of wage gains in unionized jurisdictions on wages paid by nonunionized jurisdictions in close proximity or by other jurisdictions with similar characteristics regardless of proximity.[22] To the degree that there are important spillover effects on other jurisdictions when wage settlements are reached in collective bargaining, econometric studies that rely on cross-sectional data are likely to miss them. Further, as the wage-impact research has almost totally excluded fringe-benefit costs in the dependent variable used and as the cost of fringes can exceed the equivalent of one-third or more of direct wages, there is even more reason to treat the results of the impact studies as conservative estimates of what happens when unions bargain in the public sector.[23]

Still, the wage-impact studies as a group are the best empirical work around at this time. Unless and until subsequent empirical work is able to show convincingly that the wage impact of unions and collective bargaining is substantial, the basis for behaving as if public employee unions are severely damaging to the public interest is slim.

Prevailing Wage Hypothesis

Several studies have identified prevailing wages in the labor market from which a government obtains its employees as an important determinant of public employee wages, whether or not the public workers are represented by a union.[24] Indeed, prevailing wages in the private sector may be much more important than collective bargaining in determining the level of public pay, for reasons that are partly economic (public employers have to compete to get employees) and partly legal and institutional (standard practice in a jurisdiction may be to follow the pay pattern set by certain bellwether private employers).[25]

Some studies of prevailing wage practices suggest that the principle is implemented in a way that produces compensation levels for a broad array of state and local government employees which are higher than in the private sector.[26] Application of the prevailing-wage principle in government wage decisions also may produce a more equalitarian wage structure than that found in private industry. The result may be that governments "generally pay less than necessary to attract employees of average quality at the upper managerial and professional levels."[27] Notwithstanding the likelihood that many highly competent professionals and managers will remain in public service despite comparatively low compensation levels, we ought to be concerned about a process that militates against being able to pay "going rates" for superior talent.

State and Local Employee Pensions

Traditionally, eligibility for a lifetime pension benefit upon completion of a working career has been a common element of the public employee's compensation package. The pension, along with a degree of job security not generally associated with employment in the private sector, was assumed to be a fair offset for lower wages in public-sector jobs.[28] Commonly, public pension administration encountered few problems that required more than perfunctory attention from governments' top elected and professional officials. Each year, legislatures appropriated whatever was needed to cover the year's share of pension costs. In some jurisdictions, appropriations simply equalled the actual benefits to be paid during the year; in other instances, appropriations reflected at least nominally the actuarial cost of benefits accrued during the year by active employees. As long as work-force size, benefit levels, and the number of retirees did not grow too rapidly and the jurisdiction's financial condition remained stable, the fiscal implications of the pensions did not appear to be significant.

During the 1970s, however, a variety of forces have been at work to put the spotlight on public employee pension programs.[29] Among the most important of these forces were:

o Sharp increases, both absolutely and relative to employee wages, in the current appropriations for employee retirement programs;[30]

o Revelations about fiscal disasters in private industry pension plans that led to federal regulation of private pension plans and a congressional commitment to study public pension plans and determine whether they required similar regulations;[31]

o Regular and large improvements in Social Security benefits[32] which, when coupled with comparatively generous state and local government pension benefits, gave some long-seniority retirees from state and local government jobs a publicly financed retirement income that exceeded preretirement income;[33]

78

o Recognition that periodic pension benefit improvements were providing a path to substantial compensation gains for state and local government employees, often unchecked by much immediate impact on operating budgets;[34]

o Recognition by fiscal specialists, credit rating agencies, municipal bond underwriters, and investors that mounting long-term pension obligations were capable of impairing credit quality;[35]

o Widespread concern with the accuracy and completeness of state and local government accounting and financial reporting;[36] and

o Fear of a wave of state and local government fiscal crises which would be intensified by, if not primarily attributable to, excessive pension liabilities.[37]

State-Local Pension Benefit Levels

Public pension research has begun to make substantial contributions in the last half-dozen years.[38] Owing to the absence of an easily accessible data base, much of the work to date has been of the case-study variety. It has been heavily descriptive, and it has concentrated on building up the inventory of facts about specific governments' pension plans.[39]

Mundane as much of the first wave of public pension research has been, this state-of-the-art work was a necessary first step in identifying the major policy questions that would require close attention. For example, analysis of actual plan benefits and operations helped to explain why pension costs were rising so rapidly and why research concerned with the cost of public employees could not safely overlook the pension component of compensation. Among the most salient revelations that have emerged from this work are:

o Variations in benefit levels are substantial across states and municipalities; large cities with their own pension plans are likely to provide some of the most generous benefits available in the public sector; and public employee pensions are typically better than private employee pensions.

o The gap between public and private pension levels shrinks but doesn't disappear when allowance is made for the fact that most public employees must bear part of the cost of their pensions while most private plans are completely employer-financed.

o Public employees are permitted to retire earlier (without benefit reductions) than private employees.

o As most public plans do not reduce benefits for new retirees when social security payments are increased, the result now frequently is that new retirees with long seniority receive more than they earned just prior to retirement.

o Public plans typically include a provision for automatic increases in retirees' benefits when the cost of living increases (although few plans fully maintain a retiree's real income), whereas most private plans do not guarantee any postretirement-income adjustments and make them only on an ad hoc basis.

The fact that some public pension benefits are excessive in relation to both private-sector pension benefits and any reasonable general standard (e.g., Can there be any rational defense for a pension that pays a first-year retiree well above 100 percent of his preretirement income?) has stimulated research efforts that are intended to yield prototype plan designs which would meet predetermined benefit objectives.[40] While we are still a long way from truly rational pension plan design on a universal basis, state and local governments generally are manifesting their reluctance to add to benefits simply because their employees want a feature that some other employee groups have already.

State-Local Pension Costs and Financing

Research concerning costs and other financial aspects of public employee pensions has been especially hampered by data inadequacies. Although most public plans periodically arrange for actuarial valuations of pension liabilities and determination of required contributions, the information produced in such endeavors is seldom designed to assist policy makers and others interested in assessing a plan's financial condition and the cost implications to the sponsoring government. Recently, some actuaries and other pension-finance specialists have criticized the nature of conventional actuarial reporting and the ambiguous measures of costs and liabilities to which actuaries have been wedded.[41] In response, research has been undertaken to develop optimal funding criteria or targets against which a plan's condition at any moment can be measured, funding methods that will produce the results implicit in the criteria, and report formats that will serve the needs of public officials, taxpayers, employees, and the municipal finance community.[42]

Our knowledge about the condition of specific public pension plans is also gradually improving as a result of case studies.[43] But there is a vast amount of ground still to be covered before we know how many financial time bombs are out there. Research will continue to be slow in producing results until the volume and nature of data improve substantially,[44] and until the techniques for evaluating the fiscal condition of pension plans become less cumbersome.

Notwithstanding data and methodological difficulties, there have been two efforts since 1975 to assess on an aggregate basis the fiscal condition of state and local government pension plans and to project the future expenditures needed to maintain state-local plans.[45] In the more elaborate of the two studies,[46] it was concluded that state-local plans were substantially underfunded (in 1975) and that plan assets would be declining by the year 2000—even if annual state-local contributions continued to follow past growth trends. Were state and local governments to shift immediately to a so-called full-funding basis, required contributions would nearly double as soon as 1980. Although the study does not directly address the question of what substantial contribution increases would do to states' and local governments' financial conditions, its comparison of required contribution increases with projected GNP and disposable income leave no doubt that the jolt would be severe. Unfortunately, while the results of these studies are of potential importance to those who are concerned with macro issues (e.g., the condition of the capital market), they don't add much to what is known about the condition of particular state-local pension systems.

The final item on our list of recent research efforts brings this survey full circle by directly connecting public employee pensions with wages.[47] The study in question examined the relationship between wages and pensions in 41 major cities. With the aid of some complex theoretical and quantitative devices, the author found support for the hypothesis that municipalities vary the wage they will pay according to the cost of employee pension benefits. As this work is clearly *sui generis* and very recent, its implications must be viewed as highly tentative. Yet if subsequent work confirms that such trade-offs or "compensating" wage differentials do commonly exist, then statements of the type "it is the high pension costs of public employees which are bankrupting municipalities"[48] are rendered meaningless. Furthermore, "these findings imply that increasing current funding requirements of public sector pension plans is likely to reduce the future growth of public employee wage rates."[49]

A Note About Research Needs

Public employment, collective bargaining, and compensation research with relevance to state and local government finance and financial management has made substantial strides during the 1970s. Yet there is much more to be done—beginning with the elimination of major data inadequacies. Research in the nonwage aspects of collective bargaining remains at a rudimentary level. Little is known about whether prohibition of public employee strikes serves the public interest well, nor do we know much about the costs (financial or other) that are associated with mechanisms that serve as substitutes for strikes. Although it is widely believed that collective bargaining probably impairs the quality of public service delivery or at least raises the cost, there is little evidence one way or the other about this, just as there is little known about the effects of collective bargaining on the public-sector management process.

On the pension front, most of the work remains to be done. A great deal more needs to be known about trade-offs between pension benefits and other components of employee compensation. If public employers do view compensation as a package and bargain with a stringent budget constraint on the total cost of the package, then we need not be quite so concerned (or, at least, not concerned for the same reasons) about apparently overgenerous pensions. But we will have to know in any case about the current and prospective costs of pension plans, and this will be facilitated by agreement among specialists as to what the relevant financial indicators are. Equally important, at least until the quality and timeliness of public pension plan financial reporting improves substantially, is the need for general and less cumbersome actuarial models that can be used by independent analysts to evaluate pension plans' financial conditions.

Notes

1. For example, is there a sound basis for outlawing public employee strikes? And where strikes are outlawed, what is the basis for deciding what settlement mechanism (e.g., compulsory arbitration, fact finding) to use? See David Lewin, Peter Feuille, and Thomas A. Kochan, eds., *Public Sector Labor Relations: Analysis and Readings* (Glen Ridge, New Jersey: Thomas Horton and Daughters, 1977) Chapter 5; and David Lewin, "Public Sector Labor Relations: A Review Essay," in *Public Sector Labor Relations,* ed. Lewin, Feuille, and Kochan, p. 374.

2. Lewin, Feuille, and Kochan, eds., *Public Sector Labor Relations: Analysis and Readings,* Chapter 6.

3. Walter Fogel and David Lewin, "Wage Determination in the Public Sector," *Industrial and Labor Relations Review* (April 1974), pp. 410–431.

4. The enormity of the literature is demonstrated in Ralph T. Jones, *Public Sector Labor Relations: An Evaluation of Policy-Related Research* (Belmont, Massachusetts: Contract Research Corporation and the National Science Foundation, 1975). Jones began with a bibliography of more than 700 items and eventually used more than half for his review. Lewin, Feuille, and Kochan, *Public Sector Labor Relations* contains the most comprehensive list available of work published since Jones' review.

5. Lewin, Feuille, and Kochan, *Public Sector Labor Relations,* p. 319; and Jones, *Public Sector Labor Relations,* p. 199.

6. See Text of Remarks by Jerry Wurf in *Public Sector Labor Relations: At the Crossroads,* ed. Tim Bornstein and John T. Conlon, Proceedings of 1977 Annual Conference Sponsored by the American Arbitration Association and the Labor-Management Relations Service of the U.S. Conference of Mayors (Amherst: University of Massachusetts, 1977), p. 91.

7. Fogel and Lewin, "Wage Determination in the Public Sector," p. 410; Daniel Orr, "Public Employee Compensation Levels," in *Public Employee Unions: A Study of the Crisis in Public Sector Labor Relations,* ed. A. Lawrence Chickering (San Francisco: Institute for Contemporary Studies, 1976), pp. 131–144; and Anthony M. Rufolo, "Local Government Wages and Services: How Much Should Citizens Pay?" *Business Review,* Federal Reserve Bank of Philadelphia (January/February 1977), pp. 13–20. But see, also, Bernard Jump, Jr., "Compensating City Government Employees: Pension Benefit Objectives, Cost Measurement, and Financing," *National Tax Journal* 29 (September 1976), pp. 240–242; Roy Bahl, Bernard Jump, and Larry Schroeder, *The Outlook for City Fiscal Performance in Declining Regions,* paper prepared for the U.S. Mayor's Conference (Syracuse: Metropolitan Studies Program of Syracuse University, 1978), pp. 24–39.

8. These data are reviewed in Bahl, Jump, and Schroeder, *The Outlook for City Fiscal Performance in Declining Regions,* pp. 24–39.

9. Summary of the results of the earliest of these surveys is contained in Stephen H. Perloff, "Comparing Municipal Salaries with Industry and Federal Pay," *Monthly Labor Review* (October 1971), pp. 46–50. See, for example, Bureau of Labor Statistics, Middle Atlantic Regional

Office, *Wages and Benefits of New York City Municipal Government Workers, May 1975,* Regional Report No. 51, November 1976, for a more recent version of a BLS survey.

10. Edward H. Friend and Albert Pike, III, *1975 National Survey of Employee Benefits for Full-Time Personnel of U.S. Municipalities* (Washington: Labor-Management Relations Service of the National League of Cities, 1977). However, fringes in the Friend studies are defined more broadly than in Commerce Department data. Whereas the latter include only items such as pension contributions, health insurance and the like which are furnished in addition to the salary, Friend's fringes, called "pay for time not worked," include the value of holidays, vacations, and so forth as well as more standard fringes.

An excellent study that focuses on municipal fringe benefit expenditures in one state is Norman Walzer and M. David Beveridge, *Expenditures for Fringe Benefits in Illinois Municipalities* (Springfield, Illinois: Municipal Problems Commission, 1976).

The most detailed study of state employee compensation was done by the BLS and used data for 1972 collected by the Census Bureau in the course of the 1972 Census of Governments. The results are summarized in U.S. Bureau of Labor Statistics, *State Government Employee Compensation: U.S. Summary, 1972,* Report 433 (Washington, D.C.: Government Printing Office, 1975) and individual state results are published in the Report 433 series.

11. Sean Sullivan, *State and Local Government Employee Compensation Data Needs,* Staff Report (Washington, D.C.: Council on Wage and Price Stability, 1976), p. 13. On the first page of the same report the Council observed that "we discovered that data on wages and fringe benefits for state and local government employees were so inadequate that we were unable to include an analysis of employee compensation trends in the public sector in our overall study (of collective bargaining agreements)."

12. For a summary of the trend in public employee unionism and a review of major issues raised by this phenomenon, see Neil R. Peirce, "Employment Report: Public Employee Unions Show Rise in Membership, Militancy," *National Journal* (August 30, 1975), pp. 1239–1249.

13. This is discussed in Jones, *Public Sector Labor Relations,* pp. 197–198.

14. Jones, *Public Sector Labor Relations,* pp. 201–205; Marvin B. Johnson, *Wages, Employment Productivity and Unions in the Local Public Sector,* (Detroit: Metropolitan Fund, Inc., 1977); Fogel and Lewin, "Wage Determination in the Public Sector," p. 431; and Lewin, "Public Sector Labor Relations: A Review Essay," p. 374.

15. William J. Baumol, "Macroeconomics of Unbalanced Growth: The Anatomy of Urban Crisis," *American Economic Review* 57 (June 1967), pp. 415–426.

16. Johnson, *Wages, Employment Productivity and Unions in the Local Public Sector,* p. 13; Fogel and Lewin, "Wage Determination in the Public Sector;" and David Lewin, "The Prevailing-Wage Principle and Public Wage Decisions," *Public Personnel Management* (November/December 1974), pp. 473–485.

17. This view is reflected in Harry H. Wellington and Ralph K. Winter, Jr., *The Unions and the Cities* (Washington: The Brookings Institution, 1971).

18. Fogel and Lewin, "Wage Determination in the Public Sector," p. 415.

19. Good reviews of these studies can be found in Jones, *Public Sector Labor Relations;* Johnson, *Wages, Employment Productivity and Unions in the Local Public Sector;* and Lewin, "Public Sector Labor Relations: A Review Essay."

20. In only one instance has an attempt been made to compare the effects of unions in the public sector and in the private sector. That study found mixed evidence: Bus drivers in the public sector were found to earn 9 percent to 12 percent more than drivers in the private sector; no difference was found to exist between unionized construction workers in the public and private sectors nor between a broader group of public sector and private sector employees. See Daniel S. Hamermesh, "The Effect of Government Ownership on Union Wages," in *Labor in the Public and Nonprofit Sectors,* ed. Daniel S. Hamermesh (Princeton: Princeton University Press, 1975), pp. 227–255.

21. Jones, *Public Sector Labor Relations,* pp. 213–214.

22. For evidence that employee groups in large cities keep a close eye on the earnings of their counterparts in other large cities across the country and that compensation levels are thought to matter in bargaining, see Damon Stetson, "New York City Employees Lag in a Study on Total Compensation," *New York Times* (January 1, 1978). The study discussed in the article was

prepared by a consultant to New York City unions and purported to show that New York City employees' compensation was in line with (and in some cases below) employee compensation in other large cities.

23. But in some highly original work, Edelstein has found some evidence of a tradeoff between municipal employee wages and pensions. See the section of this essay entitled *State and Local Employee Pensions.*

24. See n. 16, above.

25. The most complete application of the principle may be in California state government. As a result of 1974 legislation, the State Personnel Board makes recommendations concerning "total compensation" with the "objective to provide an equitable and balanced program of total compensation for the State's civil service employees when compared to prevailing salaries and benefits provided by other employers in California," California State Personnel Board, *Report to the Governor and Legislature* (Sacramento: California State Personnel Board, January 10, 1975), p. 5.

26. Fogel and Lewin, "Wage Determination in the Public Sector," p. 428.

27. Ibid., p. 430.

28. James A. Maxwell, "Characteristics of State and Local Trust Funds," *State-Local Finances in the Last Half of the 1970's,* ed. David J. Ott et al. (Washington: American Enterprise Institute, 1975), p. 39; Louis H. Kohlmeier, *Conflicts of Interest: State and Local Pension Fund Asset Management* (New York: The Twentieth Century Fund, 1976), pp. 5, 7; and "Public Employee Pensions in Times of Fiscal Distress," *Harvard Law Review* 90 (1977), p. 997.

29. Robert Tilove, *Public Employee Pension Funds,* A Twentieth Century Fund Report (New York: Columbia University Press, 1976), Chapter 1.

30. Although this description fits a great many states and municipalities, we lack comprehensive data about trends in state-local pension contribution rates. However, it is possible to get a crude notion of the trend by comparing data on government contributions to employee retirement systems, as reported in U.S. Bureau of the Census, *Finances of Employee-Retirement Systems of State and Local Governments* with data on payroll (personal service expenditures) as reported in U.S. Bureau of the Census, *City Government Finances.*

31. William C. Greenough and Francis P. King, *Pension Plans and Public Policy* (New York: Columbia University Press, 1976), pp. 66–67; Kohlmeier, *Conflicts of Interest: State and Local Pension Fund Asset Management;* Tax Foundation, *Employee Pension Systems in State and Local Government,* Research Publication No. 33 (New York: Tax Foundation, Inc., 1976), Chapter 7; and U.S. Congress, House Committee on Education and Labor, *Interim Report of Activities of the Pension Task Force of the Subcommittee on Labor Standards,* 94th Cong., 2nd sess., March 1976.

32. Alicia H. Munnell, *The Future of Social Security* (Washington, D.C.: The Brookings Institution, 1977).

33. Bernard Jump, "Compensating City Government Employees: Pension Benefit Objectives, Cost Measurement, and Financing," pp. 244–247; and *State and Local Employee Pension Plans: Watching for Problems* (Columbus, Ohio: Academy for Contemporary Problems, 1976), pp. 5–6.

34. For the New York City version of this phenomenon, see Bernard Jump, *Financing Public Employee Retirement Programs in New York City: Trends Since 1965 and Projections to 1980,* Occasional Paper No. 16 (Syracuse: Metropolitan Studies Program of Syracuse University, 1975).

35. Advisory Commission on Intergovernmental Relations, *City Financial Emergencies: The Intergovernmental Dimension* (Washington, D.C.: Government Printing Office, 1973), pp. 4, 6, 64–66; Roy Bahl and Bernard Jump, "Projecting the Fiscal Viability of Cities," in *Fiscal Choices of State and Local Governments,* ed. George Peterson, (Washington, D.C.: Urban Institute, forthcoming); and Nuveen Research, *Public Employee Pension Funds: Impact on State and Local Credits* (New York: John Nuveen & Co., Incorporated, 1976).

36. Sidney Davidson et al., *Financial Reporting by State and Local Government Units* (Chicago: Center for Management of Public and Nonprofit Enterprise, Graduate School of Business, University of Chicago, 1977).

Coopers and Lybrand and the University of Michigan, *Financial Disclosure Practices of the American Cities: A Public Report* (New York: Coopers and Lybrand, 1976), especially p. 27.

37. The popular media have contained many near hysterical reports about impending state-local fiscal crises caused by excessive and underfunded pensions. A recent and fairly moderate version of this genre is "Behind the Squeeze on Public Pension Plans," *U.S. News and World Report* (March 20, 1978), pp. 80–83.

38. For a listing of a wide variety of materials about public pensions, see U.S. Department of Labor, Office of Policy, Planning and Research, Pension and Welfare Benefit Programs, *Public Pension Plans: A Bibliography,* mimeographed, Washington, D.C. (May 1977).

39. Examples are Tilove, *Public Employee Pension Funds;* New York State Permanent Commission on Public Employee Pension and Retirement Systems, *Recommendations for a New Pension Plan for Public Employees: The 1976 Coordinated Escalator Retirement Plan* (New York: The Commission, 1976); Jump, "Compensating City Government Employees: Pension Benefit Objectives, Cost Measurement, and Financing"; Jump, *State and Local Employee Pension Plans: Watching for Problems;* Jump, "District of Columbia Pensions: The Adequacy of Benefits and The Case for Actuarial Funding, in *Hearings, Part 3, Pension Systems,* U.S. Congress, Senate Committee on the District of Columbia, 94th Cong., 2nd sess., March 1976, pp. 141–167; Jump, "Teacher Retirement Systems," *Journal of Education Finance* (Fall 1977), pp. 143–157; Tax Foundation, *Employee Pension Systems in State and Local Governments;* Philip M. Doyle, "Municipal Pension Plans: Provisions and Payments," *Monthly Labor Review* (November 1977); State of Michigan, Department of Management and Budget, Office of Intergovernmental Relations, *Benefits of Michigan Local Government Retirement Systems* (Lansing: State of Michigan, Department of Management and Budget, 1977); and *Financing of Michigan Local Government Retirement Systems* (Lansing: State of Michigan, Department of Management and Budget, 1977).

40. Howard E. Winklevoss, Dan M. McGill et al., *Public Pension Systems: Fundamentals of Plan Design and Funding, Part I, Plan Design* (Philadelphia: Winklevoss & Associates, Inc., January 1978), preliminary draft of a report prepared for the National Science Foundation.

41. Jump, "Evaluating the Financial Condition of Public Employee Pension Plans: Some Guidelines for the Unwary," *Governmental Finance* (February 1978), pp. 3–9; and Winklevoss, McGill et al., *Public Pension Systems: Fundamentals of Plan Design and Funding, Part II, Plan Funding.* The threat of Federal legislation that would mandate the disclosure of a variety of state-local fiscal information has not been without effect in the matter of pension finances. Similarly, the Municipal Finance Officers Association's *Disclosure Guidelines for Offerings of Securities by State and Local Governments* contains guidelines relating to what should be reported about a jurisdiction's pension obligations. For a recent review of activity on this front, see Anthony M. Mandolini, "Accounting and Reporting for Public Employee Retirement Systems," *Governmental Finance* (February 1978), pp. 10–15.

42. Winklevoss, McGill et al., *Public Pension Systems: Part II, Plan Funding.*

43. See, for example, Jump, *Financing Public Employee Retirement Programs in New York City;* The Mayor's Management Advisory Board, *Pensions: A Report of the Mayor's Management Advisory Board* (New York: The Mayor's Management Advisory Board, April 1976); and statement of Cedric W. Kroll, in *Hearings, Part 3, Pension Systems,* U.S. Congress, Senate Committee on the District of Columbia, 94th Cong., 2nd sess., March 1976, pp. 81–90.

44. According to the preliminary summary of the House Pension Task Force's report (scheduled for release in April 1978) of the results of its survey of public employee retirement systems, "Serious deficiencies exist among public employee retirement systems at all levels of government regarding the extent to which important information is reported and disclosed to plan participants, public officials, and taxpayers."

45. J. Richard Aronson, "Projections of State and Local Trust Fund Financing," Chapter 4 in *State-Local Finances in the Last Half of the 1970s,* ed. David J. Ott et al.; and Alicia H. Munnell and Ann M. Connolly, "Funding Government Pensions: State-Local, Civil Service and Military," in *Funding Pensions: Issues and Implications for Financial Markets,* Federal Reserve Bank of Boston, Conference Series No. 16 (Boston: Federal Reserve Bank of Boston, 1976), pp. 72–133.

46. Munnell and Connolly, "Funding Government Pensions."

47.   Robert H. Edelstein, *An Economic Analysis of the Public Sector Funding of Large City Pension Systems,* Draft Final Report prepared for the National Science Foundation (Philadelphia: Winklevoss & Associates, 1978).

48.   Ibid., p. V. 2.

49.   Ibid.

Accounting, Auditing and Financial Reporting

James M. Williams

With the present emphasis on all aspects of financial disclosure, governmental accounting and financial reporting is receiving greater attention than ever before. Citizens, governmental officials, and the financial community are increasingly concerned with the type, quality and reliability of the information that is being provided them.

The impetus for this renewed emphasis was primarily the New York City fiscal crisis. "New York" and the concomitant crises in other local governments prompted many to scrutinize the financial management practices of state and local governments and question their accounting systems, auditing procedures and reporting mechanisms.

Dramatic increases in government spending have also drawn attention to governmental accounting, auditing and financial reporting. The tide of fiscal conservatism has been rising and with it have come demands to cut back spending and stabilize or reduce property taxes. The passage of the Jarvis-Gann Amendment in California and the taxpayer revolts in other states are illustrative of the fervor of the proponents of less government.

These two events have resulted in concern with present quality and needed improvements in accounting, auditing and financial reporting. New research interest has focused on generally accepted accounting principles and related standards—specifically, how to meet them and how to improve them.

Renewed interest in governmental accounting and financial reporting has led to an important discovery: There has been an absence of serious research directed to accounting in the public sector. In a recent working paper on municipal accounting research, it was charged that the paucity of serious work constitutes a professional scandal.[1] The author declared that it was unconscionable for academic accountants to pay little heed to the problems of municipal accounting. Another observer, writing in 1976, called governmental accounting and reporting the "neglected step-child" of academic researchers, governmental managers, auditors and standards-setting bodies.[2] He described the status of governmental accounting research, in the context of all accounting research, as miniscule, sporadic, but increasing in recent years.

James M. Williams is a Manager with the services to State and Local Government Division of Ernst & Whinney in Cleveland, Ohio. The author wishes to thank Catherine Lavigne Spain for her assistance in the preparation of this essay.

The research that has been undertaken consists of a variety of conceptual analyses, case studies and literature reviews. The emphasis has been on solving a given problem or in recommending a particular approach. Survey methods have seen increasing use to find out what other governments are doing or to determine opinions, such as user needs. Some researchers have called for increased use of empirical research methods, which seem both likely and productive.[3]

Interest in the issues is great and growing all the time. As the profession continues to receive more attention and resources, serious research efforts will flourish. This essay will review recent research efforts with particular emphasis given to the institutions in which research is conducted. It will also identify key issues for future research.

Research Institutions

Prior to a discussion of the major research thrusts, it is necessary to have some understanding of the complexities of the research institutions. There are essentially two sources of research: the academic accounting community and the authoritative bodies.

The Academic Community

This group has focused its research attention on business accounting problems. The American Accounting Association (AAA), which is the leading accounting academic or basic research organization, has sponsored few studies and printed few articles in its journal on topics concerned with governmental accounting and financial reporting. However, the association's committees have been active in the area and have made significant contributions.

One researcher analyzed the academic governmental (nonprofit) accounting research between 1966–1977. Three components of academic literature were analyzed: two respected journals, American Accounting Association committees, and doctoral dissertations. The researcher concluded:[4]

Incisive research methods are needed to demonstrate the preferability and feasibility of the normative proposals made in the nonprofit accounting literature. For research purposes, the normative assertions should be regarded as hypotheses to be tested. It is not clear yet how the preferability and feasibility of these hypotheses are to be operationally tested so as to produce generalizable conclusions and policy-relevant results. These methodological problems confront not only nonprofit accounting, but also other branches of accounting, and applied social sciences in general. It appears that researchers' greatest challenge is to conceptualize and empirically measure the benefits and costs of alternative accounting systems (both extant and proposed). Since economics has made relatively more progress in analyzing costs and benefits, perhaps information economics could supply accounting researchers with the necessary tools to make the problems more tractable.

Another researcher suggested three areas for profitable application of empirical public-sector research: describing current practice, evaluating proposed alternatives and *ex post* testing and evaluation.[5]

The academic community's public-sector research efforts are in the formative stages, which consist of summarizing what has been accomplished to date and identifying key issues believed to be most valuable for future research. A conference on municipal accounting and reporting was convened in 1976 to bring together 60 authorities in governmental finance from various disciplines. A report of the conference identified 30 major issues within the four workshop areas:[6]

o Information requirements of investors and other users of financial reports;
o Issues of fund accounting;

87

○ Issues of auditing; and
○ Regulation of municipal reporting.

A related development is taking place at the University of Arizona where an interdisciplinary group, known as the Committee for Research in Public Sector Reporting, has been established.[7] Its purpose is to identify contemporary issues in public-sector reporting, fund research on these issues and facilitate access to relevant data. The committee will also facilitate the exchange of information among the various individuals interested in public-sector reporting in a working paper series, a biannual conference, and a newsletter.

Another effort under way at the University of Alabama is worth noting.[8] An exhaustive index of accounting literature, both present and past, is being compiled. It will encompass all accounting research—textbooks, dissertations, periodicals, pamphlets, opinions, and Securities and Exchange Commission releases.

The Authoritative Bodies

Unlike other research areas in government finance, authoritative bodies such as committees, councils and boards concerned with standards setting abound in this field. In conjunction with these activities, basic research and analysis is conducted to facilitate the formulation of standards.

Authoritative bodies are considering extensive changes which will affect state and local government accounting and financial reporting. These bodies are conducting research and will capitalize on present external research findings. The documents emanating from these bodies should also stimulate further research opportunities. Through this interrelationship, research can have a direct impact on policies and practices of governmental units that follow the accepted standards. As for their deliberations and pronouncements, however, the authoritative bodies must necessarily make their decisions on a conceptual and expert opinion basis.

Principles and practices currently in use in this area have evolved primarily from the activities of two groups—the National Council on Governmental Accounting (NCGA) and the American Institute of Certified Public Accountants' State and Local Government Accounting Committee. The pronouncements of these two groups jointly comprise the authoritative literature applying generally accepted accounting principles (GAAP) to state and local governments.

The National Council (formerly Committee) on Governmental Accounting began issuing its pronouncements in 1934. Its most recent pronouncement (1968) is *Governmental Accounting, Auditing, and Financial Reporting*, which is commonly referred to as GAAFR or the "blue book."[9] It is NCGA's authoritative publication on state and local government accounting and financial reporting.

In 1974, the American Institute of Certified Public Accountants (AICPA) published an industry audit guide entitled *Audits of State and Local Governmental Units* (ASLGU).[10] ASLGU generally endorsed GAAFR's principles but also added some alternatives.

Critics of financial reports based on GAAFR and ASLGU principles suggest that they do not meet the needs of certain user groups with legitimate interests in the financial affairs of government. Researchers and others interested in the area have called for significant research and, in some cases, drastic changes in governmental accounting and financial reporting.[11]

The Financial Accounting Standards Board (FASB), the standards-setting body recognized by the AICPA, is also concerned about nonbusiness (governmental and private nonprofit) accounting concepts and objectives. It has sponsored and published a research report by Robert N. Anthony entitled *Financial Accounting in Nonbusiness Organizations: An Exploratory Study of Conceptual Issues*, which presents the pro and con arguments for 16 conceptual issues without recommending how they should be resolved.[12] The study served as the basis for the FASB's discussion memorandum, "An Analysis of Issues Related to Conceptual Framework for Financial Accounting and Reporting: Objectives of Financial Reporting by Nonbusi-

88

ness Organizations," which is intended to solicit public comments.[13] The current FASB formal agenda will not involve any evaluation of the specific nonbusiness standards that constitute GAAP.

Thus, changes in accounting principles applicable to governmental units are receiving increased attention. It is a time for widespread consideration of the conceptual issues of governmental accounting and financial reporting. As described above, the NCGA has traditionally prescribed the application of GAAP to governments. The AICPA became involved in the process by issuing ASLGU. The FASB is exploring the objectives and conceptual issues of all nonbusiness organizations.

Who should establish standards? That is, whose pronouncements should be followed by a governmental unit preparing financial statements? Certainly, everyone should be involved in addressing the issues, but everyone cannot pronounce standards. This is an issue which must be resolved.

As previously stated, GAAFR and ASLGU constitute the application of GAAP to state and local governments. Auditors' opinions are (or should be) expressed in conformity with GAAP, but state and local legal requirements often differ from GAAP. In such cases, many governmental officials have followed the law and ignored GAAP—instead of showing both as required by GAAFR and ASLGU.

Since "New York," pressures to follow GAAP have increased and more governments are doing so. However, many doubt the effectiveness of this "voluntary" compliance. Some have advocated federal enforcement, although state and local officials believe this alternative to be unacceptable.[14] In resolving the other issues of accounting principles, the question of enforcement is a significant concern.

Recent Research

Major research thrusts can be classified into four categories. They are: improving standards, changing the reporting model, auditing issues, and disclosure. A discussion of each of these areas follows.

Improving Standards

The NCGA has undertaken a major research project intended to improve governmental accounting and reporting. The first phase of the project involves the restatement of GAAFR to provide immediate guidance by updating, clarifying, amplifying and reordering its 1968 principles. The NCGA has already issued two exposure drafts in this project: "GAAFR Restatement Principles" and "Grant Accounting and Reporting by State and Local Government Recipients."[15]

Another significant research effort, which is being conducted under the auspices of the NCGA State Accounting Task Force, is the State Accounting Project.[16] This ambitious, long-overdue research will be accomplished by state personnel and representatives from 13 national public accounting firms with the assistance of all of the relevant national state associations and the financial support of the National Science Foundation. The three-year project first involves a detailed field survey of the accounting and financial reporting practices of each state. This survey is presently under way. After the data are compiled and reviewed, development will begin on preferred accounting and financial reporting practices.

The GAAFR Restatement and State Accounting Projects will provide input to the NCGA's Subsequent Research Phase. This effort, planned for 1979–1980, will attempt to develop a conceptual framework for governmental accounting and financial reporting. Issues and problems will be analyzed and researched in order to consider significant changes in recommended requirements.

The AICPA's State and Local Government Accounting Committee is revising the industry audit guide to aid AICPA members in auditing governmental units. It is considering drastic changes, particularly in the areas of measurement focus, entity and financial reporting format. The Committee will consider the positive and negative elements of various accounting principles, discuss the problems of implementing these principles and devise solutions to these problems. The revised volume will present the recommendations of the Committee regarding the most effective accounting and auditing procedures for state and local government.

The Financial Accounting Standards Board has considered evaluating the specific nonbusiness standards that constitute GAAP, and commissioned the Anthony study described earlier to outline the issues the board would have to address if it decided to publish a set of generally accepted accounting principles for nonbusiness organizations. The project also attempts to identify users and their uses of financial statements and the concepts that are helpful in meeting user information needs.

The ultimate research outcome of the authoritative bodies is difficult to predict. Each is considering streamlining and simplifying the financial statements in order to make them more useful to general-purpose users. Major changes in standards and research findings that can significantly affect policy and practices will be considered. By all indications, this subject will continue to receive increasing productive research interest.

Significant research has been undertaken which is applied and practitioner-oriented. Increasingly, governments are striving to improve their accounting and financial reporting. The actual motivation to make these positive changes has been beneficially studied.[17] The findings are used to help motivate officials to improve performance.

As one would expect, these efforts concentrate on case studies, literature reviews and surveys. The survey approach usually attempts to determine what other governmental units are doing. The objective of these studies is to assist individual governmental units in implementing changes which would help the unit meet existing standards and accounting and reporting needs.

Changes in the Reporting Model

One major recent research area is a dissatisfaction with the existing governmental accounting and financial reporting model. A typical theme is that governmental accounting is too complex and needs a financial reporting format much more like commercial accounting.

There are several major questions surrounding the financial reporting model which research has attempted to clarify. The first asks what should be the accounting entity.[18] Identification of the appropriate reporting entity can be approached on several levels. GAAFR identifies the fund (or fund group) as the basic accounting entity and calls for separate financial statements for each one. This approach stems from an emphasis on legal compliance with restrictions on resources and stewardship. Many, however, advocate a single set of consolidated statements for the "government as a whole." The problem is to find the proper balance between aggregation (consolidation) and detail. Some researchers recommend the use of consolidated statements for the various funds to obtain a complete picture of the financial affairs of the unit.

Another entity question involves the treatment of "related" organizations—boards, commissions, authorities, districts and retirement systems. When should they be reported as part of the "parent" governmental unit and when should they be reported as independent governmental units? From still another viewpoint, some have advocated integrating all governmental units delivering services within a geographical area into a single reporting entity.[19]

Another issue requiring resolution is how governments should measure their operations—costs, expenditures, or both. This issue is complex and confusing and at the heart of much of the criticism of present GAAP.

GAAFR calls for reporting *expenditures,* the cost of goods and services acquired or the flow of financial resources, for all governmental (other than commercial-type) operations. Others call for recording *expenses* (the cost of services provided) for all operations. It is believed that this information is essential for evaluating the results of operations and changes in governmental equity. Resolution of the measurement basis issue would provide the framework for addressing more specific elements, such as depreciation, pensions and leases.

There is also confusion about the recognition and definition of revenues. The definition of revenues and the timing of their recognition are related to the measurement of operations. Under the flow of financial resources approach, GAAFR and ASLGU emphasize "measurable" and "available." Others believe that either "earning" the revenue or the period for which the operations are intended to be financed is more appropriate.[20]

The NCGA's "GAAFR Restatement Principles Exposure Draft" separates transfers and long-term debt proceeds from revenues. Others would limit use of "revenues" to the amount earned by providing goods and services.[21]

Another area attracting research interest involves the identification of users of financial reports and their information needs.[22] This is necessary before addressing more specific issues. The significance of the answers to these questions is overwhelming. Armed with related research findings, financial reporting concepts and details can be considered on a more informed basis. Potential users also must be identified and their specific information needs isolated.

The GAAFR financial reporting model presumes a sophisticated user with a need for detailed financial information. Critics suggest that present GAAP is oriented toward providing management information, but many top managers and elected officials find it difficult to understand and use. Many suggest that financial reports should instead be primarily targeted for citizens and taxpayers who need less detailed information in a less technical format. Related research is needed to determine the appropriate roles for general-purpose, special-purpose and interim financial reports.

Another concern is how budgetary and legal requirements relate to financial reporting. GAAFR and ASLGU require inclusion of budgetary data in financial statements for some funds. Both also require reporting in conformity with GAAP and reporting legal compliance. Many have questioned requiring budgetary and legal compliance data for general-purpose financial reporting.[23] They consider this data to be "managerial" or "internal." They believe that it should be reported in special-purpose reports, completely separate from general-purpose financial reports.

The major areas described above should be fertile fields for research because continued study and experimentation with these formats will facilitate the proper evaluation of proposals to change financial reporting. In addition to these concerns, other produtive areas are emerging.

Auditing Issues

A new frontier in governmental auditing and auditing research began with "broad scope" auditing. Standards for this type of auditing were articulated in 1972 by the U.S. General Accounting Office.[24] These standards defined and described the elements of a broad-scope audit: (1) financial and compliance, (2) economy and efficiency and (3) program results or effectiveness.

Significant research efforts have concentrated on performing broad-scope audits and improving the capability of governmental audit organizations to conduct these audits. The methodology has concentrated on case studies and surveys. Government internal auditing research has experienced increasing interest. With growing acceptance by state and local governments, research into broad-scope audit standards and experience should continue to provide guidance to governments beginning or improving an audit operation.[25]

It is generally agreed that governments should accomplish their objectives as completely as possible and at the least cost. In fact, there is increasing pressure on governments to do so. Concepts of "economy," "efficiency," "effectiveness" and "program results" are being advocated. The increase in public demand for accountability and productivity in government has fostered interest in the performance audit as a tool for evaluating service levels and management activities through its emphasis on economy and efficiency and program results. Unlike the financial audit, this procedure determines whether or not the entity is managing its resources effectively and deriving the desired results and benefits from its programs. Research in this area is typically practitioner-oriented in its discussions of the implementation and management of a performance audit.

Disclosure

Disclosure is the process by which a governmental unit conveys information about itself to others outside of the government. Municipal financial reports, budgets, and official statements are some of the devices which a unit uses to provide information. Previously, these reports have been designed to comply with legal and budget provisions. However, the lack of adequate disclosure, exemplified by "New York," has stimulated interest in tailoring the type and amount of information disclosed to the needs of various users.

Little work has been completed in this area beyond identifying users and cataloging their needs. Some researchers have attempted to provide empirical evidence against which suggested disclosure practices could be evaluated.[26] As it currently stands, most efforts are devoted to exploring suggested reporting changes designed to improve disclosure.

The Municipal Finance Officers Association has taken the lead in this area. The Association began work in 1974 on a research project which was to culminate in the design of a set of disclosure standards. A publication presented guidelines for use in providing information to investors in connection with offerings of state and local governments.[27] The guidelines represent the consensus of the industry on the information which it deems desirable to have available in making investment decisions.

The MFOA disclosure guidelines have been and currently are the subject of several researchers' interest.[28] The guidelines are being assessed for their ability to accomplish the objectives they set out to meet—promoting uniformity and comparability among municipal security offerings and describing a minimum set of standards. Particular attention is being directed to the importance of information appearing in municipal documents from the perspective of individuals responsible for preparing reports, attesting to the reports and using them.[29]

Determining the degree of adherence to specified standards is another important research activity. Studies have already investigated the degree to which governmental units comply with generally accepted accounting principles. Consideration of federal regulation of municipal securities offerings and sales has prompted further research on the effectiveness of MFOA's voluntary disclosure guidelines.[30]

Summary

The revival of interest in governmental accounting and financial reporting has had a favorable impact on research in the area. Recognition of the importance of financial reports has prompted users to seek the answers to basic questions about the construction of these reports and their objectives.

Similar concerns have affected individuals responsible for articulating accounting and reporting principles and those responsible for preparing the reports. They too have begun to ask questions about standards, standard-setting authorities, the usefulness of reports, and report formats.

These concerns have been translated into issues for research and are the focus of current research efforts by the academic community and the authoritative bodies.

The issues which have been raised are the most fundamental to governmental accounting and financial reporting. In the past, the interest of accountants has been directed to commercial issues with little or no attention given to public-sector problems. Under the leadership of the NCGA, which is the only national organization concerned exclusively with governmental issues, and with the support of the AICPA, government accounting and financial reporting has become an important research field.

Some have criticized current research for being nonempirical. This may be a valid criticism but it seems unfair if one takes into account that this is a relatively new area and more empirical work is coming all the time. In their attempt to produce answers to the basic questions, researchers have not been required to use the most sophisticated methodologies. The charge that their work is nonempirical should not be misconstrued as an attack on their competence or on the relevance of their work, but should be viewed as a challenge to meet in their future research endeavors.

Notes

1. Michael H. Granof, "Municipal Accounting Research: Some Observations," Working Paper 77–46 (Austin, Texas: University of Texas, School of Business, April 1977).

2. Robert J. Freeman, "Governmental Accounting Research and Standards-Setting: The Role of the NCGA," *Governmental Finance* (May 1976).

3. Granof, "Municipal Accounting Research;" and David H. Luthy, *Municipal Financial Reporting: The Importance of Selected Items of Information and a Measure of Consensus,* Working Paper (Logan: Utah State University, 1978).

4. James L. Chan, *Academic Research in Nonprofit Accounting: A Review of the Literature (1966–1977),* Working Paper No. 3 (Sarasota, Florida: American Accounting Association, Public Sector Section, 1977), pp. 9–10.

5. Robert J. Freeman, "Criteria for Policy-Oriented Municipal Accounting and Reporting Research: A Charge for the Future," in *Municipal Accounting and Reporting: Issues for Research,* ed. Michael H. Granof (Chicago: Alexander Grant and Co., 1976).

6. Granof, *Municipal Accounting and Reporting.*

7. Russell Barefield, "Committee for Research in Public Sector Reporting," *PSR Newsletter* (Tucson: University of Arizona, College of Business and Public Administration, November 1977).

8. Maurice S. Newman and John O. Mason, Jr., "Alabama Professional Accounting Research Information System" (University, Alabama: College of Commerce and Business Administration, University of Alabama, 1977).

9. National Committee on Governmental Accounting, *Governmental Accounting, Auditing, and Financial Reporting* (Chicago: Municipal Finance Officers Association, 1968).

10. Committee on Governmental Accounting and Auditing, American Institute of Certified Public Accountants, *Audits of State and Local Governmental Units,* Industry Audit Guide (New York: American Institute of Certified Public Accountants, Inc., 1974).

11. Coopers & Lybrand and the University of Michigan, *Financial Disclosure Practices of the American Cities: A Public Report* (New York: Coopers & Lybrand, 1976); James M. Patton, "Accounting for Nonprofit Organizations: A Critical Analysis of Recent Recommendations for Changing Generally Accepted Accounting Principles," Working Paper (Pittsburgh: University of Pittsburgh, March 1977); and Touche Ross & Co., *Public Financial Reporting by Local Government: Issues and A Viewpoint* (New York: Touche Ross & Co., 1977).

12. Robert N. Anthony, *Financial Accounting in Nonbusiness Organizations: An Exploratory Study of Conceptual Issues,* Research Report (Stamford, Connecticut: Financial Accounting Standards Board, April 1978).

13. Financial Accounting Standards Board, "An Analysis of Issues Related to Conceptual Framework for Financial Accounting and Reporting: Objectives of Financial Reporting by Nonbusiness Organizations," Discussion Memorandum, Stamford, Connecticut, 1978.

14. U.S. Congress, Committee on Banking, Housing and Urban Affairs, Subcommittee on Securities, *Municipal Securities Full Disclosure Act of 1976, Hearings Before the Subcommittee on Securities* (Washington, D.C.: Government Printing Office, 1976).

15. National Council on Governmental Accounting, "GAAFR Restatement Principles Exposure Draft" (Chicago: Municipal Finance Officers Association, February 1978) and "Grant Accounting and Reporting by State and Local Government Recipients Exposure Draft" (Chicago: Municipal Finance Officers Association, April 1978).

16. Jonathan Gaciala, "State Government Accounting and Financial Reporting Practices," research project funded by the National Science Foundation and conducted by the Council of State Governments, Lexington, Kentucky, forthcoming.

17. Ibid.; and Lloyd F. Hara, "County Audit Survey Project," research project funded by the Association of Government Accountants to obtain data on county auditing programs, forthcoming.

18. James M. Patton, "An Experimental Investigation of Some Effects of Consolidating Municipal Finance Reports," Working Paper (Pittsburgh: University of Pittsburgh, 1976); Sidney Davidson, David O. Green, Walter Hellerstein, Albert Madansky and Roman L. Weil, *Financial Reporting by State and Local Government Units* (Chicago: The University of Chicago, Center for Management of Public and Nonprofit Enterprise, 1977); James A. Hogan and Anthony J. Mottola, *Financial Disclosure Practices of the American Cities II: Closing the Communications Gap* (New York: Coopers & Lybrand, 1978); and Walter Johnson, "A Proposed Experimental Approach to Reporting Governmental Activity to the General Public" (Columbia: University of Missouri, 1978).

19. Hogan and Mottola, *Financial Disclosure Practices.*

20. Davidson et al., *Financial Reporting by State and Local Governmental Units.*

21. Anthony, *Financial Accounting in Nonbusiness Organizations.*

22. Davidson et al., *Financial Reporting by State and Local Governmental Units;* John H. Engstrom, "An Investigation into the Accounting Information Needs of Participants in the Municipal Budget Process" (Ph.D. dissertation, Indiana University, 1977); and Anthony, *Financial Accounting in Nonbusiness Organizations.*

23. Davidson et al., *Financial Reporting by State and Local Governmental Units.*

24. Comptroller General of the United States, *Standards for Audit of Governmental Organizations, Programs, Activities & Functions* (Washington, D.C.: Government Printing Office, 1972).

25. Felix Pomeranz, Alfred J. Cancellieri, Joseph B. Stevens and James L. Savage, *Auditing in the Public Sector* (Boston: Warren, Gorham & Lamont, 1976); Robert Atkisson, "Internal Auditing in Local Governments" (Altamonte Springs, Florida: Institute for Internal Auditors, 1978); Harry Fuchs, "State Government Audit Practices as They Relate to the Acceptance and Use of the GAO Audit Standards" (Washington, D.C.: U.S. Government Accounting Office, 1978); and Margaret C. K. Gibbs and George Gibbs, "The Broad Scope Audit," California State College, San Bernardino, California, forthcoming.

26. Jerold L. Zimmerman, "The Municipal Accounting Maze: An Analysis of Political Incentives," paper presented at the Conference on Measurement and Evaluation of the Economic Efficiency of Public and Private Nonprofit Institutions, University of Chicago, May 1977.

27. Municipal Finance Officers Association, *Disclosure Guidelines for Offerings of Securities by State and Local Governments* (Chicago: Municipal Finance Officers Association, 1976).

28. John E. Petersen et al., "Searching for Standards," *Duke Law Journal* 1976 (January 1977); Samuel B. Chase, Jr., "Improving Disclosure for Municipal Securities" (Washington, D.C.: Golembe Associates, 1976); Kay Anderson, *Municipal Disclosure Standards Sourcebook* (New York: Council on Municipal Performance, 1978); and Robert W. Ingram, "A Review of MFOA Disclosure Guidelines," *Governmental Finance* (May 1978).

29. James M. Patton, "Usefulness of Municipal Accounting and Financial Reporting Practices," Working Paper (Pittsburgh: University of Pittsburgh, May 1976); Hogan and Mottola, *Financial Disclosure Practices;* and David H. Luthy, *Municipal Financial Reporting.*

30. Coopers & Lybrand and the University of Michigan, *Financial Disclosure Practices of the American Cities.*

Intergovernmental Finance

George F. Break

If fiscal research is stimulated by rapid growth in the programs to be studied, intergovernmental grants should soon be basking in the warm glow of expert attention. Particularly since the adoption of federal revenue sharing in 1972, economists have been turning their attention to grant programs more and more. Clearly the incentives for research are there. Equally clearly, so are the problems.

In addition to the usual scarcity of reliable and relevant data, research studies of intergovernmental finance encounter two special, and difficult, problems.

The first is the lack of a clearly articulated set of goals to be achieved by the use of different grant instruments. To be sure, numerous goals have been suggested, and much ingenuity has gone into the design of different kinds of grant programs. The trouble, rather, lies in the nature and suitability of the linkages between the two. Where grants can claim a firm status as the best potential instrument—as a means of dealing with interjurisdictional spill-outs of program benefits, for example—it is especially difficult to specify the precise kind of grant design required. Where grant designs can be precisely specified, on the other hand, there are usually several superior instruments, all better suited to achieving the objective at hand than any grant program.

The second problem is the lack of any generally accepted theoretical model of government behavior. Here, at least, much progress has been made in recent years, and empirical studies today, unlike their predecessors of only a few years ago, typically rest on some carefully developed theoretical foundation. The trouble is that more than one kind of foundation can be provided, and the research results are likely to depend on what choice is made.

Everyone knows, of course, that public policy research is difficult. As Henry Aaron has said in a different connection: "The quality of the work and of the data on which the answers are based varies from superb to awful, but it is improving."[1] Exactly the same comment applies to research on intergovernmental finance. There is comfort for everyone in this state of affairs. The general public should be pleased that the trend is definitely upwards, and the expert will be delighted that there is still much to be done. Indeed, that may always be the case, for as Aaron has also noted, "Few findings that bear on enduring issues of public policy can be expected to remain generally accepted for very long."[2]

This brief discussion of recent research on intergovernmental finance cannot begin to cover all of the studies that have been done, or are under way in that area. Instead,

---

George F. Break is Professor of Economics at the University of California, Berkeley.

the focus will be on the major kinds of economic effects that intergovernmental grants can generate and on the main kinds of research design that are appropriate for the identification and measurement of those effects. Particular studies will then be used to illustrate these issues. The paper closes with a discussion of future research needs and directions.

The Price Effects of Grants

Whenever a grantor offers to share part of the cost of a well-defined state or local government program,[3] one effect is to lower the tax price at which state or local residents can acquire additional units of that particular program service. The reactions of the consumers of that service can then be studied using the standard model of utility maximization, subject to a budget constraint found in economic theory. That model, of course, was developed for application to private goods markets where consumers take prices as given and are free to adjust the quantities purchased to their own tastes. In public goods markets, in contrast, quantities are the same for everyone once the choice of program level has been made, but tax prices can and do vary from one individual to another. Some adaptation of the consumer choice model is therefore necessary to specify how consumer demands for public goods are translated into governmental budgetary decisions. The most common mechanism is the so-called median voter model based on the revelation of consumer demands by a simple-majority voting process.[4]

Two recent studies using that model provide a clear picture of its potentialities. The first, by Larry Orr, deals with the Aid to Families with Dependent Children (AFDC) program, using data for all states and the District of Columbia for the period 1963–72.[5] An important aspect of the study is its test of the hypothesis that income redistribution is a public good in the sense that taxpayers derive positive utilities from increases in the personal income of poor families. The firm establishment of such an hypothesis about taxpayer attitudes, toward which Orr's findings provide an important boost, would be of great policy significance. It would, for one thing, remove the long-established constraint that welfare programs must be financed by ability-to-pay, and not by benefits-received, principles. It would also establish income redistribution as a local public good, one that could under the right circumstances be varied from one region of the country to another in line with local taxpayer tastes.[6]

Equally important for the design of intergovernmental finance systems is Orr's finding that AFDC matching grants have a significant marginal price effect on benefit levels, but only an insignificant income effect. As he notes, these findings imply, for example, that "the institution of a federally financed benefit floor which eliminated federal matching at the margin while holding constant—or even increasing—the average federal share of benefits would reduce benefit levels by about 16 percent."[7]

A second study using a consumer utility-maximization model, by Martin Feldstein, examines the role that intergovernmental grants might play in adapting local school finance to a judicial requirement, such as that enunciated in *Serrano vs. Priest* (1971), that per pupil expenditures on education bear no significant relationship to school district wealth.[8]

In a system of complete local financing of schools there would undoubtedly be a strong positive relationship between district expenditures and district wealth measured, say, by per pupil taxable property. Numerous empirical studies, including Feldstein's, have confirmed this proposition. District demands for school services, however, should also be inversely related to the effective tax price of those services, and as already noted, tax price can be changed by the use of suitably designed state matching grants. In the present instance, the effective tax price should be made to vary directly with district wealth, and if these interdistrict price variations are large enough, their spending effects could precisely offset the countervailing effects of wealth variations so that, on the average, school expenditures would not be related to district wealth.

Clearly, a high (negative) price elasticity of district demand and a low (positive) wealth elasticity of demand would permit the achievement of wealth neutrality in school finance with only a small amount of price discrimination built into the state's matching school grant formulas. This, indeed, is the result obtained by Feldstein in his empirical analysis of the school expenditures of 105 towns in Massachusetts in 1970.[9]

That the implicit price effects of matching grants constitute a potentially important intergovernmental fiscal tool is clearly established by these two studies alone.[10] It is still a very big step from that recognition to the design of the right kind of price-effect grant. For one thing, to be certain of generating such effects, the matching grant must be open-ended, allowing recipients to claim as much of the grantor's funds as they wish provided that they match them with the required amounts of their own money. For grantor governments to be willing to expose their own budgets to such contingencies they must be highly certain about how much they are likely to have to provide in matching funds. It is doubtful that empirical studies of the price elasticity of grantee demands yet provide the solid evidence needed to allay grantor fears of this kind, and it may well be that they never will. The temptation to make matching grants closed-ended is clearly great, and most of our existing programs are of that kind. This in turn means that there very well may be no implicit price effect at the margin, and hence that the grant programs cannot be analyzed in the ways just described.

The dilemma then is clear. The scarcity of true price-effect grant programs inhibits research into the effects of that policy instrument, and the scarcity of research findings about price elasticities inhibits the establishment of such grant programs. The one way out may lie in the combination of experimental open-ended grant programs with concurrent systematic research evaluations.

Income Effects of Grants

By increasing the fungible resources available to the recipient government, most grants generate income effects. These can be observed most clearly when the grants are completely general and completely unrestricted, and the establishment of general revenue sharing in 1972 greatly expanded research opportunities in this area. Two questions have been the main focus of attention—how the funds should be allocated to recipients and how the recipients use the funds they receive.

One important body of research on the design of grant-allocation formulas begins with the proposition that funds should be allocated directly in relation to fiscal need and inversely in relation to fiscal capacity, and then proceeds to derive measures of these two grantee characteristics. Three main kinds of derivation may be distinguished: normative, average, and behavioral.

The normative approach searches for ideal measures of a region's ability to bear tax burdens and its need for public services of various kinds. There being no clear consensus on these matters, pragmatists have turned instead to the average, or typical, practice of existing governmental units for their answers. The best-known example of this approach is the Advisory Commission on Intergovernmental Relations' (ACIR) representative tax system measure of fiscal capacity.[11]

Skeptical of the representativeness of averages in a diverse world, economists have criticized the subjectivity of both of the preceding approaches and have turned to actual human behavior as the only potential source of objective measures. Briefly stated, their argument is that the observed expenditures of any state or local government are determined partly by its fiscal capacity, partly by its fiscal needs, and partly by a miscellaneous group of socioeconomic factors. If the quantitative effects of each of these determinants can be measured by a multiple regression equation that accounts for most of the observed variation in state and local expenditures, the analyst is then in a position to isolate one factor for special study by holding all the other determinants constant in a statistical sense. Specifically, to measure the relative fiscal capacities of a group of local governments, all of the determining variables other than the fiscal capacity variable are set at their mean values for the group, and expenditures of each locality are estimated from the regression equation using the actual value of the fiscal capacity variable for that community. These estimated expenditure values are then used as the measure of relative fiscal capacity for the group.

The argument, in short, is that two communities have the same fiscal capacity if, apart from any differences between them in fiscal need, taste, or any other noncapacity factor, they choose to spend the same amounts on government services. A similar procedure can then be used to derive an index of relative fiscal needs. Two of the best examples of this general approach are a study of local school expenditures in Massachusetts in 1970 by Helen Ladd and an analysis of the fiscal needs and resources of New York State schools by Harvey Brazer and associates.[12]

Each of the approaches just described has its obvious strengths and weaknesses, and no consensus has yet emerged. This being the case, research interest has centered on simulations of the impact effects on different government units of the use of different allocation formulas for unrestricted general grant funds. Ladd has shown that her behavioral measure of fiscal capacity is significantly different from the standard measures, and John Akin has used the same approach to criticize the ACIR's representative tax system measure.[13] That the ACIR measure would allocate general revenue sharing funds differently from the per capita personal income measure currently in use has been shown both by the ACIR itself and in the Brookings Institution's research studies on *Monitoring Revenue Sharing*.[14] Still more comprehensive comparisons of the effects of alternative fiscal capacity measures are presented in an unpublished manuscript by Robert Reischauer.[15] Numerous studies of alternative allocation formulas for the federal government's general revenue sharing program are summarized in two volumes of the National Science Foundation's reports on that program.[16]

Simulations of the impact effects of alternative fund distribution formulas are only the first step in a comprehensive research study of unrestricted general grants. The next step is to estimate the effects of these additional funds on the behavior of all recipient governments. This is a particularly challenging task because it involves comparing what the grantees are in fact doing with what they would have done if they had not received the grant funds, or with what they would do if they received additional grants.

Undeterred by the ambiguities inherent in any comparison of actual with hypothetical situations, researchers have taken several approaches to this problem. Telephone interviews of community leaders and members of the general public have been conducted, and scientific sample surveys, based either on mailed questionnaires or personal interviews, have been made of the views of state and local officials.[17]

Sorting out individual perceptions of reality from the reality itself is a problem with these studies that many economists would regard as critical. Political scientists, on the other hand, might argue that it is the perceptions themselves that really matter and hence that the problem is not critical at all. Be that as it may, economists have applied their own behavioral models of state and local government to the problem. Some have been based on John Crecine's computer simulation model of municipal budgeting, while others have used multiple regression analysis that attempts either to explain state and local government expenditure choices with general revenue sharing grants as one of the determinants or to predict future expenditure and revenue levels with and without the presence of revenue sharing grants.[18] One general conclusion has been that the official reports made to the Office of Revenue Sharing on the uses of funds are, not surprisingly, unreliable guides to the true uses. Other valuable findings concern the major determinants of differential behavior in spending general revenue sharing money which can then be used to estimate the effects of changes in the distribution formulas.

Economists' estimates of the use of grant monies are, of course, no more reliable than are the underlying models used to generate their results. An interesting compromise methodology is the coordinated use of a carefully selected panel of fiscal experts to monitor the behavior of revenue sharing recipients during the first years of the program's existence. This was the approach adopted for the Brookings Institution's studies, two volumes of which have been published.[19]

One behavioral reaction to revenue sharing is of particular interest to economists because it provides a partial test of the realism of some of the theoretical models used to describe, and to empirically estimate, state and local government operations. This is the division of grant funds between tax reduction and expenditure increases. Consumer utility maximizing models, on the one hand, predict that a $1 increase in per capita personal income given directly to each household would have exactly the same effects on state or local government spending as would a general revenue sharing grant equal to $1 per capita given directly to the governmental units in question. Bureaucratic or producer utility maximizing models, on the other hand, predict that grants would stimulate government spending significantly more than would equal sums of money given directly to taxpayers. Money, in other words, tends to stick wherever it is first received. That these "flypaper effects" do indeed exist to an important degree is the message of several well-designed research studies of that question.[20] Important as these findings are for economic model builders, they may be of even greater interest to policy makers and to the general public since they imply that federal grants, for example, do stimulate state and local government spending much more than would an equal amount of federal tax reduction.

A final set of revenue sharing effects is of particular interest to political scientists and sociologists. These are the effects of the program on the processes by which state and local government budgetary decisions are reached, on civil rights, and on employment practices toward minority groups. Researchers have not neglected these questions. They have been a part of the Brookings monitoring studies from the beginning, and several of the NSF-sponsored projects have dealt explicitly with process and related effects.[21]

Special Grant Effects

The pure price and income effects of grants are only the beginning of the search for the full story of intergovernmental finance. Closed-end conditional grants which have been the most important kind of federal grant—they were 61 percent of total federal grants in fiscal 1974, but that ratio has been declining in recent years—do not fall into either of the categories just discussed but generate a set of mixed effects. Much research, of varying quality, has been done here, and it is not easy to assess the significance of the diverse findings. Fortunately, several excellent surveys, critiques and annotated bibliographies are available.[22] These categorical grants, however, may or may not continue to be the dominant form of federal grants-in-aid.

In his 1971 State of the Union Message, President Nixon proposed the consolidation of some 130 existing categorical grants into six broad block-grant packages to be called Special Revenue Sharing. The areas suggested were education, law enforcement, manpower training, transportation, and urban and rural community development. For policy analysts, the change involved a great deal of uncertainty. In his 1976 survey of the empirical literature on intergovernmental grants, for example, Edward M. Gramlich remarked, "I know of no study that could have convincingly predicted the effects of converting categorical aid to special revenue sharing in any one of the six areas proposed."[23] The field, it seems, was wide open for researchers, and they showed no hesitation to enter. The ACIR led off with a short analysis of special revenue sharing in December 1971,[24] inaugurated in the spring of 1974 a 14-volume series of studies of the whole federal aid system (including five studies of special revenue sharing[25]) and in early 1976 held a roundtable discussion of block grants.[26] The Brookings Institution extended its monitoring research methodology to the Community Development Block Grant Program,[27] and numerous independent researchers selected their own areas of special interest.[28] The level of activity is encouraging, and it remains only to see how useful the results will be. Few programs, in any case, have had the distinction accorded to special revenue sharing of having its progress from the very beginning studied by carefully-designed longitudinal research methods.

A spin-off of the general revenue sharing program, authorized by Title II of the Public Works Employment Act of 1976, is the Antirecession Fiscal Assistance (ARFA) Program. Originally designed to provide relatively unrestricted aid funds to high-unemployment state and local governments through fiscal 1977, the program was extended for an additional year at a maximum budgetary authorization of $2.25 billion.

These short time horizons made policy evaluations difficult, but some research studies have already been published and more are under way. The main issues are the usual ones of the appropriateness of the program's goals and the suitability of the instruments used to achieve those goals. As a 1977 report to Congress by the Comptroller General noted, the program appears to be more responsive to long-term secular decline of cities and regions than it is to its stated purpose of moderating short-term cyclical fluctuations.[29] Presumably, each goal calls for its own special set of instruments, and the Comptroller General's report raises questions about the effectiveness of an antirecessionary aid program that uses regional unemployment data to determine both when aid funds will be distributed (triggering) and how much money each jurisdiction is to receive (targeting).

One alternative targeting mechanism that has been suggested and analyzed is some measure of the impact of a national recession on state and local governmental abilities to continue to provide their normal levels of services, the questions being how superior this alternative might be to the present distribution formula and what effects, if any, its adoption might have on the fiscal behavior of state and local governments.[30] Another issue is the nature of the trade-off between the employment-generating effects of the ARFA program and its efficiency in ameliorating state-local budgetary disruptions created by recessions.[31]

A difficult problem that has to be faced in any research study of intergovernmental grants, as for many other public programs, is the degree of confidence that should be placed in the statutory, as distinct from the operational, features of the program. It is well known that government programs are not always operated exactly in the way that the law says, or at least implies, that they should be. Converting these qualitative impressions into hard evidence is no easy task, but researchers have recently been attempting to do so with some very interesting results.

Martin McGuire, for example, has developed a theoretical model that permits him to disentangle and identify the true price and income effects of closed-end categorical grants in such a way that empirical estimates of the magnitude of these effects can be derived from the observed behavior of the recipients of the grant funds.[32] The idea here is that the statutory matching share of the grantee, for example, may not accurately indicate the true matching share. In practice the latter will be determined by a complex bargaining and adjustment process between grantor and grantee administrators who are likely to have varying degrees of discretion about which program expenditures will be matched in what specific degrees. Anyone relying solely on the statutory matching ratio, therefore, may be led far astray. McGuire's empirical estimation of his model focuses on two important issues. One is the extent to which restricted grant funds may be converted by the grantee into fungible resources, and the other is the extent to which grants stimulate more government spending than would equal increases in private-sector incomes. Both the fungibility and flypaper effects are shown to be important for the programs studied.[33]

Project grant programs, because of the nature of the application and approval process, may also produce discrepancies between statutory and effective matching ratios. This phenomenon has been documented by Howard Chernick for the Department of Housing and Urban Development's basic water and sewer facilities program between 1966 and 1971.[34] Even more interesting for economists is Chernick's evidence that the project administrators appeared to be varying matching shares so as to stimulate a greater amount of grantee spending than could have been achieved, with the same expenditure of federal funds, by the use of uniform shares for all grantees.

Unrestricted federal grants may impart to state and local government spending a stimulus that is several times that of an equal-sized reduction in federal taxes—estimates place the marginal propensity to spend on state-local services in the neighborhood of .05 to .10 for changes in disposable personal incomes, but at anywhere from .25 to .85 for changes in federal unrestricted grants. However, there is still much policy concern over the extent to which federal grants of all kinds substitute for state and local funds rather than being added to them. Maintenance-of-effort designs may be used to try to strengthen the stimulating effects, but as long as the formulas are tied to pre-grant spending levels, the effectiveness of these policies is likely to decline steadily with the passage of time. Another device is to target the grant funds in ways that can be monitored and enforced by the grantor. The operation of such controls may be facilitated if the aided group of people may readily be compared with an unaided group. Calling such a design a "differential add-on grant," Martin Feldstein has analyzed its use in Title I of the Elementary and Secondary Education Act and found it to stimulate more local spending than would a traditional type of block grant for education.[35]

Whatever the relative stimulating powers of different grant designs may be, they also may differ in the speeds with which their effects are generated and the extent to which initial effects may be offset later by a complex set of countervailing interactions set in motion by the grant program. That the impact and final equilibrium effects of grants may differ significantly is obviously an unsettling possibility for policy makers to contemplate.

If the two sets of effects do differ, it is no longer safe to rely on simple impact simulations to evaluate alternative grant designs. Complex behavioral models must be tested and used, and nowhere is that a more difficult problem than for groups of local governments operating in a single metropolitan area. A promising beginning in the development of such models has been made, for example, by Robert Inman who concludes from his analysis of five alternative school aid instruments applied to 59 local school districts in the New York metropolitan area in fiscal 1969 that the impact effects of aid tend to overestimate the final equilibrium effects by 20 to 60 percent.[36] In general, he finds that the impact effects occur mostly in the first year of the program's operation and that most of the indirect reaction effects occur during the following four years. These are important results which clearly merit further study for different programs and for different parts of the country.

Conclusions

Research on intergovernmental grants has clearly produced some valuable results. Much could also be accomplished simply by extending established methods of analysis to new data and by refining existing theoretical and econometric models in various ways. More risky but more exciting research, here as elsewhere, will concentrate, however, on new areas and methods. A few of the opportunities that beckon are the following.

    a. The development of more relevant, detailed, and precisely measured data sets. The Feldstein study of differential add-on grants provides an excellent example of what can be done with such assistance.

    b. The use of smaller observational units in econometric estimation of grant effects. Many past studies have had to use states or local governments as their behavioral units when households were the obvious proper choice. Progress here, of course, depends on the prior development of better data sets.

    c. The development and testing of alternative theoretical models of governmental behavior to see which ones are most reliable at what times and in what places. Consumer utility maximization models used to be compared with bureaucratic utility maximization models and with more complicated ones that deal with the existence of several different competing groups, each maximizing its own utility subject to various kinds of constraint and restraint.[37]

d. The extension of empirical studies beyond the direct impact effects of grants to the whole complex set of interacting indirect effects. One important question here is the extent to which the final effects of particular grant programs differ from their impact effects. Another concerns the effects of grant programs on the behavior of nonaided governmental units.[38]

e. Systematic comparisons of alternative research methodologies designed to identify the kinds of programs and questions that each can deal with most effectively. As experience with general revenue sharing is gained, it should be possible to make a relative evaluation of the Brookings Institution's longitudinal monitoring methodology compared to the use of some of the standard types of pooled cross-sectional econometric analyses.

f. A shift of emphasis from the general to the specific in dealing with questions of grant design and effect. The former, of course, is more glamorous for the researcher, but the latter is more useful for the policy maker.

g. More research on the specification and measurement of grant program objectives and on the evaluation of alternative grant designs as means toward these goals. Benefit-cost analysts will recognize their own *raison d'être* in this prescription, but many policy makers will be skeptical of its potential accomplishments. It will be up to the researchers to convince them otherwise.

Notes

1. Henry H. Aaron, *Politics and the Professors: The Great Society in Perspective* (Washington, D. C.: Brookings Institution, 1978), p. 164.

2. Ibid., p. 165.

3. For a good example of what can happen when open-ended matching grant programs are not well-defined, see Martha Derthick, *Uncontrollable Spending for Social Services Grants* (Washington, D. C.: Brookings Institution, 1975).

4. See, for example, William S. Comanor, "The Median Voter Rule and the Theory of Political Choice." *Journal of Public Economics* 5 (January/February, 1976), pp. 169–177.

5. Larry V. Orr, "Income Transfers as a Public Good: An Application to AFDC," *American Economic Review* 66 (June 1976), pp. 359–371.

6. Mark V. Pauly, "Income Redistribution as a Local Public Good," *Journal of Public Economics* 2 (February 1973), pp. 35–58.

7. Orr, op. cit., p. 370. For similar findings derived by the use of a different kind of theoretical model, see Frank A. Sloan, "A Model of State Income Maintenance Decisions," *Public Finance Quarterly* 5 (April 1977), pp. 139–173.

8. Martin S. Feldstein, "Wealth Neutrality and Local Choice in Public Education," *American Economic Review* 65 (March 1975), pp. 75–89.

9. Ibid., p. 85.

10. See also Edward M. Gramlich and Harvey Galper, "State and Local Fiscal Behavior and Federal Grant Policy," *Brookings Papers on Economic Activity* 1 (1973), pp. 15–65.

11. Advisory Commission on Intergovernmental Relations, *Measures of State and Local Fiscal Capacity and Tax Effort* (Washington, D. C.: Advisory Commission on Intergovernmental Relations, 1962); and *Measuring the Fiscal Capacity and Effort of State and Local Areas* (Washington, D. C.: Advisory Commission on Intergovernmental Relations, 1971).

12.   Helen F. Ladd, "Local Education Expenditures, Fiscal Capacity, and the Composition of the Property Tax Base," *National Tax Journal* 28 (June 1975), pp. 145–58; Harvey E. Brazer et al., *Fiscal Needs and Resources: A Report to the New York State Commission on the Quality, Cost and Financing of Elementary and Secondary Education*, processed (November 1971); and W. Douglas Morgan, "An Alternative Measure of Fiscal Capacity," *National Tax Journal* 27 (June 1974), pp. 361–65.

13.   Ladd, "Local Education Expenditures"; John S. Akin, "Fiscal Capacity and the Estimation Method of the Advisory Commission on Intergovernmental Relations," *National Tax Journal* 26 (June 1973), pp. 275–91; and Allen D. Manvel, "Tax Capacity Versus Tax Performance: A Comment," *National Tax Journal* 26 (June 1973), pp. 293–4.

14.   Advisory Commission on Intergovernmental Relations, *Measuring the Fiscal Capacity*, Appendix G; and Richard P. Nathan, Allen D. Manvel and Susannah E. Calkins, *Monitoring Revenue Sharing* (Washington, D. C.: Brookings Institution, 1975), pp. 137–40.

15.   Robert D. Reischauer, *Rich Governments—Poor Governments: Determining the Fiscal Capacity and Revenue Requirements of State and Local Government*, Brookings Staff Paper, processed (December 1974).

16.   National Science Foundation, Research Applied to National Needs, *General Revenue Sharing*, 5 vols. (Washington, D. C.: National Science Foundation, 1975), vol. 1: Summaries of Formula Research; and vol. 3: Synthesis of Formula Research.

17.   National Science Foundation, *General Revenue Sharing*, vol. 2: Summaries of Impact and Process Research.

18.   National Science Foundation, *The Economic and Political Impact of General Revenue Sharing* (Washington, D. C.: National Science Foundation, 1976), note especially the papers by Gail R. Wilensky and Robin Barlow; and *General Revenue Sharing*, vol. 2: Summaries of Impact and Process Research, note especially the paper by Tom Anton, entitled "Understanding the Fiscal Impact of General Revenue Sharing;" and Patrick D. Larkey, "Process Models and Program Evaluation: The Impact of General Revenue Sharing on Municipal Fiscal Behavior—A Summary," National Tax Association, *Proceedings of the Sixty-Ninth (1976) Annual Conference on Taxation* (1977), pp. 167–78.

19.   Nathan et al., *Monitoring Revenue Sharing*, Appendix A. The second volume in the series is Richard P. Nathan, Charles F. Adams, Jr., and Associates, *Revenue Sharing: The Second Round* (Washington, D. C.: Brookings Institution, 1977).

20.   Gramlich and Galper, "State and Local Fiscal Behavior;" Nathan et al., *Monitoring Revenue Sharing*, and *Revenue Sharing: The Second Round;* and Martin C. McGuire, "A Method for Estimating the Effect of a Subsidy on the Receivers Resource Constraint: With an Application to U. S. Local Governments 1964–1971," processed, University of Maryland, Department of Economics.

21.   National Science Foundation, *General Revenue Sharing*, vols. 2 and 4.

22.   Advisory Commission on Intergovernmental Relations: *Federal Grants: Their Effects on State-Local Expenditures, Employment Levels, Wage Rates* (Washington, D. C.: Advisory Commission on Intergovernmental Relations, 1977), pp. 45–53; John Eric Fredland, *Determinants of State and Local Expenditures: An Annotated Bibliography* (Washington, D. C.: Urban Institute, 1974); and Edward M. Gramlich, "The Effect of Federal Grants on State-Local Expenditures: A Review of the Econometric Literature," National Tax Association, *Proceedings of the Sixty-Second (1969) Annual Conference on Taxation* (1970), pp. 569–93, and "Intergovernmental Grants: A Review of the Empirical Literature," Paper presented at the International Seminar on Public Economics Conference, Berlin, January 1976.

23.   Gramlich, "Intergovernmental Grants."

24.   Advisory Commission on Intergovernmental Relations, *Special Revenue Sharing: An Analysis of the Administration's Grant Consolidation Proposals* (Washington, D. C.: Advisory Commission on Intergovernmental Relations, 1971).

25.   Advisory Commission on Intergovernmental Relations, *Safe Streets Reconsidered: The Block Grant Experience, 1968–1975*, Parts A and B (Washington, D. C.: Advisory Commission on Intergovernmental Relations, 1977); *The Partnership for Health Act: Lessons from a Pioneering Block Grant*, (Washington, D. C.: Advisory Commission on Intergovernmental Relations, January 1977); *Community Development: The Workings of a Federal-Local Block*

Grant (Washington, D. C.: Advisory Commission on Intergovernmental Relations, March 1977); *The Comprehensive Employment and Training Act: Early Readings from a Hybrid Block Grant* (Washington, D. C.: Advisory Commission on Intergovernmental Relations, June 1977); and *Block Grants: A Comparative Analysis* (Washington, D. C.: Advisory Commission on Intergovernmental Relations, forthcoming).

26. Advisory Commission on Intergovernmental Relations, *Block Grants: A Roundtable Discussion* (October 1976).

27. Richard P. Nathan et al., *Block Grants for Community Development* (Washington, D. C.: U. S. Department of Housing and Urban Development, 1977); and "Monitoring the Block Grant Program for Community Development," *Political Science Quarterly* 92 (Summer 1977), pp. 219–44, Brookings General Series Reprint 326.

28. Victor Bach and James Hartling, *Central Cities and Community Development Block Grants: A Comparative Study of Local Experience* (Austin, Texas: LBJ School of Public Affairs); Richard deLeon and Richard LeGates, *Redistribution Effects of Special Revenue Sharing for Community Development*, processed, University of California, Davis, Institute of Governmental Studies, 1976; Richard P. Nathan et al., *Where Have All the Dollars Gone? Implications of General Revenue Sharing for the Law Enforcement Assistance Administration* (Washington, D. C.: U. S. Department of Justice, 1976); and Nonna A. Noto, "Simplifying Intergovernmental Transfers: The Lessons of Community Development Block Grants," *National Tax Journal* 30 (September 1977), pp. 259–67.

29. Elmer B. Staats, *Anitrecession Fiscal Assistance—An Evaluation*, Report to the Congress (Washington, D. C.: U.S. General Accounting Office, 1977).

30. Margaret Jess and Dennis Zimmerman, "Targeting Anti-Recessionary Assistance to States: An Evaluation of PL 94-369," National Tax Association, *Proceedings of the Seventieth (1977) Annual Conference on Taxation* (1978).

31. Edward M. Gramlich, "Evaluating Countercyclical Revenue Sharing," paper presented at Brookings Conference on the Economic Stimulus Program, Washington, D. C., November 1977.

32. Martin McGuire, "An Econometric Model of Federal Grants and Local Fiscal Response," in *Financing the New Federalism*, ed. Wallace E. Oates (Washington, D. C.: Resources for the Future, 1975), pp. 115–38.

33. McGuire, *A Method for Estimating*.

34. Howard Chernick, "Economics of Bureaucratic Behavior: Allocation of Federal Project Grants" (Ph.D. dissertation, University of Pennsylvania, 1976).

35. Martin S. Feldstein, *The Effect of A Differential Add-On Grant: Title I and Local Education Spending*, Discussion Paper 562 (Cambridge, Massachusetts: Harvard University, Institute of Economic Research, 1977).

36. Robert P. Inman, "Micro-Fiscal Planning in the Regional Economy: A General Equilibrium Approach," *Journal of Public Economics* 7 (April 1977), pp. 237–60.

37. See, for example, Randall Bartlett, *Economic Foundations of Political Power* (Glencoe, Ill.: Free Press, 1973); and Douglas G. Hartle, *A Theory of the Expenditure Budgetary Process* (Toronto: University of Toronto Press, 1976).

38. John C. Weicher, "Aid, Expenditure, and Local Government Structure," *National Tax Journal* 25 (December 1972), pp. 573–83.

State-Local Intergovernmental Finance

Harold A. Hovey

Introduction

This essay discusses research relating to state and local interactions in financial areas. The subject matter is treated in three principal categories:

o State grant program issues and impacts;
o State regulation of local fiscal affairs; and
o State actions shifting local financial responsibilities.

From either a state or local perspective, the subject matter of those three categories is critical. State intergovernmental spending accounted for almost 40 percent of total state spending in 1975.[1] From a local perspective, state aid accounts for about a third of local revenues.[2] The sheer magnitude of state grant spending makes the nature and allocation of those grants an often-debated topic at the state and local levels. An understanding of the financial situation of any particular local government or group of them (e.g., central cities) requires an understanding of the patterns of state financing as well as financing through federal and local sources.

Legally, local governments are creatures of the states, which have the legal power to establish and alter boundaries and even to abolish local units or assume their functions. States can prescribe how much local governments can borrow, what tax sources they can use and the functions on which they may and may not spend funds. Thus, a discussion of how particular local governments finance certain functions is often simply a discussion of state law.

Either as an exercise of inherent power or as strings attached to grant programs, states can mandate expenditures of local governments. For example, for school districts states can mandate the length of the school year, the permissible size of classes, and the pay of teachers.

These relationships suggest intergovernmental financial relationships among state and local government as a key research topic in state and local finance. Unfortunately, this subject matter does not develop much of a literature when compared to federal grant programs of roughly equivalent magnitude. There are a number of reasons for the difference:

o In some situations, the development of theory for national-level decisions provides a basis for understanding the same issues and phenomena when they arise on a state-by-state basis. For example, discussion of the alternative merits of categorical assistance versus block grants and revenue sharing at the federal level provides the basic arguments for the same issues at the state level.
o There is a larger and centralized audience for research findings and a larger quantity of interested researchers dealing with issues regarding the federal grant system. Much of what is done at the state and local levels remains in the hinter-

Harold A. Hovey is a Consultant specializing in the management problems of state and local governments.

lands and does not appear in national circulation.

o There simply is more research money available at the federal level through the Congress and the staffs that support it and through Executive Branch agencies than is available at the state and local levels. For example, on the order of $5 million has probably gone into research on federal general revenue sharing. It is unlikely that one-third that amount has been spent in evaluation of state general revenue sharing programs.

Such literature as there is tends to be based upon quite limited data, because researching the detailed laws and spending patterns of 50 states is obviously much more time-consuming than research about the federal government. The literature often deals either with a specific state or group of states or with the type of aggregates that can be developed using data from the Census of Governments.

When detailed data are used, they are usually found in studies that are developed to fill the policy-making needs of a single state. These studies often take forms (e.g., testimony before legislative committees, task force reports, staff reports) that are not copyrighted and not disseminated beyond the state in which they are created.

State Grant Programs

Shared Revenues

A number of states have revenue sharing programs. Some of these are akin to the federal general revenue sharing in that recipients have considerable freedom to decide how to use the funds. Others use the shared-revenue concept, with the local entitlements being a function of the yield of some revenue source, but have an element of earmarking of the proceeds. For example, it is very common for states to share motor vehicle registration fees, drivers' license fees and gasoline tax revenues with local governments. The local governments are commonly required to segregate the receipts and use them exclusively for road construction and maintenance.

At the national level, it is difficult to find studies of state shared-revenue programs for the understandable reason that good data are difficult to come by. The Bureau of the Census collects information on state assistance to local governments every five years as part of the Census of Governments. However, doing very much with these data on a multistate basis is difficult for these reasons:

o It is difficult to sort out components of state aid that were financed in whole or in part with federal funds;

o It is difficult to distinguish situations in which the state contracts with local governments from those in which a grant is involved; and

o The diversity of state aid arrangements means that they do not neatly fall into such classifications as formula and nonformula.

The most comprehensive attempts to cope with these data will be found in the first chapter of the Advisory Commission on Intergovernmental Relations study cited earlier. (See note 1.)

At the state and local levels, studies of shared-revenue programs are common, although these are more likely to be done by staff members of state agencies and contractors than by the types of persons who would publish findings as part of an organized literature. Such studies as there are tend to focus upon need for shared revenues and the ability of the state government to provide revenue. The author knows of no study of state shared revenues parallel to the many federal attempts to learn the impact on various functional areas of general revenue sharing.

The formula used to distribute shared revenues is a source of much controversy within the states. These issues occasionally give rise to published reports.[3]

Categorical and Block Grants

Most state assistance to local government takes the form of earmarked grants. The most common areas for such grants are health and welfare and education.

Assistance to local government in any categorical field presents a number of common questions including:

- What will be used as the indicator(s) of need—population, number of students, number of vehicle registrations, "merit" as determined from competitive applications, etc.;
- What will be used, if anything, as the measure of local ability to pay—wealth, tax base, income, etc.;
- What will be required of the recipient government by way of matching or minimum effort; and
- What will be the administrative provisions of the grant—accounting and auditing, performance standards, etc.?

The most extensive literature on these types of issues will be found in the school-finance area. The concentration on this area occurs because of the large amounts of money involved at the state level and considerable recent litigation on school finance. This literature is reported in the essay by Allan Odden elsewhere in this volume.

Each functional area of state grants tends to develop a mini-literature consisting primarily of studies within a single state for a single function.[4] It is also not uncommon to find studies, such as those in educational finance, which compare and contrast formula approaches in a single function in a number of different states.[5] It is rare for anything to be found on the administrative requirements of state grant programs on either a cross-program or cross-state basis. The Municipal Finance Officers Association's analysis of recent research indicated one example of a comparison of programs within a state[6] and one multistate comparison of productivity encouragements.[7]

The issue of how much to spend on various grant programs also tends to produce a literature in every state. Local school systems, libraries, highway engineers, mayors and county commissioners constantly produce studies on why more funding is needed for various activities. State officials in turn publish documents tending to show that less than the requested funding is necessary and, sometimes, that more local funds should be used in financing the function. Often, this literature is uniquely related to conditions in the particular state in which it originates and is of primary value outside the state only to others wishing to conduct similar analyses.

Another common source of research is the constant flow of general local government financing studies. These studies tend to be conducted either in connection with potential overhaul of the local government financing structure as part of statewide tax revision proposals or in connection with commissions on local government which states periodically create. The general approach of these studies is to examine the finances of local government in terms of adequacy to support expenditures, disparities among local governments, the regressivity of the resulting tax structure, and the relative financial roles of state and local taxpayers.

While these studies of local finance, and the problems that give rise to them, are not new, the passage of Proposition 13 in California and continuing litigation on school-aid formula issues will probably lead to an outpouring of research in the next several years. Many of the issues involved are quite complex, combining elements of limitations on local taxing powers, assistance distribution formulas, and changing state roles in financing of locally administered functions.

Much less common are studies that seek to analyze the overall patterns of state grants relative to particular geographic areas. While it is easy to find literature that has policy prescriptions for state officials (e.g., what state governments should do to help cities), it is much more difficult to find data on a multistate basis. The cross-state studies that are available tend to be anecdotal rather than quantitative treatments of state aid patterns.[8]

Practically every state has one or more geographic areas whose residents argue about discrimination in state grant programs and the location of state facilities in the same way as various regional representatives are participating in the Sunbelt-Snowbelt debate nationally. In Michigan, some representatives of the Upper Peninsula are arguing for secession. In Illinois, residents of the West Central portion of the state dub the area "Forgottonia." Attempts to prove discrimination in the fiscal impacts of state action are generally confined to observation of the location of state facilities and simple financial flow studies. These studies contrast the amount of state revenue raised in particular areas with the amounts returned in services and grants.

To date, attempts to perform this same type of study for state aid and facility locations on a multistate basis have not been successful. For example, in the discussion of the development of an urban program for the Carter Administration there was considerable discussion about whether states discriminate against central cities in their aid program distributions and other policies. Partly because of definitional problems (e.g., what does "discriminate" mean in the context of a grant-in-aid formula?) and partly because of data problems, those data were simply not available to illuminate policy formulation.

The Impacts of Assistance

There is much less evaluation literature at the state and local levels than at the federal level, although interest in evaluation—particularly in state legislative staffs—is increasing. Where evaluation of the activities supported by state grant funds does take place, the evaluation tends not to be tied directly to the assistance provided. For example, a number of state officials have become interested in the productivity of elementary and secondary school systems. However, this interest tends to result in overall evaluations of school systems, rather than evaluation of the impact of a particular state grant program.

As a result, little is known in general about the impacts of state grants on local behavior. For example, does increased assistance per pupil in elementary and secondary education or public health tend to: (1) cause higher factor costs, particularly employee wages; (2) cause higher output; or (3) allow lower taxes by paying for output and factor costs that would otherwise be paid for by local taxes? There has been some conceptual work on topics like these,[9] but little data analysis has taken place.

State Regulation of Municipal Fiscal Affairs

The New York City financial crisis triggered considerable interest in state regulation of municipal financial affairs. In recent years, a number of states have established or strengthened agencies responsible for making sure that local governments did not experience financing crises. Research on state supervision of municipal financing has been undertaken by the Municipal Finance Officers Association and the Advisory Commission on Intergovernmental Relations.[10]

Within the field of public finance there is a substantial literature dealing with the question of what tax and user-charge sources of revenue are most appropriate. This tax policy literature is highly relevant to choices made by state governments regarding, for example, the access of local governments to taxes on sales and income.

A much less understood field is the impact of state mandating of expenditures on local governments. This subject has been recently explored in a pioneering report of the Advisory Commission on Intergovernmental Relations (ACIR).[11] Generally, comparisons are available on mandating in particular functional areas (e.g., elementary and secondary education), but little information is available on a cross-cutting basis.

State, Regional and Community Roles

State Assumption

One of the approaches to providing services which prove financially burdensome to particular communities (e.g., central cities and rural areas) is for a state to assume management and financing of activities that were previously carried out at the local level. States have been assuming a number of costs that were formerly local, with the major example being welfare costs. With the exception of many studies and reports by ACIR relating to this general subject, there is an insignificant literature on state assumption generally. However, there are studies of individual assumption decisions in various functional areas.

Regions and Special Districts

Another way to solve some of the problems which are addressed by state assumption is to shift management and financing responsibility from a unit of government covering a relatively narrow geographic area to one serving a broader area. ACIR alone has produced a literature on this subject also, which can be supplemented by a variety of works by economists on exernalities associated with particular services and by regional planners and others on appropriate organization and roles for sub-state districts. In some cases, specific proposals have been costed for particular areas.[12]

A more limited way to achieve broadening of financial responsibility is to make no change in service responsibility but to share a regional tax base among municipalities on the basis of some factor(s) other than the location of the taxable activity. A Minnesota experiment with the regional tax sharing concept is beginning to produce a literature involving analysis of the potential for the application of the concept elsewhere.[13]

New Emphases on Development

In recent years, federal attention has turned more and more to the problems of central cities. This interest has included increasing recognition of the role of the private sector and the possibilities of using public funds to stimulate private job creation rather than as funding for transfer payments and public facilities. Much of this emphasis is reflected in the urban policy proposals offered by President Carter in the spring of 1978.

State governments have traditionally maintained economic development activities ranging from some planning of growth to a variety of tax abatement and industrial location incentives.[14] These traditional interests in economic development generally have recently been combined with interest in the fate of key urban areas in the policy planning processes of a number of states. At the state level, the result has been the development of urban-oriented development strategies in such states as Michigan, California and Massachusetts. There is also substantial state interest in using some form of state or regional development banking institution to promote economic development.[15]

Interest in this area is likely to be stimulated by the Carter Administration's proposal for "state incentive grants," which was offered as part of the urban policy message. The concept of the incentive grants is that the states would compete for a limited quantity of federal funds, with state proposals being judged by their effectiveness in reaching and dealing with the economic problems of distressed areas, particularly central cities.

Research Needs

In general, it seems likely that persons working on intergovernmental fiscal relations in particular functional areas have a considerable quantity of research available, although they may perceive it as being insufficient to meet all of their needs. Information is routinely swapped by functional specialists in state and federal governments and by the consultants and academics associated with them on such matters as school-aid formula options and highway-financing patterns.

What is generally missing at the level of individual states are looks at grant programs and other state actions affecting intergovernmental fiscal matters across functional areas. It would seem that additional information on the geographic impacts of such programs, on administrative solutions in one program that could solve problems in a program in another functional field, and on other cross-cutting subjects would be of assistance to state decision makers.

For federal-level decision makers and students of urban problems, the most significant research gap would appear to be in the understanding of state actions affecting the financial conditions of central-city governments and other jurisdictions, such as school districts and counties, serving central-city areas. This concern should also extend to urban places (e.g., Newark and East St. Louis) that are not central cities of their SMSAs but which share central-city problems.

As a beginning, it would be desirable to know how state governments are treating those places now in terms of their distribution formulas for state revenue sharing, sharing of earmarked taxes, earmarked state aid for such functions as education and pass throughs of federal grant programs. In this context, analysis of the impact of actual state policy changes on city financing in recent years would be quite helpful.

Such research would be useful to both federal and state policy makers. In addition, state policy makers need a national perspective on state alternatives for dealing with urban fiscal problems so that they can more intelligently select among those alternatives. Federal policy makers need this same perspective for the purpose of deciding whether and how federal programs can be used as leverage for encouraging more effective state actions to solve urban fiscal problems.

Notes

1. Advisory Commission on Intergovernmental Relations, *The States and Intergovernmental Aids* (Washington, D.C.: Government Printing Office, 1977), p. 2.

2. Ibid., p. 7.

3. An example is Garth N. Jones, *Alaska's Revenue Sharing Alternatives* (Springfield, Virginia: National Technical Information Service, 1975).

4. For example, North Carolina Department of Human Resources, *Mental Health Aid Distribution in North Carolina* (Raleigh: North Carolina Department of Human Resources, 1976).

5. For example, Council of State Governments, *State Subsidies to Local Corrections: A Summary of Programs* (Lexington, Kentucky: Council of State Governments, 1977).

6. Texas Advisory Commission on Intergovernmental Relations, *State Administration of Grants-in-Aid to Localities: Improved Procedures for Texas* (Austin: Advisory Commission on Intergovernmental Relations, State of Texas, 1977).

7. D. David Brandon is conducting a study for the National Science Foundation of the application of productivity incentives in state-local aid formulas.

8. For examples, see Harold A. Hovey, *State Urban Development Strategies,* State Planning Series No. 5 (Washington, D.C.: Council of State Planning Agencies, 1977); and William E. Bivens, III, *State Development Strategies for Rural Communities,* State Planning Series No. 6 (Washington, D.C.: Council of State Planning Agencies, 1977).

9. Edward M. Gramlich and others have developed a draft paper with a theory of how governments will respond to grants-in-aid in relation to the power of employees.

10. John E. Petersen, Lisa A. Cole, and Maria L. Petrillo, *Watching and Counting: A Survey of State Assistance to and Supervision of Local Debt and Financial Administration* (Washington, D.C.: Municipal Finance Officers Association, 1977).

11. Advisory Commission on Intergovernmental Relations, *State Mandating of Local Expenditures* (Washington, D.C.: Government Printing Office, 1977).

12. For example, Joseph Slavet and Katherine Bradbury, *Financing State and Local Services* (Lexington, Massachusetts: D.C. Heath, 1975).

13. For a good discussion of the Minnesota tax-sharing plan, see National Council on Urban Economic Development, *Tax Base Sharing,* Information Service Report No. 5, April 1976; and

Wallace O. Dahl, "An Evaluation of Minnesota's Fiscal Disparity Act," paper presented to National Association of Tax Administrators, June 1976.

14. See Council of State Governments, *State Growth Management* (Lexington, Kentucky: Council of State Governments, 1976).

15. For examples of state action, see Martin Katzman and Belden Daniels, *Development Incentives to Induce Efficiencies in Capital Markets* (Boston: New England Regional Commission, 1976).

State-Local Public Finance Theory

William H. Oakland

The literature on state and local finance theory is tremendously diverse, defying comprehensive review by a short essay such as this Consequently our strategy is to summarize the state-of-the-art and recent contributions in three broad areas of inquiry:
1. The optimal structure of government for the delivery of state and local public services;
2. The theory of the expenditure behavior of a state or local government unit; and
3. The incidence of state and local property taxes.

While each of these issues is important in its own right, they share the property of being highly relevant to the question of governance in our large urban areas—perhaps the leading policy issue of the day. Furthermore, since each of the areas has been examined with the use of modern analytic techniques and models, the essay should provide insight into methodological issues as well. Finally, as the reader will quickly recognize, the issues are highly interdependent. The question of optimal government structure, for example, cannot be resolved without a knowledge of how government units behave. Thus, it would not have been possible to treat one of the areas of inquiry without the others in any event.

Optimal Government Structure

Why aren't all government services provided by a single government? How do we decide which functions to allocate to the various levels of government in a federal system? How are government services most efficiently provided at the metropolitan level? What role, if any, can intergovernmental grants play in improving the workings of our system of government? These are among the questions which have been addressed by public finance theorists with respect to the optimal organization of government. Together they fit into the body of literature which has come to be known as the theory of fiscal federalism.[1]

Among the principal building blocks of the theory is the hypothesis that government units tend to provide services uniformly to their constituents. Such uniformity may be due to the collective nature of the government service itself, as in the case of defense, or it may reflect institutional considerations, such as court restrictions. Whatever its source, however, service uniformity coupled with diversity of citizen tastes provides a powerful motive for decentralized provision. At the same time,

William H. Oakland is Professor of Economics at Tulane University, New Orleans, Louisiana and Associate Fellow in Economics and Public Finance at the Academy for Contemporary Problems in Columbus, Ohio.

however, there are significant limitations on the benefits from decentralization, the most important of which is the reason why certain goods and services are provided by the public sector in the first instance—the collective nature of the goods themselves. If the unit of provision is excessively small, many of the benefits of its public services will accrue to nonresidents. Unless guided by altruistic motives, therefore, such governments will tend to ignore nonresident benefits and hence provide nonoptimal levels of public services.

The preceding remarks make it clear that decentralization has both benefits and costs which need to be balanced to determine an optimum.[2] The wider the set of individuals who can benefit from a public service, the greater the gains from centralization. Since most public services differ in the degree to which they can be shared, it follows that the optimal degree of decentralization will vary from service to service. Because of decision-making costs and economies of scale in administration, however, the optimum will not be characterized by a different set of governments for each public service. Rather, a geographic hierarchy of governments, not unlike the federal system of the United States, is likely to emerge.

The preceding comments notwithstanding, there are two major functions for which there is broad agreement that the central government should bear prime responsibility—stabilization and distribution. In both cases, it is not so much a question of balance as of feasibility which precludes decentralized provision. A regional stabilization policy would prove futile because of economic interdependence. For example, mobility of capital would thwart any attempt to reduce the interest rate within a small region. By the same token, the ability to relocate may also neutralize efforts to redistribute income within a region. Here, however, mobility is somewhat limited in the short run so that efforts to redistribute may enjoy initial success. Nevertheless, as some would argue that New York City demonstrates, in the long run those who are redistributed against can simply migrate to other regions. While international migration poses similar problems for a national redistribution policy, cultural and language considerations make emigration a much less serious threat.

Implicit in the discussion of the advantages of decentralization was the assumption that as governments become smaller they also become more responsive to the tastes of their constituents. This proposition is far from obvious and has led to one of the most hotly contested issues of urban public finance theory—the relative merits of metropolitan governance.

The principal support for decentralized urban governance is based upon a proposition initially developed by Tiebout[3] and later refined by Hamilton.[4] Essentially, the Tiebout hypothesis states that individuals, by the choice of their community of residence, are able to obtain a package of public services and taxes which closely conform to their preferences. To be operational, the mechanism requires that the number of communities be large. Moreover, if the size of a community is sufficiently large to avoid any benefit spillovers between jurisdictions, the outcome can also be shown to be optimal. In effect, individuals are able to make their demands for public services effective by voting with their feet.

Early critics of the Tiebout mechanism argued that the outcome did not constitute an equilibrium position as long as local public services were not financed by head taxes.[5] If services were financed by property taxes, for example, individuals would have an incentive to seek out communities with a greater per capita tax base so as to enjoy lower taxes. But such movements would distort the original match between preferences and public services and consequently render the outcome suboptimal. As Hamilton recognized, however, this problem would be avoided if communities had the power to exclude those who relocate simply to obtain bargain public service prices.[6] The zoning power can achieve precisely such results and maintain the system of homogeneous communities envisaged by Tiebout.

Other critics have not so much questioned the logical consistency of the model as they have challenged its empirical relevance.[7] They point to the reality of modern urban governance where every significant urban area contains at least one large political jurisdiction—the central city. Decentralization, if it exists, is confined to the suburbs. At best, they argue, the Tiebout mechanism is available only to middle- and upper-income white households and is applicable to a limited set of urban public services. The poor are confined to the central city by the very zoning mechanism used to buttress Tiebout's argument.

Moreover, many urban public services do not satisfy Tiebout's stringent condition on the scope of beneficiaries. Instead they yield benefits which accrue to most or all residents of the metropolitan area—e.g., transportation, water and sewer services, public health activities, cultural and recreational services. For historical reasons, the responsibility for providing such services has been vested with the central city. However, because of a persistent outmigration of middle- and upper-income classes, the ability of the central city to finance such services is continuously eroding. Hence, there is little reason to believe that such services are provided efficiently or equitably.

In effect, then, these critics charge that the Tiebout mechanism is largely irrelevant as a principal criterion for governance in a metropolitan area. As a substitute they propose the following paradigm.[8]

For reasons spelled out below, the fiscal climate confronting middle- and upper-income groups in the central city is distinctly inferior to that prevailing in the suburbs. As a result, such families tend to relocate from city to suburbs. However, this only widens the fiscal disparity for those who remain. Consequently, the suburbanization of above-average families is a self-reinforcing process, threatening to turn the city into a ghetto for poor minorities. This outcome is to be contrasted with the favorable consequences of population redistribution in the Tiebout model.

The key ingredient to this line of argument is the unfavorable fiscal climate in the city relative to the suburbs. In part, this reflects the fact that city residents alone must bear the tax burden for services with an areawide constituency.[9] More important, however, is the clustering of poor in the central city, perhaps because of exclusionary zoning by suburban communities. Since local governments finance most services by taxes which tend to rise with a family's income—e.g., the property tax—those with above average incomes in effect subsidize the services provided low income families. In effect, above-average income residents of the central city must pay a "poor" tax which is totally absent in suburban communities. As would be expected, such efforts to redistribute income are thwarted by migration.

The preceding view has not been without its detractors. Some argue that other factors, such as transportation cost reductions and the higher cost of new housing, are more important for the flight to the suburbs.[10] Others, such as Hamilton, have taken the position that city-suburban fiscal disparities are at least partially neutralized by the capitalization process.[11] In other words, lower central-city property values can offset the higher fiscal costs of residing in the city. While there is validity to both of these objections, few analysts would deny that fiscal factors have played some role in the demise of the central city.[12] And this effect is directly the consequence of decentralized governance in urban areas.

Clearly, metropolitan government would eliminate fiscal incentives for relocation within the urban area. The greater centralization of government, of course, raises the question of responsiveness. Since opposition to metropolitan government is widespread and is frequently voiced by central-city and suburban residents alike, the question of responsiveness should not be dismissed. A great deal of the uncertainty here could be resolved by a careful study of expenditure patterns in urban areas which differ significantly with respect to centralization—say a Houston as compared with a Detroit.[13]

Metropolitan government, however, is not the only mechanism for dealing with the perverse fiscal incentives which plague current governance arrangements in many urban areas. A system of grants from higher levels of government can also do the trick. Recall that the fundamental problem arises because of the public-sector costs associated with the geographic concentrations of poor households. A grant from, say, the federal government to central cities to cover these costs would relieve nonpoor city residents of this burden and hence eliminate their fiscal incentive to flee to the suburbs. Such an arrangement is a natural extension of the principle that programs of income redistribution should be the responsibility of the central government.[14] Unfortunately, however, this type of program changes the terms for which local governments can procure public services and therefore may distort local expenditure programs. Whether it does depends upon the way in which expenditure decisions are made—a subject to which we now turn.

Expenditure Behavior of Local Governemtns

Until quite recently the behavior of governmental institutions remained largely outside the realm of economic inquiry. Policy analysis consisted mainly of identifying situations where private behavior was suboptimal. By assumption, enlightened government officials would take appropriate action to eliminate the imperfection. All of this changed quite abruptly during the decade of the sixties. Inspired by the seminal work of Buchanan and Tullock,[15] analysts extended the principles of economic inquiry to the political system. Just as businessmen were postulated to maximize profit, politicians were assumed to maximize votes and bureaucrats to maximize budgets. What emerged was essentially a new subdiscipline which bridged the fields of economics, political science, and sociology and which is referred to as the Theory of Public Choice.

While a survey of the public choice literature is beyond the scope of this essay, its development has had a profound influence on the theory of public finance, particularly as it relates to the behavior of public expenditure. The earliest attempts to explain expenditure patterns by state and local governments were cast in the traditional mold in which public officials pursued the social interest. Accordingly, public budgets were hypothesized to be determined through a constrained maximization process in which some measure of social welfare is maximized subject to a constraint on total community resources.[16] The arguments of the social welfare function were usually taken to be per capita consumption of private and public goods by community residents. Total community resources were measured as the sum of per capita incomes plus any grants received from higher levels of government. As the reader should easily recognize, this specification is quite similar to that used to explain individual consumer behavior. In fact, in most analyses it is identical. Consequently, all of the properties of the household demand function were assumed to be applicable to expenditure behavior with respect to local public services.

Among the most interesting applications of this model is to the Theory of Grants. Because benefits to nonresidents are assumed to be ignored by the community decision maker, public services which have such benefits will tend to be underprovided. Applying the theory of consumer behavior, such underprovision can be offset by: (1) increasing the total resources available to the community, and/or (2) reducing the cost of the particular service to the community. These have come to be known as lump-sum and matching grants, respectively. Lump-sum grants have income effects only and hence are a relatively ineffective way of stimulating expenditure. Matching grants have both an income and a price effect. Thus, for a given amount of grant outlay, matching grants are more stimulative than lump-sum grants. While these results are straightforward, they are of considerable relevance to such issues as the relative merits of general versus categorical grants.

Another implication of the expenditure model which has gone unnoticed until quite recently is the implication that lump-sum grants have effects equivalent to other sources of increase in community resources. Thus, it makes no difference for community expenditures on public goods whether a community is given a lump-sum grant of $1 per capita or enjoys an increase in, say, wage income of $1 per capita. Moreover, these both have equivalent effects to a $1 per capita reduction in central government taxes. Hence, a federal lump-sum grant which is financed by an equivalent increase in federal taxes should have no impact upon the behavior of the community.

The latter prediction, however, seems at odds with observed behavior. During the debate on general revenue sharing it was not uncommon to find state or local political leaders favoring the program even though it could be shown that their constituents would pay more in federal taxes than they would enjoy in grant revenues. Furthermore, there is econometric evidence that the proposition is false.[17] Specifically, it is generally found that grants have a substantially more stimulative effect than increases in income. This has come to be known as the "flypaper theory" of government grants—i.e., money sticks where it first hits.[18]

Because of this apparent inconsistency with the facts, theorists have sought to modify the underlying theory of expenditure behavior. Some analysts have recast the welfare function in terms of tax burden and public services.[19] This approach is not necessarily inconsistent with the traditional model since the latter can be easily translated into a tax-burden framework. However, the new approach shifts the locus of attention from community well-being to the utility of the political decision maker. Since the political process can be expected to be somewhat imperfect, the two points of view can be expected to diverge. In particular, it is no longer necessary to assume that lump-sum grants have effects equivalent to those of other increases in community resources.

While the tax-burden approach is consistent with the "flypaper effect," it has the drawback of being somewhat superficial. Just whose utility is being maximized is left unspecified, as is the underlying political process. An alternative approach to the problem which has been recently suggested is to assume that expenditure decisions are controlled by the median voter.[20] Such a framework is virtually identical to the traditional model, with the exception that median voter variables are substituted for community variables. Given these parallels, one could conjecture that "flypaper" responses would be ruled out. Such a conjecture is correct if the median voter's perception of grant-in-aid funds is accurate. However, in this model the median voter is assumed to perceive the marginal tax price of public services as being equal to the average tax price. The existence of any lump-sum grant renders such a perception incorrect. In effect, lump-sum grants are believed to have price effects. This model's usefulness, therefore, turns on the empirical validity of such an illusion.

The Incidence of the Property Tax

The final issue to be considered by this essay is the question of the incidence of the property tax. Until fairly recently, most public finance theorists held the view that the property tax was borne by consumers of those products produced by the taxed property. Like most consumption taxes, therefore, the incidence of the property tax was believed to be regressive. The only exception is the tax on land which was held to be borne by landowners. Nowadays, however, most economists would reject the first view while some are beginning to question the validity of the second.

The attack on the conventional view of property tax incidence came from two distinct sources. On the one hand, Mieszkowski[21] analyzed the problem within a general-equilibrium framework similar to that used to examine corporation tax incidence. On the other hand, Hamilton[22] examined the question within the context of the Tiebout model. We treat these models in turn.

Mieszkowski suggested that the conventional model suffered from two major deficiencies: (1) its partial equilibrium methodology, and (2) its tracit assumption that the property tax is applied to only a very small segment of the aggregate capital stock. Because of the first weakness, the conventional model overlooked the fact that as capital fled the taxed sector there would be a general reduction in the rate of return to capital. Of course, if the fraction of capital subject to tax were small, the reduction in the rate of return would be small. However, this does not mean that the reduction in earnings is small *relative* to the tax receipts. Indeed, if one employs the assumptions of Harberger[23] in his analysis of the corporation income tax, these magnitudes would be *equal*. Hence, it would be reasonable to assert that owners of capital paid the entire property tax.

One might object to the latter conclusions on the grounds that the prices of those goods whose capital is taxed have also risen in price. And under plausible conditions, the extra cost to consumers is at least as large as the tax burden. Shouldn't one conclude that the property tax is borne by *both* owners of capital and consumers of the taxed sectors' products? If so, then the conventional view is at least partially correct.

This is where Mieszkowski's second point comes into play. He argues that the property tax is more nearly a general tax on capital than a selective tax. As evidence he points to the virtually universal use of the property tax by local government and the widespread practice of taxing the real capital of business enterprise in addition to housing real estate. Now, if the tax is completely general and imposed at equal rates in all areas, no price increases can result. For capital has no place to flee to escape the tax. Hence, the total and sole burden of the property tax is upon owners of capital.

Since the property tax is not entirely general, some forms of capital being exempt, and since tax rates are not everywhere equal, the latter conclusion must be modified somewhat. As before, the rate of return to capital will be equalized in all areas and in all uses and so owners of capital will suffer the full brunt of the tax. However, some excise effects will also be present. Wherever effective rates of tax are high, the prices of outputs will increase and/or prices of other inputs will decrease. Hence, some burden will be felt by *some* consumers and *some* suppliers of other factors. However, where effective tax rates are low, the reverse will be true. It is not the case that consumers *as a whole* bear a burden of the property tax, nor do suppliers of other factors *as a whole*. Thus, the overall progressivity of the property tax will mirror the incidence of ownership of capital—i.e., fairly progressive.

A somewhat different approach to property tax incidence is taken by Hamilton.[24] Instead of rejecting the assumption that the property tax is only a partial tax on capital, Hamilton goes further and assumes the tax to apply only to housing capital. Furthermore, unlike other approaches, he explicitly considers local public services which are assumed to be financed exclusively through the property tax. Arguing that households select a community on the basis of both services and taxes and that communities engage in minimum housing-size zoning to keep out those seeking public-service bargains, Hamilton concludes that the property tax essentially serves as a benefit charge—i.e., the price of local public services. Accordingly, incidence becomes synonymous with consumption of public services and the property tax is neutral with respect to housing consumption.

While this model may appear to be at odds with that of Mieszkowski, the two can, in fact, be easily reconciled. It is only necessary to observe that fiscal differentials are the key variables in both models. Hamilton's basic results are unaffected if the *average* rate of the property tax is borne by owners of capital and Mieszkowski's model need only be reformulated in terms of net benefits (i.e., tax costs less service benefits) instead of tax rates alone.

As the preceding discussion makes clear, the theory of property tax incidence has undergone a considerable restructuring in recent years. This has largely been the result of a general restatement of the problem in general-equilibrium terms. Experience shows that such a transformation often produces dramatic results. There is no better example of this than the recent finding of Feldstein that a tax on land value or land rent can actually increase the market value of land![25] Presumably, similar surprises will emerge with respect to other state and local theory concepts as our knowledge of general-equilibrium models progresses.

Notes

1. Perhaps the best statement of the economic theory of federalism is given in Wallace E. Oates, *Fiscal Federalism* (New York: Harcourt, Brace, Jovanovitch, 1972).

2. Some writers have added a third consideration which needs to be brought into the balance—economies of scale. However, scale economies refer to the unit of *production,* not *provision.* The issue under discussion relates to the latter, not the former. See Jerome Rothenberg, "Local Decentralization and the Theory of Optimal Government," in *The Analysis of Public Output,* ed. J. Margolis (New York: Columbia University Press, 1970), pp. 31–64.

3. See Charles Tiebout, "A Pure Theory of Local Public Expenditure," *Journal of Political Economy* (October 1956), pp. 416–24.

4. See Bruce W. Hamilton, "Zoning and Property Taxation in a System of Local Governments," *Urban Studies* (June 1975), pp. 205–11.

5. Ibid.

6. Ibid.

7. See, for example, William Neenan, *Political Economy of Urban Areas* (Chicago: Markham, 1972); and Richard Netzer, "State-Local Finance and Intergovernmental Fiscal Relations," in *The Economics of Public Finance,* ed. Blinder, et al. (Washington, D.C.: Brookings Institution, 1974). For a good discussion of the issues, see David Bradford and Wallace Oates, "Suburban Exploitation of Central Cities and Government Structure," in *Redistribution Through Public Choice,* ed. Harold Hochman and George Peterson (New York: Columbia University Press, 1974), pp. 43–90.

8. This mechanism is nicely described in William Baumol, Philip Howrey and Wallace Oates, "The Analysis of Public Policy in Urban Models," *Journal of Political Economy* (Jan/Feb 1971), pp. 142–53, and tested by David Bradford and Harry H. Kelejian, "An Econometric Model of the Flight to the Suburbs," *Journal of Political Economy* (May/June 1973), pp. 566–89.

9. To the extent that the state or the federal government provides financial assistance, residents of the suburbs contribute.

10. See, for example, Edwin S. Mills, *Urban Economics* (Glenview, Illinois: Scott-Foresman, 1972).

11. See Bruce W. Hamilton, "Capitalization and Intrajurisdictional Differences in Local Tax Prices," *American Economic Review* (December 1976), pp. 743–53.

12. Whatever capitalization occurs is likely to be incomplete. See William Oakland, "Central Cities: Fiscal Plight and Prospects for Reform," paper presented before the Committee on Urban Economics, Columbus, Ohio, May 5–6, 1977.

13. The costs of centralization may not be small. Bradford and Oates ("Suburban Exploitation") estimate the costs of shifting provision of education to the state level to be a staggering 50 percent of the education budget.

14. For a discussion of this principle, see William Oakland, "A Rationale for Federal Government Intervention in Housing: Distortions Arising From Present Fiscal Arrangements at the Local Government Level," in *Housing in the Seventies Working Papers* (Washington, D.C.: Government Printing Office, 1976), pp. 459–73.

15. See James Buchanan and Gordon Tullock, *The Calculus of Consent* (Ann Arbor: University of Michigan Press, 1976).

16. See Lester C. Thurow, "The Theory of Grants-in-Aid," *National Tax Journal* (December 1966), pp. 373–377; and James A. Wilde, "Grants-in Aid: The Analytics of Design and Response," *National Tax Journal* (June 1971), pp. 143–55.

17. See Edward Gramlich, "Intergovernmental Grants—A Review of the Empirical Literature," in *The Political Economy of Fiscal Federalism,* ed. Wallace Oates (Lexington, Massachusetts: Lexington Books, 1977).

18. This term first appears to have been coined by Harvey Galper and Edward Gramlich, "State and Local Fiscal Behavior and Federal Grant Policy," *Brookings Papers on Economic Activity* 1 (1973).

19.   See Stephen M. Barro, *Theoretical Models of School District Expenditure Determination and the Impact of Grants-in-Aid,* monograph R-867-FF (Santa Monica: Rand Corporation, 1972).

20.   See P. Courant, Edward Gramlich, and Daniel Rubinfeld, "The Stimulative Effects of Intergovernmental Grants," paper presented at the Committee of Urban Public Economics (COUPE), New York, New York, November 10–11, 1977.

21.   See Peter M. Mieszkowski, "The Property Tax: An Excise Tax or a Profits Tax," *Journal of Public Economics* (Spring 1972), pp. 73–96.

22.   See Hamilton, "Zoning and Property Taxation."

23.   See Arnold C. Harberger, "The Incidence of the Corporation Income Tax," *Journal of Political Economy* (June 1962), pp. 215–40.

24.   See Hamilton, "Zoning and Property Taxation."

25.   See Martin Feldstein, "The Surprising Incidence of a Tax on Pure Rent: A New Answer to an Old Question," *Journal of Political Economy* (April 1977), pp. 349–61.

Revenue and Expenditure Forecasting by State and Local Governments

Roy W. Bahl

The instability of state and local government economies has placed a premium on effective fiscal planning at the state and local levels. In the Northeast and industrial Midwest, the economic base is in decline as jobs continue to shift to the faster-growing South and Western regions, and central cities in this region are doubly damned in that they continue to lose jobs to their surrounding suburbs. In the face of this decline, it is important to evaluate the level of resources available in the near future and to estimate the expenditure implications of likely claims against these revenues, e.g., the effects of public employee union demands.

The need for effective fiscal planning is no less pressing in the growing regions. Suburbanization, industrialization, and pressures to "catch up" in the quality of public services delivered and in the levels of public employee compensation paid all are pushing state and local government budgets upward. Long-term fiscal planning in the growing areas may ameliorate some of the fiscal difficulties which lie ahead. A painful lesson learned from governments in the older region is that expenditure commitments are long-lived and not easily reversible. For example, New York City's debt burden and pension obligations are examples of commitments made at a time when the economy was more able to support a higher level of public sector activity.

This importance notwithstanding, the state of the art in revenue and expenditure forecasting is primitive.[1] While some state governments have sophisticated revenue-forecasting schemes that project for a five-year period,[2] few if any have a similar technique for expenditures. At the local level there are very few attempts to carry out any systematic revenue and expenditure forecasts. A recent survey by the Urban Consortium included 28 cities and six counties with populations of more than 500,000 and received an 82 percent response. While the survey was able to identify the existence of some systematic techniques, 72 percent of the respondents stated that the forecasts were primarily extrapolation, ". . . taking into account recent trends and adjusting these trends based on current information on future trends."[3]

Because the problems associated with forecasting revenues and expenditures—particularly expenditures and particularly at the local government level—are indeed formidable, there has been a paucity of research on the subject. The purpose of this paper is to explore, albeit in a summary fashion, the major problems associated with

Roy W. Bahl is Professor of Economics and Director, Metropolitan Studies Program, The Maxwell School, Syracuse University.

revenue and expenditure forecasting and in that context to review the state of the literature. In the final section we mention the broader question of budgetary forecasting, i.e., a model which simultaneously takes into account the effects of exogenous factors on revenues and expenditures. Before reviewing the problems and prospects for revenue, expenditure, and budgetary forecasting, we consider the alternative approaches which have been taken to project the outlook for state and local governments.

The concern in this review is with forecasting for an intermediate period—approximately five years. The one-year forecast, such as that used to develop the annual budget, is not the issue here since it is not clear that such projections cannot be better done without systematic models.

Techniques For Projecting Local Government Fiscal Viability

A proper forecast of the fiscal viability of a local government would be derived from analysis of both the current situation and that projected for the future, and it would reflect consideration of both the financial and the economic structure of the local area.[4] Most importantly, it would be based on an underlying theoretical model which would enable evaluation of fiscal health with respect to clearly defined criteria. Three general avenues of state-local fiscal evaluation have been followed by various analysts: comparative quantitative analysis, comparative case studies, and aggregate state-local sector analysis.

Comparative Quantitative Analysis

The absence of a normative theory of public output has led economists to concentrate their attention on the more positive question of what determines municipal expenditure, revenue, and debt levels. From this concern has grown a series of studies which attempt to find a statistical relationship between the level of these fiscal-outcome indicators and the social, economic, and demographic characteristics of the community. These "determinants" studies are almost all cross-section, and usually employ a straightforward multiple regression technique.[5]

Though there is much virtue to the determinants approach, it may be critiqued on grounds that it does not permit analysis and projection of the fiscal status of individual local government units. At best, it allows one to determine how a particular local government unit compares to others at a given point in time. Such results do not enable analysis of how the current cash-flow position of a government is likely to be changed by future economic or demographic developments. Moreover, exogenous but important factors such as the national inflation rate are not even considered in a cross-section model, since these are assumed to affect all governments equally. Finally, the determinants model is often estimated at a very aggregated level (e.g., expenditures are usually taken as the single output proxy) so that underlying financial indicators and even factor cost differentials are not usually considered.

For these reasons, plus others relating more purely to measurement and data problems, the determinants approach may be quite readily rejected as a foundation for a model that can identify, through estimation of budgetary outlooks, those jurisdictions that are likely to face a cash-flow crisis.

Case Studies

Case studies of local government fiscal viability have many of the characteristics necessary for projections of budgetary conditions. They may be detailed and take into account the factor important to a specific city, and they may consider both the short-term cash flow and long-term economic factors.[6]

There can be little question but that a kind of case-study approach is necessary to accurately evaluate and project the behavior of the local government fisc. However, a missing ingredient in most case studies which have been carried out is the use of a well-defined and comparable model.

Sector Projections

A third approach is to project the fiscal position for the entire state-local sector. While there are not a great many fully developed and systematic projection exercises that are routinely carried out for the state-local sector, less ambitious aggregate studies are fairly common. Two of the more important major aggregate studies of recent vintage are those prepared by the Tax Foundation[7] and by the American Enterprise Institute.[8] Though now a bit dated, these studies agreed in two important respects: that the state-local sector will be in surplus by 1980, and that fiscal problems will relate more to specific urban areas with "special" difficulties.

Although one could raise several objections to the assumptions on which these studies are based and to the optimism of their conclusions,[9] the relevant issue in the present context involves whether aggregative sectoral analysis runs the risk of obscuring more than it reveals about the condition of particular jurisdictions. The point is that sectoral analysis focuses exclusively on the *net* budgetary position of the entire sector rather than on the budgetary position of individual governments. Notwithstanding the utility of knowing about the aggregate budgetary position of the entire state and local sector, particularly in connection with questions involving the capital market's ability to accommodate the financial requirements of governmental and private users of capital and other highly aggregative policy issues, such information is of little value in evaluating the fiscal outlook of single jurisdictions or in comparing conditions among several jurisdictions. In other words, the outlook for a particular city is not likely to be enhanced simply because the outlook for the aggregate of cities is bright.[10]

Revenue Forecasting

Developing a model for revenue forecasting requires dealing with four important problem areas: (1) cleaning the tax revenue series of discretionary changes in the rate and base, (2) identifying a proper independent variable(s), (3) developing an appropriate model for purposes of estimation, and (4) forecasting intergovernmental revenues. Because of one or the other of these problems, fiscal forecasting research has been centered on state government sales and personal income taxes to the neglect of the largest major revenue sources in the state-local sector—the property tax and intergovernmental flows.

Cleaning the Tax Series

The problem of cleaning a revenue yield series of all discretionary changes is a serious impediment to developing a forecasting model, even in the relatively easy sales and income tax cases.[11] Three approaches to cleaning the series have been used. The first was developed by Prest in estimating the elasticity of the personal income tax in the United Kingdom.[12] He roughly estimates *automatic* growth by using information on how much of each year's tax increase is due to legal changes. The method does not adequately adjust for the effects of any given year's discretionary change on revenues generated in all future (or past) years; hence it is too rough for use on state and local government tax forecasting.

An alternative approach, a so-called constant structure method, would simulate the tax yield in all past years if under the current structure.[13] Though based on the simplifying assumption that past tax structure changes have not affected the aggregate level of income, this approach has been widely used.[14] The third approach cleans the series while estimating the elasticity coefficient by introducing a dummy variable for years in which major discretionary changes have taken place.[15] The difficulty with this approach is that discretionary changes in rate and base occur much too frequently and the dummy variable may only be used for major discretionary changes.

The problem of cleaning the series is even more complicated in the case of the property tax, since it is not clear what constitutes a discretionary change. Certainly changes in the statutory tax rate are discretionary, but less clear are the cases of improvements in assessment practices and changes in the equalization rate.

Choosing the Independent Variable

To develop a forecast, tax revenue and tax base growth must be related to the growth in some variable which reflects local economic growth. The common choice for an independent variable is personal income in the community (so common is the choice that the income elasticity of tax revenues is referred to in shorthand manner as *the* elasticity of tax revenues). Despite this common practice, there are serious flaws with personal income as the independent or predictor variable. First, available measures of personal income are subject to major omissions, hence may not accurately reflect fiscal capacity. Second, data on personal income are generally two years out of date, and forecast income data are not readily available. Finally, the personal income independent variable is subject to the criticism that it is not available on a small area basis, i.e., city or county.

For these reasons, some have suggested that a better indicator of local economic activity might be the aggregate level of private employment.[16] There are a number of reasons for choosing the employment base rather than the income base as a gauge of the level of economic activity. First, employment data are collected and reported on an industry basis and in a form that is more consistent, comprehensive, and detailed than that for income data. Second, the principally used measure in virtually all the analyses of core-city decline is employment loss. Third, employment is the measure most commonly applied in the analysis of urban structure and urban economic base changes.[17] Finally, labor and capital are the primary mobile inputs in the productive process in urban areas, and of the two, at least measurement ease would dictate the choice of the employment unit.[18]

Defining the Model

A third major problem in developing revenue forecasting techniques is the defining of an appropriate model. The traditional model estimates tax revenue growth as a function of growth in some indicator of local or state economic activity. This approach does not allow for a feedback effect, e.g., for the effects of taxes on the level of personal income. It may, however, express taxes as a function of a number of independent variables, usually in a single-equation model.[19] A variant on this approach is Auten and Robb's work on Missouri, where the model explicitly allows for the interaction of various taxes but not for the feedback effects.[20]

The alternative is to specify a simultaneous-equation model which does allow for the feedback effects. Simultaneous-equation models have several advantages as a forecasting methodology. The flexibility provided by a multiple-equation system can allow for greater realism in modeling revenue functions, and such models are easily adaptable for simulation by changing the exogenous variables within the several equations over a range of values.[21] However, the advantages of simultaneous models do not come without additional costs. Data requirements are in most instances massive and a substantial investment must be made to build, estimate, and update the model. As a result, there are few examples of the use of this technique at the local government level. Oddly, the larger models tend not to treat the public sector in as great a detail as does the traditional model. Much less attention is paid to particulars of the tax structure, and large models seem to have less ability to capture the revenue effects of changes either in the underlying economic base or in the structure of the tax itself.

Projecting Intergovernmental Flows

The fourth problem with revenue forecasting is developing a proper treatment of intergovernmental flows. These obviously require a different approach since they cannot be extrapolated or linked to a specific local variable such as personal income.

Direct federal or mandated federal pass-through funds might be projected from formulae and estimated appropriation size; at least some degree of certainty can be placed on the estimates. State aid flows are more difficult to estimate since they are more variable, depending on the fiscal position of the state government. In states where such transfers are important, one is led to the inescapable conclusion that a local government revenue forecast requires a state government revenue forecast.

Expenditure Forecasting

The expenditure forecasting problem is qualitatively different than the revenue forecasting problem. In the tax revenue case, the issue is one of projecting the natural growth in the tax bases to determine how much revenue will be generated at a given rate structure. In the expenditure case, the forecast requires assumptions about desired levels of services, the productivity of workers, the cost of labor and materials, the level of employment, capital improvements, and the level of fringe benefits. By comparison with the revenue side, there would seem considerably more room for discretion on the part of the local government. For that reason, the expenditure forecasting problem is considerably more difficult than the revenue forecasting problem.

There is little by way of a literature arguing a systematic, analytic approach to expenditure forecasting.[22] However, there are related analyses of expenditure determinants,[23] the demand for state and local government employment,[24] and the determinants of municipal wage rates[25] which are useful in enumerating the factors that underlie expenditure growth. The most reasonable of the systematic projections of long-term expenditure growth take these determinants as a starting point and simulate alternative expenditure outcomes.

When this approach is taken, an early issue which arises is the need to separate the "controllables" from the "noncontrollables." While this has stirred some debate, for projection purposes there has been general agreement on the following list of short-term noncontrollables: service and repayment of existing debt,[26] pension obligations, mandated transfer payments, negotiated wage and fringe increments, and the increased price of essential government purchases. These items may be directly built into the projections.

Other expenditure items are more controllable, though some (e.g., certain police services) are so essential that they become noncontrollables. Still it is possible to adjust the larger components of expenditures, particularly labor costs, for different levels of wage rate, benefit, and employment increase.

A second major problem is how to treat inflation. There are no good indexes of prices paid by local governments for labor and nonlabor services, and the development of such indexes is a laborious task.[27] Yet some portion of local government cost increase is surely due to price increases and has to be captured in the projections.

A third difficulty is projecting the variables that drive the simulation. These usually include community income, negotiated wage rates in the private sector, school enrollment rates, the regional inflation rate, etc. Clearly, this type of data is most difficult to forecast and to relate in a systematic way to expenditure increase.

Budgetary Forecasting

Revenue and expenditure forecasts may be combined to project a range of possibilities for the overall fiscal deficit/surplus facing a state or local government. By combining the most likely sets of assumptions, the most likely budget position could be forecast. Viewed another way, from a range of outcomes it should be possible to determine the conditions under which substantial budget deficits will occur and the nature of the relationship between the state and local government budgetary positions.

There are two techniques open for budgetary forecasting. The first is to determine expenditures and revenues simultaneously in the context of a full econometric model.[28] The second is to combine separate revenue and expenditure analyses in a consistent manner and simulate alternative outcomes. Given the state of the art and the great generality of full econometric models in forecasting the state and local government budget, this piecemeal approach would seem the most appropriate next step.

Notes

1. No distinction is made here between forecasting and projecting. Either term is taken to refer to a best estimate of the fiscal outcome under alternative assumptions about the growth in factors affecting that outcome.

2. For a review of alternative techniques used, see R. Berney and B. Fredrichs, "Income Elasticities for State Tax Revenues; Techniques of Estimation and Their Usefulness for Forecasting," *Public Finance Quarterly* (October 1973), pp. 409–425.

3. The Urban Consortium, "A Process for Revenue and Expenditure Forecasting in Local Government," mimeographed (Washington, D.C.: The Urban Consortium, 1977).

4. In this section, I draw from Roy Bahl and Bernard Jump, "Projecting the Fiscal Viability of Cities," in *Fiscal Choices of State and Local Governments,* ed. George Peterson (Washington, D.C.: Urban Institute, 1978).

5. Reviews of the determinants literature may be found in Roy Bahl, "The Determinants of Public Expenditures: A Review," in *Functional Federalism: Grants-in-Aid and PPB Systems,* ed. Selma Mushkin and John Cotton (Washington, D.C.: George Washington University, State-Local Finance Project, 1968); George Wilensky, "Determinants of Local Government Expenditures," in *Financing the Metropolis: Public Policy in Urban Economics,* ed. John Crecine (Beverly Hills, California: Sage, 1970); John E. Fredland, "Determinants of State and Local Expenditures: An Annotated Bibliography" (Washington, D.C.: Urban Institute, 1974).

   Recent studies include Thomas E. Borcherding and Robert T. Deacon, "The Demand for the Services of Non-Federal Governments," *American Economic Review* 62 (December 1972), pp. 891–901; and T. C. Bergstrom and R. P. Goodman, "Private Demands for Public Goods," *American Economic Review* 63 (June 1973), pp. 280–296.

6. See Advisory Commission on Intergovernmental Relations, *City Financial Emergencies: The Intergovernmental Dimension* (Washington, D.C.: U.S. Government Printing Office, 1973); and David Stanley, *Cities in Trouble* (Columbus, Ohio: Academy for Contemporary Problems, 1976).

7. Tax Foundation, *The Financial Outlook for State and Local Government to 1980* (New York: Tax Foundation, 1972).

8. David J. Ott, Attiat F. Ott, James A. Maxwell, and J. Richard Aronson, eds., *State-Local Finances in the Last Half of the 1970s* (Washington, D.C.: American Enterprise Institute for Public Policy Research, 1975).

9. Some of these objections are set forth in Roy W. Bahl, Bernard Jump, and David Puryear, "The Outlook for State and Local Government Fiscal Performance," in *The Future of State and Local Government Finances, Hearings before the Subcommittee on Urban Problems of the Joint Economic Committee,* 94th Congress, 2nd sess., 1976

10. Alternatively, the sectoral projection model could be useful if it were built up from estimates of the budgetary position of individual state and local government units. Such an undertaking would be massive and to the author's knowledge has not been carried out.

11. The various approaches to cleaning a tax revenue series are outlined in Roy W. Bahl, "Revenue Forecasting in Less Developed Countries," mimeographed (Washington: D.C.: International Monetary Fund, 1971).

12. Alan Prest, "The Sensitivity of the Yield of the Personal Income Tax in the United Kingdom," *The Economic Journal* 76 (September 1962), pp. 576–596.

13. Robert Harris, *Income and Sales Taxes: The 1970 Outlook for States and Localities* (Washington, D.C.: Council of State Governments, 1966).

14. See, for example, Michael Wasylenko, "Estimating the Elasticity of State Personal Income Taxes," *National Tax Journal* 28 (March 1975), pp. 139–42.

15. John B. Legler and Perry Shapiro, "The Responsiveness of State Tax Revenue to Economic Growth," *National Tax Journal* 21 (March 1968), pp. 46–56; and Neil Singer, "The Use of Dummy Variables in Estimating the Income-Elasticity of State Income Tax Revenues," *National Tax Journal* 21 (March 1968), pp. 200–204.

16. Roy Bahl and David Greytak, "The Response of City Government Revenues to Changes in Employment Structure," *Land Economics* 52 (November 1976), pp. 415–434.

17. See Edgar Hoover and Raymond Vernon, *Anatomy of the Metropolis* (Cambridge, Massachusetts: Harvard University Press, 1959); and David Birch, *The Economic Future of Cities and Suburbs,* CED Supplementary Paper Number 30 (New York: New York Committee for Economic Development, 1970).

18. Charles Tiebout, *The Community Economic Base Study,* CED Supplementary Paper Number 16 (New York: New York Committee for Economic Development, 1962).

19. See, for example, Lee Madere, "Municipal Budget Projections: New Orleans, La.," mimeographed, U.S. Department of Housing and Urban Development, Washington, D.C., forthcoming.

20. Gerald E. Auten and Edward H. Robb, "A General Model for State Tax Revenue Analysis," *National Tax Journal* 29 (December 1976), pp. 422–435.

21. Robert H. Milbourne, "Econometric Forecasting in Wisconsin: Personal Income Tax Collections," *Presentations on Revenue Estimating Procedures* (Chicago: Federation of Tax Administrators, 1976).

22. Roy Bahl and Richard Gustely, "Forecasting Urban Government Expenditures," *Proceedings of the Sixty-Seventh Annual Conference of the National Tax Association* (Columbus, Ohio: National Tax Association, 1974); and Claudia Scott, *Forecasting Urban Government Expenditures* (Lexington, Massachusetts: Lexington Books, 1971).

23. Roy Bahl, "The Determinants of Public Expenditures;" John E. Fredland, "Determinants of State and Local Expenditures;" and Jesse Burkhead and Jerry Miner, *Public Expenditure* (Chicago: Aldine Publishing Company, 1971).

24. Ronald Ehrenberg, "The Demand for State and Local Government Employees," *American Economic Review* 63 (June 1973), pp. 366–379; and Orley Ashenfelter, "Demand and Supply Functions for State and Local Employment: Implications for Public Employment Programs," mimeographed (Princeton, New Jersey: Princeton University, 1972).

25. R. Baird and John Landon, "The Effects of Collective Bargaining on Public School Teachers' Salaries: Comment," *Industrial Labor Review* 24 (April 1972), pp. 410–417; and James C. Ohls and T. J. Wales, "Supply and Demand for State and Local Services," *Review of Economics and Statistics* 54 (November 1972), pp. 424–430.

26. However, as is so vividly illustrated by the New York case, even debt-repayment schedules can be altered in the long run. The concept of a controllable versus a noncontrollable expenditure, therefore, must be handled very carefully.

27. David Greytak and Bernard Jump, Jr., *The Impact of Inflation on the Expenditures and Revenues of Six Local Governments, 1971–1979,* Metropolitan Studies Program, The Maxwell School, Syracuse University (Syracuse, N.Y.: Syracuse University, 1975); and David Greytak, Richard Gustely and Robert Dinkelmeyer, "The Effects of Inflation on Local Government Expenditures," *National Tax Journal* 27 (December 1974), pp. 583–598.

28. J. C. Hambor, M. R. Norman, and R. R. Russell, "A Tax Revenue Forecasting Model for the State of Hawaii," *Public Finance Quarterly* 2 (October 1974), pp. 432–50.

The State-Local Sector and The Economy: Overall Performance and Regional Disparities

Robert W. Rafuse, Jr.

The two sets of issues addressed in this essay have been the objects of intermittent attention in the professional literature for decades. Only in the past two or three years, however, have the overall cyclical behavior of the state-local sector and the existence of regional disparities in employment, income, and fiscal levels and trends become the subjects of national policy debate and matters of major concern to researchers.

The fiscal performance of the state-local sector as a whole over the business cycle became an issue with major policy implications in 1975 as the full dimensions of the recession began to be appreciated. The search for federal policies to spur recovery coincided in that year with rising concern among state and local officials about the impacts of soaring unemployment and continuing inflation on their fiscal outlooks. The result was a decision by the Congress to use state and local governments as the vehicle for three major programs to combat the recession: expanded public service jobs, public works, and countercyclical fiscal assistance patterned after general revenue sharing.

The decision to take this route rather than the traditional one of tax cuts and increased direct federal spending testifies to the importance of two primary factors. The first is the power of the coalition of state-local organizations that four years earlier had mobilized to gain the enactment of revenue sharing. The second is an idea — that the fiscal behavior of the state-local sector in a recession is perverse; that, by cutting expenditures and raising taxes to maintain balanced budgets, the sector contributes to a worsening of an already serious economic situation.

Concern about regional economic and fiscal disparities flowered in 1976 in the "Sunbelt-Frostbelt" controversy. The existence of disparities among the regions is nothing new. Fifty years ago, by any measure, they were far more substantial than they are today. What was new in 1976 was the special strains on the economies of manufacturing-based areas induced by the worst recession in decades, and the peculiar sensitivity to formula-design issues produced by a decade of burgeoning federal grant-in-aid programs. The result was a flurry of technical (and not so technical) analyses of recent trends in and prospects for regional disparities. The publicity given

Robert W. Rafuse, Jr. is Deputy Assistant Secretary for State and Local Finance, U.S. Department of the Treasury.

to these analyses prompted a massive effort to mobilize regional interests, initially with a view to influencing the design of federal policies. As the immediate flare-up cooled, efforts were also initiated to mobilize regional interests for the design and implementation of self-help development strategies.

This essay provides a general review of recent developments involving both sets of issues. The first section summarizes the controversy over the cyclical behavior of the state-local sector, reviews the recent record, and outlines a general theory suggested by that record. The second section reviews selected contributions of recent research on regional disparities.

The State-Local Sector and the Business Cycle

This section begins with a discussion of the history of the "perversity hypothesis." A brief review of the behavior of the state-local sector in the national income accounts since the early 1970s follows, and the section concludes with an outline of a theory of state-local cyclical behavior that is suggested by recent developments.

The Perversity Hypothesis

One of the earliest, and clearly the most influential, articulations of the hypothesis that the fiscal behavior of the sector tends to aggravate cyclical swings in the economy was that by Alvin H. Hansen and Harvey S. Perloff in 1944:

the taxing, borrowing, and spending activities of the state and local governments collectively have typically run counter to an economically sound fiscal policy. These governmental units have usually followed the swings of the business cycle, from crest to trough, spending and building in prosperity periods and contracting their activities during depression. [1]

Thus Hansen and Perloff concluded that, since:

states and localities have in fact *followed* the swings of the cycle and have thereby *intensified* the violence of economic fluctuation, . . . unless their fiscal systems are planned in relation to the federal stabilization program, they are likely to nullify in large measure the national countercyclical activities. [2]

Since the Hansen and Perloff study was completed more than 30 years ago, there have been a number of analyses of the behavior of state and local governments over the business cycle. For example, a 1964 study by the author of this essay concluded that

. . . the fiscal behavior of the state and local governments over the cycle [has] . . . been a significant factor in moderating the seriousness of the post-war recessions and in promoting recovery. During each expansion period, state and local government finances have been expansionary, but their strongest expansionary thrust has tended to fall in the early stages of the expansion with a tapering-off appearing in the later stages of the boom. [3]

For a decade following publication of the Rafuse and Sharp results, the cyclical behavior of state-local finances received no further consideration in the technical literature. Then, in late 1975, as the worst recession since World War II was reaching what was to prove to be its trough, the Subcommittee on Urban Affairs of the congressional Joint Economic Committee published a staff study that effectively resurrected the perversity hypothesis. [4] Among its conclusions were estimates that the recession was cutting state-local employment by more than 140,000 positions, and forcing the enactment of $3.6 billion in tax increases and $3.3 billion in expenditure cuts below current service levels. These results appear to have been instrumental in persuading the Congress to enact the Public Works Employment Act of 1976, which provided for $2 billion in public works grants and $1.25 billion in funding for an Antirecession Fiscal Assistance (ARFA) program, also known as countercyclical revenue sharing. [5]

128

One of the primary reasons state-local fiscal behavior between World War II and 1963 was cyclically stabilizing was the existence of significant lags in the sector's fiscal responses to fluctuations in the economy. The lagged responsiveness of state-local finances to fluctuations in the gross national product (GNP) is well illustrated by the national income accounts data since 1973.[7]

In 1972 dollars, the GNP peaked in the fourth quarter of 1973 and declined steadily through the first quarter of 1975. Between the second quarter of 1975 and the end of 1977, real GNP rose at an average annual rate of 5.7 percent.

State-local purchases of goods and services continued to grow throughout the 1974-75 decline in the GNP and for three quarters past the trough. For a year thereafter, beginning in the first quarter of 1976, however, real state-local purchases were stagnant. In fact, they were nearly one percent lower in the first quarter of 1977 than five quarters earlier. Stagnation ended in the second quarter of 1977, when growth in real state-local purchases resumed strongly. It is clear that the sector did not make a strong contribution to the economic recovery. Indeed, at the end of 1977, real state-local purchases were only 5.6 percent higher than at the trough of the recession, nearly three years earlier, a period when the real GNP rose 16.3 percent.

This behavior is especially curious when it is compared with similar periods following the GNP troughs of previous recessions. During the comparable 11-quarter period following the GNP trough of the 1969-70 recession, the increase in real state-local purchases (12.2 percent) exceeded that in real GNP (12.0 percent).[8] The rise in real state-local purchases (15.3 percent) exceeded that in the real GNP (14.6 percent) by an even larger margin during the 11 quarters following the trough in the recession of 1960-61.

The most likely explanation for the behavior of state-local purchases since the 1974-75 recession is the peculiar performance of the sector in construction. State-local contract construction in real terms weakened in 1973 but strengthened in 1974, reaching its recent peak (at an annual rate of $28 billion) in the second quarter of that year.[9] This was followed by moderate decline to the recession trough. Outlays held fairly steady through the remainder of 1975 at an annual rate of about $25 billion, a rate only 5 percent lower than that sustained during 1973 and 1974.

In the fourth quarter of 1975, however, a six-quarter (accelerating) decline in real contract-construction spending began. The decline was interrupted by a 10.3-percent rise in real outlays in the second quarter of 1977. But this was followed by a 2.5-percent decline in the third quarter, no change in the fourth, and a 10.1-percent drop in the first quarter of 1978. By early 1978, the real value of state-local contract construction was less than 75 percent of its average in 1975.

Had real state-local contract construction purchases merely remained constant at the level achieved in the fourth quarter of 1975, total state-local purchases in 1972 dollars would have risen steadily throughout 1976 and 1977 at an average annual rate of 3.1 percent (the same as that sustained during 1972 and 1973). This compares with the actual rate of only 2.0 percent over the period, which was achieved only with the very strong growth (in nonconstruction outlays) during the last three quarters of 1977.[10]

The only other important category of state-local expenditures in the national income accounts is transfer payments to persons, which account for substantially less than 10 percent of total outlays.[11] Between 1960 and 1973, state-local transfers, adjusted to a constant-purchasing-power basis,[12] grew at an average annual rate of 7.5 percent. In striking contrast to what might have been expected, between the prerecession peak in the fourth quarter of 1973 and the end of 1977, real state-local transfers rose at an annual rate of only 1.4 percent.

On the same price-deflated basis used in the preceding discussion of expenditures,[13] state-local revenues (excluding federal grants-in-aid) peaked with the GNP in the fourth quarter of 1973. Deflated own revenues declined at an average annual rate of 3.0 percent until the GNP trough, when they resumed strong growth at a rate that averaged 4.8 percent per year through the end of 1977. This compares favorably with the 4.9-percent rate achieved during the entire 1960-73 period, when discretionary revenue-raising activity by state legislatures and local governments was more intense than it has been in the past three years.

Between 1960 and 1973, federal grants-in-aid—adjusted for the decline in the buying power of the funds over the period—grew at an average rate of nearly 10 percent per year. Although much attention has been focused on the efforts of the federal government to fight the recession and to accelerate recovery by increasing grants to state and local governments, the fact is that the real value of federal grants rose at an average annual rate of only 7 percent between the fourth quarter of 1973 and the fourth quarter of 1977. Moreover, the quarter-to-quarter changes in real federal grants have been increasingly erratic since 1973. Some of these shifts, ranging in size up to +$5.9 billion in 1976 and -$6.7 billion in 1967, have been far larger than the quarterly changes in any of the other fiscal variables, suggesting that the federal government has been a major destabilizing factor in the recent behavior of the state-local sector.

An overall characterization of the fiscal behavior of state and local governments during the past five years may now be obtained from an analysis of the patterns of quarter-to-quarter changes in the four primary fiscal variables discussed above. If the net increase in the two categories of receipts (federal grants and own receipts) exceeds the net increase in the two expenditure categories (purchases and transfers), a "surplus" exists, and the change in fiscal behavior may be characterized as restrictive, or contractionary. Such a "surplus" also appears when receipts increase and expenditures decline, and when receipts decline less than expenditures.

Conversely, a "deficit" occurs when expenditures increase more than receipts, when expenditures increase and receipts decline, and when expenditures decline less than receipts. The existence of a "deficit" suggests that the state-local fiscal behavior was expansionary during the quarter.[14]

From the first quarter of 1973 through the first quarter of 1975, the state-local sector was expansionary. The average "deficit" in 1974, however, was only slightly more than half as large as it was in 1973. In the second quarter of 1975, the sector moved into "surplus," and the magnitudes of the restrictive changes increased from quarter to quarter (except for a small "deficit" in the second quarter of 1976) until the third quarter of 1976. From the fourth quarter of 1976 through the first two quarters of 1977, the net effect of the sector was decreasingly restrictive and then increasingly expansionary. The third quarter of 1977 saw a major swing toward restriction, largely attributable to the failure of state-local expenditures to rise at anything like the magnitude of the very large increase in federal grants disbursed in the quarter. An equally large swing back toward expansion occurred in the fourth quarter of 1977, primarily because of the drop in federal grants.

A more conventional measure of the overall cyclical behavior of the state-local sector is its surplus-deficit position in the national income accounts. On a gross basis, the sector ran a surplus in every quarter of the period.[15] The major factor accounting for these surpluses is the social insurance funds of the states and local governments, which have run surpluses in every year since World War II. Between 1950 and 1977, the surpluses realized by these funds increased at an average annual rate of more than 12 percent. As these surpluses are not generally available for operating purposes, most recent analyses of state-local behavior in the national income accounts have subtracted the insurance-fund surpluses from the overall sector surpluses to yield what is called the "operating account" surplus or deficit.[16]

The state-local sector experienced declining operating account surpluses from 1972 through the cyclical peak, increasing deficits through the trough quarter, declining deficits through the recovery quarter, and generally rising surpluses since. When the operating account status is translated to quarter-to-quarter changes, the results are strikingly similar to the "surpluses" and "deficits" calculated from sector data on a price-adjusted basis, which were discussed earlier.

130

A Theory of State-Local Cyclical Behavior

The findings of the preceding section suggest some of the dimensions of a theory of the cyclical behavior of state and local governments. It is apparent that a great deal can be said about the cyclical behavior of the state and local sector on the basis of data readily available in the national income accounts.

It should also be apparent, however, that much remains obscured and unexplained by an analysis based exclusively on macroeconomic data. Much of what cannot be learned from such an analysis, moreover, is critical to the design of effective public policies for dealing with the fiscal problems of the states and local governments. Fragmentary research relating to the cyclical behavior of individual state and local governments has been undertaken in the past five years, but a definitive analysis remains to be attempted.[17]

In the long run, the fundamental reality of state and local finance is the balanced budget. The government of a growing state or locality can finance capital outlays by selling bonds, and the aggregate value of the jurisdiction's outstanding debt may rise indefinitely. However, unlike the federal government, whose debt may rise indefinitely with no untoward consequences associated with refinancing (because of its control of monetary policy), it is always understood that every particular issue of state and local debt will be liquidated from general revenues or from the revenues generated by whatever project the debt was issued to finance.

State and local governments can usually rely upon deficit finance only for capital purposes, and then only subject to the intense scrutiny of a bond market constantly on the lookout for overextension. Such governments cannot—though some have, for a time, tried to—incur operating deficits that will be financed by selling bonds, as the federal government can and does.

During a period of general economic prosperity, therefore, a state or local government's current operating expenditures are a function of available revenues.[18] Those revenues rise from year to year at a rate in relation to the growth in its economy that is determined by the nature of the jurisdiction's revenue system. The more income elastic the system, the faster the growth in current revenues. Revenue elasticity is a two-edged sword, however. A high-elasticity system produces rapidly rising revenues during a boom, but at the cost of declining revenues during a recession. A low-elasticity revenue system is not as productive during a boom, but its yield may not decline significantly during a recession.

Typically, the prudent state or locality allows in its fiscal decision making for the fact that, sooner or later, a recession or adverse local economic developments will undermine the rate of growth in its revenues. Consequently, in one or more of the many available ways, provision is made for the accumulation of financial reserves, which will be available to sustain operating budgets in the event of economic adversity.

With prudent fiscal management, therefore, the typical state or local government enters a recession with significant financial reserves. Normally, these are sufficient to sustain operations at existing or even slowly growing levels in the face of declining or moderating growth in revenues. By drawing down reserves and maintaining spending, even if not at prerecession rates of growth, the state or local government inadvertently pursues a policy that contributes to recovery of the economy from the recession.

Only if the recession turns out to be deeper or more prolonged than expected is a jurisdiction likely to exhaust its reserves and be forced to adopt policies that are inconsistent with national economic recovery, or perverse. Faced with exhausted reserves and falling revenues, a jurisdiction has two alternatives: to reverse the revenue decline by raising tax rates or adopting new sources, or to cut planned operating outlays.[19] The principal options available for cutting planned operating outlays are employee layoffs, freezes on new hiring, postponement of wage and salary increases, and deferral of nonpersonnel procurement.

131

When the recession bottoms out and the recovery process gets under way, revenues respond quickly. Unless the recession has been so serious as to require operating cutbacks whose restoration as soon as possible is politically essential, the pressures for expenditure increases are not likely to be as intense as they were before the recession. This political reality, coupled with anxiety about the strength of the recovery, is likely to result in efforts to restore depleted reserves rather than to return immediately to historical rates of growth in operating outlays.

Eventually, as recovery proceeds, reserve restoration is accomplished and current outlays begin growing at rates that finally catch up with rates of growth in revenues. Ultimately, if the expansion phase of the cycle continues long enough, expectations of expenditure growth established during the catch-up period may combine with sufficiently reduced anxiety about future recession to place demands upon rising revenues that require discretionary rate increases and new-source adoptions.[20]

The historical record of the state-local sector, including that of the past three or four years, seems generally to be consistent with this theory of cyclical behavior. There is, however, an important exception to the general theory, and that involves jurisdictions in areas that do not share the benefits of general prosperity.

The ability of a state or local government to make it through a recession without raising taxes or cutting expenditures depends upon its having (1) an extremely inelastic revenue system or (2) accumulated sufficient financial reserves during the period before the recession. Local governments that rely upon the real property tax for the bulk of their revenues are characteristic of the first situation. The jurisdiction that cannot depend upon the down-side stability of its revenues depends for the accumulation of the necessary reserves upon the strength of its economy. If that economy is not strong on the up-side of the cycle, reserves are not likely to be accumulated, and the government enters a recession facing the immediate prospect of raising taxes or cutting expenditures. Even if the recession's impact is relatively moderate, the unavailability of reserves is likely to result in procyclical responses that may not be necessary in jurisdictions more hard-hit by the recession.

Other local governments with revenue systems that are sufficiently income-inelastic to shield them from recession-induced losses may, however, be experiencing secular stagnation or even decline in their economies. For such jurisdictions, too, even the mildest recession may be sufficient to prompt cyclically perverse fiscal responses.

The fact is that a number of jurisdictions around the country fit one or the other (or even both) of these descriptions. They are, in general terms, located in areas with stagnant or declining populations and employment and, in many cases, deteriorating residential, commercial, and industrial property. The cyclical fiscal behavior of the state-local sector as a whole examined in the previous section suggests that these jurisdictions are a small minority of all state and local governments. It is clear, however, that they are the jurisdictions that are most likely to engage in procyclical fiscal behavior.[21] If there is to be a national policy whose objective is to minimize the extent of cyclically perverse behavior by state and local governments, it is also clear that some means must be found for targeting that policy on such jurisdictions.

Regional Disparities

The fiscal behavior of the state and local government sector over the business cycle is directly relevant only to a fairly narrow range of macroeconomic concerns. Far more germane to most of the major issues on the nation's policy agenda in 1978 is the question of the nature and extent of the differences in the fiscal behavior (and the underlying economic conditions that so powerfully influence fiscal behavior) of state and local governments among regions, among states, and among urban, rural, and suburban areas.

132

Regrettably, few of the national-income-account data are available on a disaggregated basis; personal income is a notable exception. Consequently, analysis of fiscal and economic issues below the national level must proceed with a data base far less comprehensive and historically reliable than that available for analysis of the sector as a whole.

This problem notwithstanding, the ingenuity of researchers has been thoroughly demonstrated in the past few years, which have seen a veritable explosion of studies, analyses, and occasional polemics on the general subject of subnational disparities in state-local economic and fiscal behavior.

As disparities among urban areas and among urban, rural, and suburban areas in given states and in different parts of the country are considered in other papers in this volume, the focus of this section is on interregional and interstate differences. These disparities have been a central fact of American economic history. However, the convergence of relative incomes in the regions toward the national average is one of the most important trends of the past half century, and most recent studies project this process to continue for the foreseeable future.

The discussion of recent developments regarding disparities begins with the appearance of the issue that triggered much of the recent attention: the famous (or infamous) "Sunbelt-Frostbelt" controversy. A brief review of this development is followed by a summary of the research that has appeared during the past two years and that is currently in progress.

The New Sectionalism Controversy: Sunbelt and Frostbelt

Ironically, the year of the nation's Bicentennial saw escalating concern about widening disparities in rates of economic growth and demographic change among certain areas of the country.[22] In this issue, some have seen the potential for the emergence of a new sectional controversy that could rival in importance such disputes as that involving the Second Bank of the United States.[23]

The focus of the controversy was on the position of the "Sunbelt" vis à vis the "Frostbelt" or the "Snowbelt".[24]

The alarm attached to evidence adduced by a number of studies of trends since 1970. These data appear to show a dramatic acceleration in migration of people and jobs from the Northeast in particular—and the Frostbelt in general—to the Sunbelt, coupled with seriously lagging economic growth in the former region and a continuing boom in the latter. One of the most important consequences of these trends, it was argued, is the increasingly desperate fiscal condition of state and local governments in the Frostbelt and the relative prosperity of governments in the Sunbelt.

Particular attention was devoted to the possible role of the federal government in exacerbating the situation, and to the potential for changes in federal policies designed to mitigate or even reverse the trends. It is this aspect of the issue more than any other that appears to have accounted for the unprecedented surge of activity in 1976 and 1977 on the part of the Frostbelt states to organize in support of such changes in federal policy.

The first in a series of journalistic treatments of the sectionalism controversy in 1976 was a five-part series of front-page articles in *The New York Times*.[25] Although predominately anecdotal in character, one of the major points made was that the federal government appears to be encouraging population and employment shifts to the Sunbelt by the regionally redistributive consequences of its tax, grant, and contracting policies.

The second contribution by a major national publication to the flowering of the controversy appeared in the *Business Week* issue of May 17, 1976, as a special report titled "The Second War Between the States."[26] The dramatic tone of the title carried through the articles, which were replete with references to a "flood tide" of migration and "breathtaking relative decline" in the "industrial North." The *Business Week* report was followed closely by an article in the *National Journal* titled "Federal Spending: The North's Loss is the Sunbelt's Gain."[27] This article pieced together

133

data on federal fiscal flows to arrive at two fundamental conclusions:

1. That major inequities exist in the "balance of payments" of the states, with some showing "enormous" surpluses and others large deficits; and
2. That there are systematic biases in the pattern of surpluses and deficits that result in "a heavy flow of federal dollars away from—rather than toward—the states and regions of the nation in the most severe economic straits."[28]

Although numerous articles in national publications have appeared since, the three cited above set the tone for the debate. Generally, most recent treatments by journalists have been more moderate in tone, but the important contributions have been in the technical literature, which is reviewed in the remainder of this section.

The Technical Literature on Disparities

The voluminous literature generated over the past two years that bears in one way or another on the issues addressed in this section is difficult to classify in any rigorous way. The following discussion is intended to provide a general overview of some of the important contributions without pretence at being either comprehensive or analytically systematic.

One of the first technical monographs to be published following the journalistic treatments discussed above is an analysis of recent trends and current relative status of the Sunbelt and the Northeast and Midwest industrial areas by Carol L. Jusenius and Larry C. Ledebur.[29] The primary thesis of *A Myth in the Making* is that the focusing of attention on the superior economic performance of the South since 1970, and especially on the lower unemployment rate of its economy in 1975 compared with that of the Northeast-Midwest, fails to account for the fact that in terms of absolute economic welfare the South still lags significantly behind the North. Moreover, the authors suggest that an alarmist psychological climate has been generated by focusing virtually exclusively on recent trends and discussing them in terms of direct comparison between the two areas. This climate of opinion may lead, in turn, to the adoption of precipitous changes in federal policies that will undermine prospects for continued growth in the South without significantly contributing to a solution to the serious problems of the Northeast-Midwest.

In March 1977, Jusenius and Ledebur completed a follow-up study that presents a vast array of indicators of relative economic development and distress in the same groups of Sunbelt and "Northern Industrial Tier" states that were the focus of their 1976 monograph.[30] The central thesis of this paper is that the framing of issues in terms of regional or sectional competition diverts attention from the key task of problem diagnosis that is a prerequisite for the design of a national policy for regional economic development. From their data, the authors conclude that:

1. No particular region's economic problems are more serious than those of any other;
2. The nature and dimensions of the economic problems of each region vary over a wide range; and
3. Unemployment is the primary problem of the North, while poverty is the South's most serious difficulty.

In August 1977, the Congressional Budget Office (CBO) published a background paper analyzing the patterns of federal spending among counties, with reference to the relative economic well-being of recipient areas.[31] Special attention is given to distinguishing between counties experiencing economic problems stemming from slow economic growth and those whose problems are rooted in low income. In general, the study finds federal spending per capita to be higher in low-growth counties than in growing counties, but it also establishes that federal outlays are larger in high-income than in low-income counties.

The regional distribution of federal grants-in-aid to state and local governments in 1975, and shifts in that distribution since 1970, are the focus of a report published in November 1977 by the Academy for Contemporary Problems.[32] Among the key conclusions reached in this study—which compares grants received by each of the four broad census regions on a per capita basis, per $1,000 of personal income, and as a proportion of state-local general revenue—are:

1. By all three criteria, interregional disparities decreased between 1970 and 1975;
2. Between 1970 and 1975, the Northeast moved from third to first in grants per capita, though in 1975 it was still below the national average on the other two criteria;
3. The Midwest lagged the other three regions in 1975 on all three criteria, but the magnitude of the lag had declined since 1970; and
4. Variations within each region are much larger than those among regions, which suggests that analysis at the regional level is really not a very productive endeavor.

In December 1977, the U.S. General Accounting Office weighed-in with yet another analysis of the distribution of federal grants-in-aid, again focused primarily upon the regions.[33] In addition to considering trends in the dollar volume of total grants (with conclusions similar to those of the other studies mentioned earlier), the report calculates an "aid/support ratio" for each region for the period 1969–75. This ratio is defined as per capita total grants received divided by normalized per capita federal personal income taxes paid in the same year. The tax payments are normalized by multiplying actual per capita taxes in a given year by the national ratio of total grants to total income taxes in that year. The results for the aid/support ratio show:

1. A pronounced general trend over the period toward convergence of the values for the regions; and
2. Throughout the period, the East North Central region was the major "net contributor to Federal aid," and the East South Central region was the primary net beneficiary.

One of the most recent analyses of trends in U.S. population and employment is that appearing in the final report of the President's Urban and Regional Policy Group.[34] The general thesis of this analysis is that the population distribution has been subject to a "thinning-out" process that is traceable to the early years of this century and that has been accelerating in recent decades. This process, the report argues, has been undermining the economic bases of the nation's older cities, but negligible attention is given to direct analysis of the fiscal problems the process has presumably generated. The lack of attention given to a systematic review of the distribution of existing federal aid and its impacts on state-local finance is a surprising omission from a report addressed to the redesign of federal policies, most of which are now and will in the future be in the form of grants-in-aid of one type or another.

Another dimension of the disparities among regions, states, and localities involves state and local tax burdens. Many of the journalistic discussions have relied upon per capita taxes collected in the various jurisdictions being compared. But this measure fails to allow for the wide variation in income levels around the nation. For this reason, the traditional technical measure of relative tax burdens has been tax effort, or the ratio of tax collections to personal income. A recent paper by John Ross and John Shannon calls the traditional measure into question on the grounds that it fails to take account of time trends in tax effort and that it tends to understate the tax effort of slow-growing states and to overstate the effort of fast-growing states.[35]

The authors suggest two alternative measures. The first adds a time dimension to the traditional ratio of tax collections to personal income. The resulting measure of "fiscal blood pressure" is expressed as a state's relative fiscal effort in 1974 (the state's fiscal-effort ratio divided by the national average ratio) combined with a measure of the relative annual average rate of change in the state's fiscal-effort ratio during years 1964–74.[36]

Unfortunately, the trade-off between the two indexes is not defined. It is clear that 120/120 is worse than 110/110, but which state is in the worse fiscal bind: one whose measure is valued at 120/110 or one whose measure is valued at 110/120?

Thus, it is not possible to convert the dual measure into one number that would permit compilation of a unique ranking of the states.

Accordingly, Ross and Shannon classify the states by four categories: high and falling, low and falling, high and rising, and low and rising. Among the four, states in the high-and-rising category are unquestionably experiencing more fiscal pressure than those in the low-and-falling category. It is not so obviously true that a similar ranking can be assigned to the high-and-falling and low-and-rising categories. Which state's situation is to be preferred, that of Arizona (107/22) or that of Virginia (90/196)?

The first measure does not come to grips with the fact that personal income provides a misleading impression for many states of their actual potential ability to raise revenue if they "made average use of all major taxable sources" (the so-called representative-tax-system definition of fiscal capacity). Thus, Ross and Shannon calculate a second fiscal pressure index. The only difference between the two measures is an adjustment in the personal income data so that they are a more accurate indicator of the potential yield in each state of a "representative" revenue system.

The two measures produce generally consistent results. States in the Northeast and Midwest have been experiencing increasing fiscal pressure, while states in the Sunbelt have been under relatively low and/or falling pressure.

A number of studies currently in progress deserve mention in this review. Glenn L. Nelson, of the Department of Agricultural and Applied Economics at the University of Minnesota, is engaged in an analysis of the determinants and impacts of the distribution of federal outlays in selected substate regions in the North Central States.

Irving Leveson, of the Hudson Institute, is completing a general analysis of the future of the U.S. economy and its regions. A number of likely alternative futures are being considered in this study sponsored by the U.S. Economic Development Administration.

Stephen P. Dresch and David A. Updegrove, of the Institute for Demographic and Economic Studies in New Haven, are wrapping up a study designed to develop analytical capabilities for identifying the regional impacts of changes in federal tax, transfer, and purchasing policies. The model (IDIOM), being developed with funding provided by the U.S. Economic Development Administration, is also intended to project the effects of other types of exogenous changes on the national and regional economies.

Finally, Janet Pack, a member of the staff of the Advisory Commission on Intergovernmental Relations, is completing an analysis of the consequences of federal tax, transfer, and investment programs on unemployment, employment, and per capita income of the regions.

Notes

1.   Alvin H. Hansen and Harvey S. Perloff, *State and Local Finance in the National Economy* (New York: Norton, 1944).

2.   Ibid., p. 199.

3.   Robert W. Rafuse, Jr., "Cyclical Behavior of State and Local Finances," in *Essays in Fiscal Federalism,* ed. Richard A. Musgrave (Washington, D.C.: Brookings Institution, 1965), p. 118. Similar conclusions were reached in another study completed about the same time by Ansel M. Sharp, "The Behavior of Selected State and Local Government Fiscal Variables During the Phases of the Cycles 1949–61," *Proceedings of the 58th Annual Conference on Taxation, November 8–12, 1965* (Columbus: National Tax Association, 1966), pp. 599–614.

4.   Ralph Schlosstein, *The Current Fiscal Position of State and Local Governments: A Survey of 48 State Governments and 140 Local Governments,* report to the Joint Economic Committee, 94th Cong., 1st sess. (December 1975).

5.   A study of the general issue of the fiscal behavior of state and local governments over the cycle and of the design of federal policies that can contribute to the effectiveness of the federal stabilization policy by mitigating the adverse, or "procyclical," effects of state and local fiscal policies was initiated in 1977 by the Advisory Commission on Intergovernmental Relations in cooperation with the Congressional Budget Office. This study, mandated by section 215 (b) of the Public Works Employment Act of 1976, is to be submitted to the Congress by July 21, 1978. See also the analysis of the Antirecession Fiscal Assistance program prepared for the Office of Revenue Sharing, U.S. Department of the Treasury by Peat, Marwick, Mitchell & Co., the Municipal Finance Officers Association, Phoenix Associates, and Harold A. Hovey, *An Analysis of the Antirecession Fiscal Assistance Program* (Washington, D.C.: Office of Revenue Sharing, U.S. Department of the Treasury, 1978).

6.   A more extensive discussion, including tabular presentations of the data, appears in an appendix by Robert W. Rafuse contained in Peat, Marwick, Mitchell et al., *An Analysis of the Antirecession Fiscal Assistance Program*.

7.   This discussion refers to data adjusted to eliminate the effects of inflation, which distort the underlying "real" relationships. This should not be interpreted as implying that inflation has not been an extremely important factor in state-local decision making over the past five years or so. In this connection, it is interesting to note the finding of the General Accounting Office's review of the impact of ARFA on 52 states and localities that "the vast majority of governments visited cited inflation as having posed the major impediment to maintaining financial stability." [Comptroller General of the United States, *Report to the Congress: Antirecession Assistance Is Helping But Distribution Formula Needs Reassessment* (Washington, D.C.: U.S. General Accounting Office, 1977), p. 11].

8.   All data in this paragraph are from Bureau of Economic Analysis, U.S. Department of Commerce, *The National Income and Product Accounts of the United States, 1929–74: Statistical Tables* (Washington, D.C.: Government Printing Office, 1977), p. 9.

9.   The data referred to in this discussion are state-local purchases of structures, which exclude construction force account compensation (for work performed by employees of state and local governments). The data for 1977 and the first quarter of 1978 are unpublished estimates by the Bureau of Economic Analysis, U.S. Department of Commerce.

10.   This diagnosis is generally consistent with that advanced by Edward M. Gramlich, who argues that the design and implementation of the Local Public Works Program provided strong incentives for state and local officials to postpone commitments of their own resources to construction in anticipation of possible federal funding. See "State-Local Budgets the Day After It Rained: Why Is the Surplus So High?" *Brookings Papers on Economic Activity* 1 (1978), pp. 191–214.

11.   Net interest paid and subsidies less current surpluses of government enterprises have both been negative items for the past 10 or more years. As they are relatively small and stable magnitudes, it is reasonable to abstract from them in the present context.

12.   Using the GNP implicit price deflator for personal consumption expenditures.

13.   Using the GNP price deflator for state-local purchases of goods and services.

14.   A "surplus" is not an infallible indication that the state-local sector was contractionary, and a "deficit" is not conclusive evidence that the sector was expansionary, but for the brief period involved they are reasonably good indicators of the direction of changes. Fiscal theory suggests that the macroeconomic consequences of changes in the four fiscal categories are not truly commensurate. A $1 billion increase in state-local tax receipts, for example, is less restrictive than a $1 billion increase in transfer payments. Moreover, the restrictive effect of $1 billion in federal grants depends upon how they are financed by the federal government—by higher federal taxes, borrowing, or by reduction in some other type of federal outlay.

15.   On this basis a deficit has not been seen since the first quarter of 1968.

16.   For a critical view of this measure as an indicator of the fiscal situation of the states, see National Association of State Budget Officers and National Governors' Association Center for Policy Research, *Fiscal Survey of the States, Fall 1977* (Washington, D.C.: National Governors' Association, 1977).

17.   The theory outlined in the next few pages is based upon the macroeconomic analysis above, the field work undertaken for the Treasury study of the Antirecession Fiscal Assistance program, and the related work of a number of economists referenced in the text.

18. See Edward M. Gramlich and Harvey Galper, "State and Local Fiscal Behavior and Federal Grant Policy," *Brookings Papers on Economic Activity* 1 (1976).

19. Unless the economic outlook is so grave as seriously to undermine confidence in the future, postponement of planned capital outlays to be financed by the sale of bonds is not likely to be contemplated, since long-term interest rates tend to be most attractive at such times.

20. This appears to be what happened during the late 1960s, when the sustained period of prosperity and the attendant enormous increases in state-local spending generated increasing cries of state-local fiscal crisis, and rising pressures for federal relief in the form of general revenue sharing.

21. See the statement prepared by George E. Peterson for presentation at hearings by the Intergovernmental Relations and Human Resources Subcommittee, House Committee on Government Operations, *Intergovernmental Antirecession Assistance Act of 1977; Hearings — March 1, 2, and 8, 1977*, 95th Cong., 1st sess., 1977, pp. 17–36. See also U.S. Department of the Treasury, "Evaluation of the Antirecession Fiscal Assistance Program," mimeographed (Washington, D.C.: U.S. Department of the Treasury, 1977), pp. 20–43. The extended discussion of the cyclical adjustment process in the latter document closely parallels that appearing in the text above.

22. For a general overview of the controversy, see Robert W. Rafuse, Jr., *The New Regional Debate*, Agenda Setting Series (Washington, D.C.: Center for Policy Research and Analysis, National Governors' Conference, 1977). See also John E. Petersen, *Frostbelt v. Sunbelt, Part I: Key Trends of the Seventies* and *Part II: Changing Federal Policies* (New York: First Boston Corporation, 1977).

23. See Daniel P. Moynihan, "The Politics and Economics of Regional Growth," *The Public Interest* 51 (Spring 1978), pp. 3–21.

24. There is an astonishing lack of consensus regarding the precise set of states in each section. See Rafuse, *The New Regional Debate*, for a description of the many definitions that have been used in the various studies.

25. February 8–12, 1976.

26. "The Second War Between the States," *Business Week*, May 17, 1976, pp. 92–114.

27. Joel Havemann, Rochelle L. Stanfield, and Neil R. Pierce, "Federal Spending: The North's Loss is the Sunbelt's Gain," *National Journal*, June 26, 1976, pp. 878–91.

28. Ibid., p. 878.

29. Carol L. Jusenius and Larry C. Ledebur, *A Myth in the Making: The Southern Economic Challenge and the Northern Economic Decline* (Washington, D.C.: Office of Economic Research, Economic Development Administration, U.S. Department of Commerce, 1976).

30. Carol L. Jusenius and Larry C. Ledebur, *Federal and Regional Responses to the Economic Decline of the Northern Industrial Tier* (Washington, D.C.: Office of Economic Research, Economic Development Administration, U.S. Department of Commerce, 1977).

31. Peggy L. Cuciti, *Troubled Local Economies and the Distribution of Federal Dollars* (Washington, D.C.: The Congressional Budget Office, 1977).

32. Charles L. Vehorn, *The Regional Distribution of Federal Grants-in-Aid*, Urban and Regional Development Series No. 3 (Columbus, Ohio: Academy for Contemporary Problems, 1977).

33. U.S. General Accounting Office, *Changing Patterns of Federal Aid to State and Local Governments, 1969–75*, Report No. PAD-78-15 (Washington, D.C.: U.S. General Accounting Office, 1977).

34. President's Urban and Regional Policy Group, *A New Partnership to Conserve America's Communities: A National Urban Policy* (Washington, D.C.: Government Printing Office, 1978), pp. 1–3 to 1–24.

35. Advisory Commission on Intergovernmental Relations, *Measuring the Fiscal "Blood Pressure" of the States—1964–1975*, Information Report M-111 (Washington, D.C.: Advisory Commission on Intergovernmental Relations, 1977).

36. For example, if state and local tax collections in 1974 were 10 percent of a given state's personal income, while the same ratio for the nation as a whole was 8 percent, then that state's

relative effort was 125 percent of the national average. If the state's fiscal effort ratio had been increasing by 2 percent per year over the 1964–74 period, while the average annual national increase was only 1 percent, then the state's relative annual rate of change was 200 percent of the national average. The resulting measure would be expressed as 125/200, which indicates that the state's fiscal pressure is above average and rising more rapidly than the national average.

Public Policy Issues in
School Finance Reform

Allan Odden

The issues related to inequities in public school finance structures no longer hinge mainly on relationships between expenditure levels per pupil and local school district wealth. It is recognized by both state policy makers and school finance scholars that the issues related to school finance are much more complicated; that they must be analyzed within the broader context of local, state and federal public finance and intergovernmental fiscal relations; and that they are importantly affected by the changing demographics of the society in general, including the increasingly fragmented politics of the public education policy-making process. This review discusses some of these complex issues, beginning with an attempt to identify different definitions and concepts of school finance equalization.

School Finance Equalization

There are at least six major issues related to school finance equalization. The first concerns definitions of equalization, including different concepts of equity in school finance. This issue also encompasses the implications of each definition for appropriate school finance programs and the effects such programs have on students as well as taxpayers. The second issue concerns wealth equalization and the growing body of research that is showing that wealth equalization is more complicated than previously considered. The third issue, land value capitalization, focuses on the long run effect that local taxes or expenditures can have on the prices of land and homes within school districts. The fourth issue relates to pupil-need equalization and the attempts to provide additional services for high-cost student populations, including the need to structure the financing mechanisms of those services to enhance and not undermine overall equalization objectives of the general aid program. The fifth issue concerns cost equalization and the possibilities for modifying school aid formulas for the varying purchasing power of the education dollar across school districts within a state. The sixth issue is the equalization of intradistrict resource distribution.

Definitions of Equity

There are numerous legal standards, as well as other definitions of equity, in school finance. It is critically important for policy makers to be aware of these different

Allan Odden is the Director of the Education Finance Center of the Education Commission of the States in Denver, Colorado.

definitions because each requires a different type of equalization formula for implementation and each will have different fiscal results, will affect students differently, and will impose different tax burdens on households.[1]

There are basically two different definitions of financial equity in school finance: fiscal neutrality and expenditure per pupil equality. The fiscal neutrality standard is not concerned with differences in expenditures per pupil *per se*, but requires only that expenditure per pupil differences not be related to differences in local school district fiscal ability. The objective of this standard is to eliminate the relationship between local wealth and expenditure levels by equalizing the ability of all school districts to raise education revenues from local and state sources at a given tax rate. In the main, therefore, this equity standard is focused more on taxpayers than on students. Appropriate school finance programs for implementing this equity standard include district power equalization, guaranteed tax base, guaranteed yield or percentage equalization programs.

The second equity standard is an "equalized expenditure" per pupil norm. It is focused primarily on students and requires that expenditures per pupil, after adjustments for different education costs and pupil needs, be equal across all school districts in a state. This standard is concerned with the gaps in expenditures per pupil between high- and low-spending school districts and requires the reduction—if not elimination—of those differences. Appropriate school finance programs for implementing this equity standard include a high-level foundation program with very limited local enrichment or a full state-assumption program.

Fiscal neutrality neither requires nor, in general, results in reductions in expenditure per pupil differences.[2] The fact that fiscal neutrality programs do not significantly reduce differences in expenditures per pupil is one consistent fact in school finance across all states that have enacted programs designed to create a fiscally neutral system. On the other hand, states that have developed and funded new school aid programs designed explicitly to reduce expenditure differences have closed expenditure gaps.[3]

Selection of an equity standard for a state's school finance structure should be one of the first tasks in the process of designing and implementing a new school aid formula. However, attention must also be given both to the point in time at which the system will be adjudged to meet the standard and the measures that will be used to make the judgments. With respect to the point in time at which the system should be evaluated, the issue is whether the aid allocation *process* or the *results* from the process are to be judged.[4] Policy makers should be aware of this distinction and make evaluations of the state's program with it in mind. It would not be unfair to state, however, that public policy research in general has been primarily concerned with results and is suspicious of a process that seems fair but produces inequitable results.

Until recently, not enough attention has been given by school finance analysts to the statistical tests used to measure the degree to which a system meets either equity standard. Yet there are a great number of conceptual issues related to the various statistical tests that can be used. There are many tests of equality; each has strengths and weaknesses. A state could score high on one equality test but low on another. Similarly, there are many tests of fiscal neutrality, each potentially ranking a state differently.[5]

An informal school finance cooperative, consisting of researchers from projects funded by the National Institute of Education and the Ford Foundation, is currently investigating these measures in more than 30 states for which the projects have a universal sample of district data. The objective of this cooperative venture is to produce a set of statistical tests to be used to assess how each state's school finance structure meets the standard of either expenditure per pupil equality or fiscal neutrality equity. By the end of 1978, it is anticipated that a "state of the states" with respect to school finance equalization under both equity standards can be reported for all states for both the 1975–76 and 1976–77 fiscal years. This information should be useful for states individually as they assess the effectiveness of their current structures, and for the federal government should it enact a federal program to encourage school finance equalization.

In summary, there are four important elements related to definitions of equity in school finance equalization:

a. Choice of a particular equity standard;
b. Design of an appropriate school finance program to implement it;
c. Determination of a point in time at which to evaluate the program; and
d. Selection of measures on which to make evaluation judgments.

Wealth Equalization

Most states continue to assess local school district fiscal capacity by assessed valuation of property per pupil. Many states modify the assessed valuation figures by assessment-sales ratios to adjust for the varying levels of assessment across assessing jurisdictions. This simple fiscal-capacity measure has come under attack in recent years for a number of reasons. First, it has been shown that income is an important determinant of school district fiscal decisions in addition to property wealth.[6] Second, there is little correlation between property wealth per pupil and income per pupil or household income in many states. Third, economic research has demonstrated that wealth equalization is a function not only of (1) total property wealth and (2) household income, but also of (3) the composition of the property tax base and (4) the structure of the equalization formula itself.[7] The effect of these factors on the local "economic price" of providing education services must be determined in order to design an equalization formula to neutralize all four elements.

The basic argument that all four factors influence local school district decisions is as follows. First, without any state equalization aid formula, districts with high property wealth are able to raise greater revenues at a given tax rate than districts with low property wealth. This argument has led to the development and use of the current set of equalization programs, based primarily on property wealth per pupil. Even with equalization formulas that neutralize wealth differences, however, districts with higher income bear a lower percentage burden in providing a given level of education than districts with lower income; i.e., the economic price in the higher-income district is less. Third, even holding total property wealth and household income constant, districts with a greater proportion of the property tax base comprised of nonresidential property—i.e., commercial and industrial property—are able to shift some of the property tax burden to nonresidential property owners. Thus, to raise an additional $100 per pupil, for example, the greater the nonresidential property tax base, the lower the price to resident homeowners for the extra expenditure. Finally, the structure of the aid formulas is important because, for foundation types of systems, the state aid is fixed as long as the district levies the minimum required local tax rate, while for percentage equalizing or guaranteed tax programs the aid is variable, depending not only on local wealth but also the local tax rate. State aid will rise as the district increases its tax rate, but the additional aid has a "price" since local dollars also will rise as the tax rate is increased.

An expanding policy analysis literature treats in detail how both state aid formulas with a "price" variable and local fiscal capacity measures other than total assessed value of property per pupil affect local district expenditure decisions.[8] In general, studies have found that, other things held constant, expenditures per pupil increased as income increased, as the proportion of the property tax base that was residential decreased, and as the "price" variable (i.e., matching rate) in the formula decreased.

Other recent studies indicate that wealth neutrality is a significantly more complicated concept than previously considered within school finance circles. While the results are not yet completely definitive, they do show that effecting wealth equalization and wealth neutrality in a state school finance structure requires investigation of at least four factors: property wealth, composition of the property tax base, household income, and the "price" component of an equalization formula.[9]

142

Land Value Capitalization

A new issue that has been raised in light of school finance reform is capitalization. Capitalization refers to the long run effect that local taxes or expenditures can have on the prices of land and homes. In general, if taxes increase in one school district or the quality of education services decreases, other things held constant (including taxes and spending levels in neighboring districts), the price of homes may decrease. Likewise, if taxes decrease or expenditures increase, prices may increase. In the real world, obviously, taxes and expenditures in all districts change simultaneously. Although capitalization is a secondary, spin-off effect, major school finance reforms that significantly change either local tax or spending levels will probably, in the long run, have an effect on the local value of land and homes.[10]

In the early 1960s, Daicoff conducted one of the first studies of capitalization that took into account both the change in taxation level and the change in service levels.[11] He found, contrary to expectations, that property values and tax rates were positively associated, i.e., that increased taxes were accompanied by higher price levels. His suggested explanation was that the negative effects of higher taxes were more than compensated for by the positive effects of higher service levels. However, other recent studies that controlled for service level differences did find evidence of classical capitalization.[12]

In one of the most sophisticated studies of this issue, Oates used regression analysis in a study of capitalization in New Jersey. He found that, although differentially high local property tax rates were negatively associated with land values, the effect was more than offset when the proceeds of the tax were used to provide increased educational services.

Bish, in a theoretical discussion of this issue related to the effects of school finance reform, suggested that a major reform would have considerable capitalization impacts. Newacheck, drawing from the results of related studies, predicted that a school finance reform in California that caused a tax increase on the order of 70 cents per $100 of assessed valuation in a particular school district could produce reductions in the value of a $100,000 home of about $3,400. And many persons in California believe that AB 65, the California school finance reform of 1977, will, over the next few years, have major capitalization effects.[13]

Pupil Need Equalization

One of the characteristics of school finance reforms in the 1970s has been increased attention to student populations that require extra educational services, such as the handicapped, the economically or educationally disadvantaged, the student for whom English is not the dominant language, and the student in vocational education programs. At the same time, many school finance analyses ignore these categorical programs. The relationship between the financing of these special services and the general aid structure, moreover, has been almost totally ignored by the court cases. Nevertheless, local, state and federal revenues for these high-cost services should be as much a part of comprehensive education finance structures and analyses as revenues for normal student services.

One of the emerging issues for the categorical funding mechanisms is the degree to which they decrease or increase wealth or income-related inequities in the provision of categorical program education services. There is some information that suggests that such inequities occur most noticeably in states in which the overall state role in funding education is low. That is, high-wealth, high-income districts seem to identify more special education needs, spend more for those services and receive greater amounts of state support for the services. Such a situation is counter to what one would expect and what other research has shown: namely, that the incidence of students needing special services is greater in low-income, poorer areas.

On the other hand, analyses of special education services in states where the state role in funding education is higher show little relationship between the wealth and

143

income characteristics of school districts and the provision of special resources. Exactly what mechanisms are operating to produce these results have not been explicitly identified at this time. But the results of research clearly suggest that the general state role, the structure of the categorical aid funding system and the equity in the provision of special education services are interacting and producing unanticipated behaviors in school districts.[14] Heightened sensitivity is needed to these potential behaviors and additional policy research is needed to insure that unintentional inequities do not occur.

Cost Equalization

Policy makers in all states know that the purchasing power of the education dollar varies, in some cases dramatically, across school districts in a state. In the past few years, there has been increased interest in developing indices that a state could use to adjust the equalization formula to account for these differences in the costs of providing education services. At the same time, there have been a number of different attempts to develop such indices, some more substantively grounded than others.

The crudest attempts to develop costs indices have been those that simply make comparisons of expenditure differences across school districts. Such attempts are seriously flawed, however, because expenditure differences are dramatically different from cost differences. Differences in education expenditures are caused by two factors: differences in the quality or level of services provided and differences in the costs of providing those services. The former are within the control of local school districts; i.e., except where explicitly limited by state law, local districts are able to choose the level of education services they wish to provide. Differences in education costs, however, are outside the control of local districts and are caused by factors such as geographical location, characteristics of the student body, and other demographic characteristics of the school district.

The development of indices that indicate the differences in education costs requires a rigorous economic model and sophisticated statistical techniques that can separate the controllable from the uncontrollable variables and that, holding constant the level or quality of services provided, base the indices on the uncontrollable variables. Cost-of-education indices based on this economic methodology are also different from, as well as more accurate than, cost-of-living indices. Clearly, the market basket of goods that is based on household expenditure patterns and used to develop cost-of-living indices is different from the market basket of goods that school districts must purchase to provide education services.

Several studies have developed cost indices using economic modeling and regression analysis. Some studies have attempted to predict average teacher salaries among districts and have then developed the indices on the basis of the uncontrollable factors accounting for differences in district average teacher salaries.[15]

Other studies have used samples of individual teachers, rather than district averages, to produce cost indices. Such a methodology allows one to pick up both inter- and intradistrict factors that may account for salary differences and is based on the fairly well developed hedonic price methodology that has been used in other economic research.[16]

The effect of using cost indices, however, is not a neutral one. Metropolitan districts in general have above-average indices, while rural districts have below-average indices. Thus, all things being equal, the use of a cost-of-education index will result in relatively greater amounts of aid flowing to metropolitan districts as compared to nonmetropolitan districts. In almost every research report, moreover, the highest cost indices have been found to occur in the central-city school districts. This can substantiate the claim that costs are higher in the cities and justify the use of cost indices to compensate city school districts for the lower purchasing power of their funds.

144

Intradistrict Equalization

School finance has for the most part concerned itself with interdistrict resource allocation issues. Nevertheless, there have been both litigation and policy research related to intradistrict resource distribution issues. The most well-known district struggling with these issues is the Washington, D.C., district, which came under court order to allocate dollars per pupil so that the differences among the schools within the district ranged within five percent of the average school. Both court briefs and subsequent research had shown that the inequality of resource distribution was closely related to socio-demographic characteristics of the schools, with the predominantly black, low-income schools receiving the lowest amounts per pupil.[17]

The issue of intradistrict resource distribution is one that, while not the top agenda item in any state, is being raised by a number of policy makers at the state and local levels. One can expect that this issue will be given more attention in the near future, especially for large-city districts.

The Politics of Education

Although many of the substantive issues surrounding school finance are economic, education finance policy is made by state legislators who must allocate the scarce resources of the states among numerous functional areas. In this light, it is important to note the changes that have occurred and are occurring in the politics of public education policy making. No longer do state legislators rely solely on the old education lobby for advice on the policy changes that need to be enacted each year. The politics of education is becoming increasingly complicated as well as fragmented, with competition both within the education circle and between educators and noneducation groups demanding other governmental services.

The new complexities in the politics of education can be viewed in a number of different ways. First, there is greater fiscal conflict between local school districts and other local governments concerning scarce local revenues, as well as intergovernmental aid. Second, there is a declining percentage of taxpayers willing to pay high education taxes. Third, teacher groups and parent groups are no longer aligned as closely as they used to be. Both the second and third factors result in an erosion of political support for public education. Fourth, courts, legislatures and governors increasingly involve themselves in the problems of school financing. Fifth, the urban-suburban cleavages have broadened, causing additional fragmentation in the general support for education. Six, there are two competitive elements within the education sector: (a) horizontal competition between general aid and the host of categorical, targeted aid programs, and (b) vertical competition between elementary/secondary education and the postsecondary sector.[18]

Within this fragmented and complex vortex of political pressures, school finance reforms are enacted by state legislators. Yet, little research of a substantive, political science, public policy-making nature has been conducted that sheds much light on the politics of school finance reform. Numerous descriptive accounts of the school finance reform events in a number of states have been reported. Although informative, these case histories do not allow rigorous comparisons across states. Berke, Shalala and Williams have made the best attempt to generalize both across states and across methods for effecting reform.[19] They showed that reform attempts via referenda were considerably less successful than legislative attempts and identified the following characteristics of successful legislative efforts to change school finance policies:

a. A two-to-four-year time period of analysis and legislative debate;
b. Occurrence of external events such as a court case, a governor's commission, or joint legislative study;
c. Strong political leadership from either the legislative or executive branch;

145

d. A reform package, including noneducational aid, of "leveling-up" in which all districts receive something; and

e. Funds to finance the reform, either from a revenue surplus or an increase in taxes.

While these generalizations are useful, what is needed, especially in light of the rapidly changing political arena, is a cross-state study of the politics of school finance reform. The results would be (1) useful to policy makers in nonreform states, (2) helpful in explaining the elements of reform apart from individual state characteristics, and (3) a contribution to the developing constructs of the politics of education.[20]

Changing Societal Demographics

Important demographic changes in the American society are occurring that have important implications for school financing policies. The first, of course, is declining enrollments which are expected to persist through the early 1980s. The impact of such declines, however, will be felt through the 1990s in the nation's high schools and postsecondary institutions. A second factor is the increasing suburbanization across the country, accompanied both by increasing racial and economic segregation and the decline of many core cities. Related to this phenomenon is the growth and affluence of the "sunbelt" and the decline of the Northeast. Another factor, and one which has received little attention, is the growth of small, nonmetropolitan towns reflecting the demise of the rural-urban migration and the beginnings of what is now a net urban-rural population shift.

These demographic changes affect education finance in many ways. The drop in the youth population has been followed by increased demands for services for senior citizens and relatively less concern for education. Continued suburbanization and interregional racial and economic fragmentation have heightened class, ethnic and economic conflict and have made the school management of these problems more difficult. Within the education sector, the fact that the management of retrenchment requires greater skill and allows a smaller margin of error has not really been acknowledged; and inefficiencies, misunderstandings and low teacher morale have occurred.

In short, much has been written on the impacts that changes in the country's demographics are having on education policy making; but there still exists precious little substantive policy analysis of what the impacts actually are and what policy makers can do about them, although the previous section indicates some of the impacts on the politics of education. The most comprehensive research projects on the impacts of declining enrollments were conducted under the sponsorship of the National Institute of Education and have been compiled in a book entitled, *Declining Enrollments: The Challenge of the Coming Decade.*[21]

One of the growing concerns surrounding the economic impacts of enrollment declines is the teacher aging problem. The limited labor market for new teachers is resulting in a teaching force that is older, albeit more experienced, more expensive because greater numbers of teachers are in the "lower right hand corner" of the salary schedule and, because of seniority and tenure laws, more constraining for school districts with respect to personnel allocation. This is essentially a result of a decrease in demand for teachers and the concomitant effects, economic as well as political, on local school districts.[22]

Although overall enrollment declines may stop in the early 1980s, they will continue in many states, have already affected high schools in many districts and are just beginning to hit the colleges and universities. The management of an education enterprise in a time of decline will continue to be a problem in many pockets of this country for some time. Additional policy research is needed at a number of levels, both (1) to assist local districts in coping with the problems created by the decline and (2) to guide state legislators as they seek to enact policies that help ease the burden of decline while also requiring the making of hard decisions when they are merited.

146

Impacts of School Finance Reforms

School finance is like many other public policy issues in that, while much research is conducted describing the nature of the problem, little attention unfortunately is given to assessing the results of a policy change until problems in it arise at some future date. Although some attention has been given to determining the impacts of school finance reforms that have been implemented, much more is needed. At this time, the National Conference of State Legislatures' *Legislator's Handbook* is still the most extensive compendium on the fiscal impacts of school finance reforms.[23]

The September 1977 Interim Report prepared for the Assistant Secretary for Policy and Evaluation at HEW entitled "School Finance in the Seventies: Achievements and Failures," concludes that few school finance reforms have been effective in reducing expenditure per pupil gaps among districts within a state.[24] For those expecting such spending gaps to have decreased, these findings are a disappointment. As mentioned earlier, however, fiscal neutrality programs were never intended to close spending differences, although many policy makers believed that such would be the case. Since the data sample on which this study is based gives biased results for individual states, however, the conclusions of the study must be treated with caution until the study is replicated with an unbiased data set.[25]

A second issue related to the results of school finance reforms concerns the programmatic changes that occur as a result of reform. In other words, how have new dollars been used at the local level? The initial studies on this topic found that about 80 cents of each new state dollar was used to provide additional services for students, while the other 20 cents was used to raise teachers' salaries.[26]

Third, there is also concern that increasing the state role in public education finance will swing control of the education process to the state level as well. Although past research has shown that there is no systematic relationship between state control and the level of state aid, state and federal rules, regulations and guidelines have produced a general shift in the past decade towards more centralization in the running of schools.[27] In an attempt to counter this shift, Florida and California enacted provisions in their school finance reforms that encouraged school districts to decentralize many planning, budgeting and programmatic decisions to the school-site level.

A last issue that can be discussed under this section concerns the impact of reforms on the residential locational decisions of households. Households decide to live in localities for a number of reasons including the local tax burden, the general cost of living in the area and the set of local government services provided, including education services. Substantial changes in these variables that could result from a school finance reform might produce changes in the residential location decisions households make and cause migrations, over time, of persons from one district to another. Such changes could exacerbate or diminish the socioeconomic fragmentation that already exists in many regions of many states, especially metropolitan areas. This issue is just beginning to receive attention in school finance circles.[28]

Collective Bargaining and Teacher Retirement Systems

The primary economic issue for collective bargaining centers on whether it increases the salaries of teachers and other education personnel and, if so, to what degree? Most of the economic research has shown that collective bargaining has small effects on school budgets, causing less than a five-percent increase, other things held constant.[29] Chambers, however, using individual teachers as the unit of analysis rather than district averages, has shown the impact to be substantially larger, on the order of 15 percent. Chambers' work also shows that the economic impact of collective bargaining is regional in nature; i.e., a district that does not engage in collective bargaining, but is located in a region that in general does bargain, is affected by the higher salary demands to a degree similar to that of the bargaining districts.[30]

147

The Rand Corporation's Policy Center for Education Finance and Governance is engaged in a study of the ways in which collective bargaining by teachers influences the environment of the classroom and the organization of the school. This research emphasizes bargaining outcomes other than wages and fringes, such as hours, working conditions, job security, and teacher power over curriculum.[31]

An additional teacher-related fiscal issue that should be, but seldom has been, part of school finance is the funding of teacher retirement systems. Not only has there been very little written on this topic, but the data to conduct empirical policy analysis on the issues are hard to come by.[32]

There are numerous issues that need to be considered in assessing the financial health of teacher retirement funds. The first concerns the governmental level at which the funds are operated and funded. Most teacher retirement systems are funded and operated locally; other public employee pension systems are operated at the state level. On the whole, state-operated funds seem to fare better. Record keeping is more extensive, funding is sounder, and investing strategies have produced greater returns.

A second issue concerns the integration of teacher retirement systems (or any state and local public pension fund) with the Federal Social Security System. In the 37 states with integrated systems, retirement levels equal, on average, 70 percent of spendable income before retirement. In the remaining 13 states, the combination of teacher retirement system pensions with social security often produces a retirement salary greater than preretirement income. This clearly makes no sense. Congress may require state and local government participation in Social Security, which will force the integration question on states not now participating.

The third issue concerning teacher retirement systems relates to how the adequacy of their funding can be assessed. Since there are no commonly accepted standards in actuarial science, it is necessary for a policy maker to look in detail at the assumptions used in determining the funding of pension systems. The two critical assumptions are those pertaining to future salary growth and to expected earnings on investments. The former requires 20-to-30-year salary projections which must be done on the basis of a series of assumptions about inflation and the size of the employment force. For the latter, the common error is an overly optimistic assumption about annual earnings. What is needed is a series of simulations of funding needs for a pension system based on alternative assumptions. This would provide the policy maker with a set of alternatives on which a more reasonable decision could be based in terms of providing an adequate funding level.

As states continue to examine fiscal issues related to education, however, it is undoubtedly time to include the financial, including the actuarial, aspects of teacher retirement systems on their agenda. States need neither pension fund bombshells nor broken promises to the retired. Attention to the structures and cost of retirement programs could save a state from facing either of these two undesirable alternatives.

Tax and Expenditure Limitations

There is a growing interest in controlling government expenditures at all levels—local, state and federal. For example, in the November 1976 elections, there were ballots in numerous states related to controlling either the expenditure growth of state governments or the total tax burden as a percentage of statewide personal incomes. Although most of these referenda were defeated, many state legislatures have enacted limitations on expenditure and tax growth. The overwhelming approval in June 1978 of the Jarvis-Gann (Proposition 13) initiative in California, which limits property taxes to one percent of market value, is a strong indication that the public is serious about halting increasing taxes and government expenditures.

In a sense, school finance has taken the lead in this new development of expenditure controls and taxation limits. One of the primary characteristics of the school finance reform enacted in the 1970s has been the simultaneous use of expenditure controls, tax limits, state aid caps, and other mechanisms to control expenditure increases and stabilize the local property tax.[33]

Apart from expenditure and tax limitations are other tax issues related to school finance structures. Although the debate on the incidence of the property tax continues, the most recent evidence indicates that the property tax imposes a greater percentage burden on low-income households than on high-income households.[34]

State policy makers, who continue to view the property tax as regressive in nature, respond by enacting and expanding state-financed circuit breaker programs of property tax relief that protect low-income households, especially those in wealthy school districts, from property tax overburdens. The policy question that links school finance to expanded circuit breaker programs, however, is how such programs interact with the school finance system. Furthermore, the equity and incidence pattern of all state taxes is of concern for school finance policy makers concerned with the taxation side as well as the distribution side of school finance structures.[35]

Low-Income and Minority Students and Urban School Finance

Simple school finance reform laws providing equalization based only on assessed valuation of property per pupil can offset gains made in providing needed education services to low-income and/or minority students, as well as exacerbate the fiscal plight of many central-city school districts. Although the impact of school finance structures on low-income and minority students could be separated from the impact on urban districts, the two issues are inexorably intertwined. A recent NCSL study has shown that, particularly for cities in the Northeast and Midwest, the population shifts that have occurred in the past decade have left city school districts with a student body that is increasingly composed of minority students from lower-income families, especially Spanish-speaking families.[36] At the same time, the property tax bases have been stagnant or declining. The result has been to increase the fiscal squeeze on city districts because, although total numbers of students have dropped, the remaining population is characterized by concentrations of students needing higher-cost education services such as bilingual education, compensatory education, or education for the handicapped.

Not all minority and low-income students are found in city school districts, however. The residence of low-income and minority students and the impacts of school finance structures on them vary significantly across states, as found in a study of these issues funded by the National Institute of Education which is to be published late in 1978. In Colorado, for example, the majority of black students were found to live in the urban districts, primarily in Denver, which is high in property wealth, while students from Spanish-speaking backgrounds were divided in essentially a bimodal distribution between the wealthier urban districts and very poor rural areas. Low-income students, moreover, had different locational characteristics.

Similarly, in California it was found that black students received the largest average education expenditures, due primarily to the urban factors in the California compensatory education program and the concentration of black students in the urban centers. Low-income concentration in California was found to be completely unrelated to low-wealth concentration. The NIE study also includes the states of Texas, New Mexico and New Jersey. The results indicate quite clearly that simple equalization formulas based on property wealth deal with only one issue—namely low wealth—and state policy makers must be aware that additional factors must be added to the basic formula to insure that low-income and minority children are not unexpectedly disadvantaged by a new equalization program.[37]

While the NIE study also shows that minority and low-income children are most highly concentrated in city school districts, city districts also face other education pressures that push up the level at which they must fund their public schools. Much has been written in the past on the municipal overburden issue, that is, the drain on the education budget created by the many noneducational services that cities are required to provide. Vincent, in a paper on urban economics given to the most recent

149

Conference of the Committee on Taxation, Resources and Economic Development, delineates these education overburden elements:[38]

    a. Declining or stagnant fiscal capacity to fund services;
    b. High concentration of low-income students;
    c. Declining enrollments causing high personnel costs and excess physical capacity;
    d. Higher concentration of special-need students;
    e. Diseconomies of scale; and
    f. High relative costs of attracting education personnel to the school system.

The overburden issues again reveal the complexities of designing fair funding structures for public schools. The push to eliminate wealth-related expenditure disparities in a state's public school finance structure can be taken as an opportunity, as it was in California during the 1977 legislative session, to develop a comprehensive state public education policy for the financing and governance of categorical and general aid programs. Cities, low-income and minority students, special student populations requiring higher-cost education services, students in low-wealth school districts, and nondisadvantaged students must all be helped by a school finance reform.

Another population group that has not received much attention in school finance circles are Indian students, both those attending public schools and those attending schools run by the Bureau of Indian Affairs or tribally controlled contract schools. The BIA has come under severe criticism recently for major problems in delivering adequate and reliable funding for Indian services, especially education.[39] In a soon-to-be-published report of the inequalities in financing BIA schools over the past four years, substantial unjustified inequality of resource distribution is found among the many schools run and/or financed by the BIA.[40] Severe problems have also been noted in the financing of education services for Indian students attending public schools.[41]

The Federal Role in School Finance

In the very short run, the general nature of the federal role in school finance will not change. It will continue to be one supporting (1) special student populations, including the handicapped, the economically disadvantaged, the bilingual and the vocational student, as well as (2) basic and applied research on many of the unsolved issues related to education finance.

Although many would like to see the federal government appropriate the funds for the current federal education programs to the full authorized level, in a sense the major problem with the federal role in the past has been the rules and regulations governing the use of federal dollars, especially in education areas in which states had developed programs to complement or augment the federal objectives.[42]

There may also be increased interest by the Congress in a specific federal role to assist the states in school finance equalization. For the past two years, this interest has been manifested through the dissemination of funds to assist states in the research and development of better equalization systems. In September 1977, congressional hearings were held to help states in equalizing educational opportunities.[43] The thrust of most of the testimony was that it was probably the right time to begin raising the issue of how the federal government could implement an equalization role. However, before a specific law or program is enacted, some hard policy analysis needs to be done to map out the status of equalization among and within the states as the basis for any federal program.

State Analytic Tools and Research Capabilities in School Finance

Numerous states and many organizations have developed the capacity to simulate and test a variety of different school finance structures. A description and "midterm" evaluation of a number of computer simulations is available in a recent Education Commission of the States publication entitled *Computer Simulations in School Finance-Reform.*[44]

After assessing some of the technical aspects and uses of simulations, the booklet comes to two conclusions. First, it is difficult to tell at this point how simulations have affected either specific school finance policies or the policy-making process itself. Second, the utility of simulations depends largely on the research knowledge on which the simulation is developed. For example, while it is simple to design a simulation with the capability of using a cost of education index, such an option is useless unless the hard research of developing district cost indices is undertaken by a state.

In this light, it is worthwhile noting a recent article by Sally Pancrazio of the Illinois Office of Education on state education agencies as research arenas.[45] The author argues convincingly that a better nexus must be developed between the university-based educational research community and the research sections of state departments of education, acknowledging that one difference in perspective is the basic research orientation of the former and the applied orientation of the latter. In terms of assessible data bases and the opportunity both to respond to and help influence the education policy concerns raised by state policy makers, state departments of education are ideally situated. However, the legislative and executive parts of state governments often have questioned the ability of state departments of education to respond to the research possibilities with which they are presented. As a way to resolve this debate, one can hope that a rigorous evaluation will be undertaken on the use of the almost $13 million in federal Section 842 funds that have been allocated, primarily to state departments of education. That amount of money is one of the largest sums ever appropriated for applied education finance research. By the end of 1978, after the state plans have been presented, the results of the use of those funds should be known.

Notes

1. As the states enacting reforms have begun to examine the results of their new programs, one of the most perplexing phenomena has been the use of inappropriate criteria to evaluate a particular program. The most common example is the disappointment of many policy makers over the ineffectiveness of power equalization or guaranteed yield programs in reducing large gaps in expenditures per pupil between high- and low-spending districts. The fact is that such programs are not intended to reduce spending gaps.

2. Alan G. Hickrod, Ben C. Hubbard et al., *The 1973 Reform of the Illinois Grant-in-Aid System: An Evaluation After Three Years* (Normal: Center for the Study of Educational Finance, Illinois State University, 1976); Allan Odden, *School Finance Reform in Michigan and Missouri: Impact on Suburban School Districts*, Papers in Education Finance, Paper No. 11 (Denver, Colorado: Education Commission of the States, September 1977); and Renee Montoya, *Impact of School Finance Reform in Colorado,* Papers in Education Finance, Paper No. 8 (Denver, Colorado: Education Commission of the States, forthcoming).

3. The best example is the New Mexico foundation program that guarantees a foundation expenditure per pupil and prohibits any local enrichment. New Mexico is the only state in the country, except for Hawaii with its full state assumption program, that qualifies under the expenditure disparity clause for counting Federal Impact Aid as local revenue. To so qualify, New Mexico has reduced the expenditure per pupil differences between the school districts at the 5th and 95th percentile to less than 15 percent.

4. Lee S. Friedman and Michael Wiseman, *Toward Understanding the Equity Consequence of School Finance Reform* (Berkeley: Graduate School of Public Policy, University of California at Berkeley, 1977).

5. Robert Berne, "Equity and Public Education: Conceptual Issues of Measurement," Working Paper No. 4 (New York: New York University, Graduate School of Public Administration, October 1977).

6. Thomas Yang and Ramesh Chaudari, *A Study of the Relationship Between Selected Socio-economic Variables and Local Tax Effort to Support Schools in Illinois* (Normal: Center for Student Education Finance, Illinois State University, 1976). See also Alan G. Hickrod, "Local Demand for Education: A Critique of School Finance Research Circa 1959–69," *Review of Education Research* (Winter 1971).

7. W. Norton Grubb and Stephen Michelson, *States and Schools* (Lexington, Massachusetts: D.C. Heath and Co., 1974); Martin Feldstein, "Wealth Neutrality and Local Choice in Public Education," *American Economic Review* 65 (March 1975); and Helen Ladd, "Local Education Expenditures, Fiscal Capacity and the Composition of the Property Tax Base," *National Tax Journal* 27 (June 1975).

8. Grubb and Michelson, *States and Schools;* Feldstein, "Wealth Neutrality;" Ladd, "Local Education;" Stephan Barro, "Theoretical Models of School District Expenditure Determination and the Impact of Grants-in-Aid," a report prepared under Ford Foundation Grant R-867-77 (February 1972); and Robert Inman, "Optional Fiscal Reform of Metropolitan Schools: Some Simulation Results with a General Equilibrium Model," mimeographed (Cambridge, Massachusetts: Harvard University, 1977).

9. Stephan Carroll, *The Consequences of School Finance Reform* (Santa Monica, California: The Rand Corporation, forthcoming); and Phillip E. Vincent and Kathleen Adams, *The Fiscal Responses of School Districts: A Study of Two States—Colorado and Minnesota* (Denver, Colorado: Education Commission of the States, forthcoming).

10. Jens Jensen, *Property Taxation in the United States* (Chicago: University of Chicago Press, 1931); and F. Woodward and R. Brady, "Inductive Evidence of Tax Capitalization," *National Tax Journal* 18 (June 1965).

11. Darwin Daicoff, "Capitalization of the Property Tax," (Ph.D. Dissertation, University of Michigan, 1961).

12. John Wicks, Robert Little and Ralph Beck, "A Note on Capitalization of Property Tax Changes," *National Tax Journal* 21 (September 1968); and R. Stafford Smith, "Property Tax Capitalization in San Francisco," *National Tax Journal* 23 (June 1970).

13. Wallace Oates, "The Effects of Property Taxes and Local Public Spending on Property Values: An Empirical Study of Tax Capitalization and the Tiebout Hypothesis," *Journal of Political Economy* 77 (November/December 1969); Robert L. Bish, "School Finance Reform and Fiscal Equalization: Reconciling Legal and Economic Approaches," mimeographed (Los Angeles: University of Southern California, December 1975); and Paul Newacheck, "Capitalization: The Price of Educational Finance Reform in California," mimeographed (Berkeley: Graduate School of Public Policy, University of California at Berkeley, June 1976).

14. William Wilken and David Porter, *State Aid for Special Education: Who Benefits?* (Washington, D. C.: National Conference of State Legislatures, October 1976); Lawrence Vescera, *An Examination of the Flow of Title I and State Compensatory Education Aid and Their Effects on Equalization in Four States: Florida, New Jersey, New York and Texas*, Papers in Education Finance, Paper No. 10 (Denver, Colorado: Education Commission of the States, February 1978); Renee Montoya, *Impact of School Finance Reform in Colorado*, Papers in Education Finance, Paper No. 8 (Denver, Colorado: Education Commission of the States, forthcoming); John Callahan and William Wilken, *National Conference of State Legislatures Report on School Finance Revision in Washington State: Special Education Finance* (Washington, D.C.: National Conference of State Legislatures, October 1975); and John Callahan and William Wilken, *Special Education in Maryland* (Washington, D.C.: National Conference of State Legislatures, June 1976).

15. Harvey Brazer and Ann Anderson, "A Cost Adjustment Index for Michigan State School Districts," *Selected Papers in School Finance 1975* (Washington, D. C.: U. S. Office of Education, 1976); Donald Frey, *The Determinants of Teachers' Salaries in New Jersey* (Washington, D. C.: National Urban Coalition, May 1976); Lawrence Kenny, David Denslow and Irving Goffman, "Measuring Differences Among the Florida School Districts in the Cost of Education: An Alternative Approach," *Selected Papers in Education Finance 1975* (Washington, D. C.: U. S. Office of Education, 1976); and W. Norton Grubb and James Hyman, "Constructing Teacher

Cost Indices: Methodological Exploration with California Unified School Districts," *Selected Papers in School Finance 1975* (Washington, D. C.: U. S. Office of Education, 1976).

16. Jay G. Chambers, Allan Odden and Phillip E. Vincent, *Cost of Education Indices Among School Districts: An Application to the State of Missouri* (Denver, Colorado: Education Commission of the States, 1976); and Jay G. Chambers, *An Analysis of Education Cost Across Local Districts in the State of Missouri 1975–76*, Papers in Education Finance, Paper No. 7 (Denver, Colorado: Education Commission of the States, 1978). These authors are currently involved in similar projects in California and Texas that will include the development of teacher and administration cost indices, an index of transportation costs (which was also done in the second Missouri study), and an energy or plant operations cost index. In addition, the authors plan to use the indices developed in an analysis of school district response to the California aid formula and the changes in it that have been enacted over the past five years.

17. *Hobson v. Hansen*, 327 Federal Supplement (1971). Other research on intradistrict resource allocation has been scant. Attempts were made to conduct such analysis for the New York City school district but the results have not been widely disseminated. Also, Lawrence Vescera, "Inside Inequality: A Study of Intra-School District Resource Allocation," *Journal of Education Finance*, forthcoming. Reported on an extensive analysis of the inequality of expenditures per pupil among schools within the Los Angeles unified school district. Although found significant differences in expenditures per pupil among schools, the differences were not systematically related to achievement levels, economic differences or racial differences.

18. James A. Kelly, "The Public Policy Context of Education Finance," *Administrator's Notebook* 26 (1977–1978).

19. Joel Berke, Donna Shalala and Mary F. Williams, "Two Roads to School Finance Reform," *Society* 13 (January/February 1976).

20. The Education Commission of the States plans to publish a booklet on the politics of school finance reform in seven states sometime in 1978.

21. Susan Abramowitz and Stuart Rosenfeld, eds., *Declining Enrollments: The Challenge of the Coming Decade* (Washington, D. C.: National Institute of Education, 1978).

22. The issue is being given some attention in Minnesota by a study being conducted by William Wilken of the National Conference of State Legislatures and in California by Jay Chambers under a Ford Foundation grant. The Chambers study is designed explicitly to uncover (1) the direct financial binds that changes in the demography of the education work force place on both local school districts and the state, (2) the implications of the changes for the equity of the distribution of education resources, (3) the potential long-term impacts on the funding of teacher retirement systems, and (4) the effect on the changing demand for various kinds of teachers.

23. John Callahan and William Wilken, *School Financial Reform: A Legislature's Handbook* (Washington, D. C.: National Conference of State Legislatures, 1976). See also, Darwin Daicoff, "An Analysis of the Kansas School District Equalization Act of 1973," *Selected Papers in School Finance 1976* (Washington, D. C.: U. S. Office of Education, 1977); Carroll, *The Consequences;* and Harvey Brazer and Ann Anderson, "Michigan's School District Equalization Act of 1973," *Selected Papers in School Finance 1976* (Washington, D. C.: U. S. Office of Education, 1977).

24. Lawrence Brown, Alan Ginsburg, Neil Killalea and Esther Tron, "School Finance in the Seventies: Achievements and Failures" (Washington, D. C: Office of the Assistant Secretary for Planning and Evaluation, U.S. Department of Health, Education and Welfare, September 1977).

25. The Interim Report Analysis was based on the stratefied sample school district data from the Elementary and Secondary General Information Survey (ELSEGIS) for 1975–76 conducted by the National Center for Education Statistics, which gives biased results for individual states.

26. Michael Kirst, "What Happens at the Local Level After State School Finance Reform," *State and Local Government*, ed. Alan K. Campbell and Roy W. Bahl (New York: The Free Press, 1976); and Stephen Barro and Stephan Carroll, *Budget Allocation by School Districts: An Analysis of Spending for Teachers and Other Resources* (Santa Monica, California: The Rand Corporation, 1975).

27. Betsy Levin et al., *Public School Finance: Present Disparities and Fiscal Alternatives* (Washington, D. C.: The Urban Institute, July 1972); Susan Furhman, *Local Control: Fear or*

Fantasy (Newark: The New Jersey Education Finance Reform Project, April 1974); and National Urban Coalition, *School Site Lump Sum Budgeting* (Washington, D. C.: National Urban Coalition, forthcoming).

28.   The Childrens Time Study Project being conducted by Charles Benson at the University of California at Berkeley is investigating some aspects of this issue in the Oakland metropolitan area: a book based on the study's results entitled *The Serious Business of Growing Up in America* will be available by the end of 1978. The study is unique in many ways because a sample of over 700 *individual* children is being followed. The study is looking at how home conditions, such as parental aspirations, expectations, and locational decisions, family structure in terms of one or two parents, student experiences and activities, and quality of education services interact to affect student education achievement. The study hopes to be able to sort out the relative effects of school versus nonschool variables on student achievement, thereby providing insight into how government dollars can be split between school finance reform and other noneducation functions to maximize the impact on pupil learning.

29.   Robert N. Baird and John H. Landon, ''The Effects of Collective Bargaining on the Public School Teachers Salaries,'' *Industrial Labor Relations Review* 25 (April 1972); David B. Lipsky and John E. Drotning, ''The Influence of Collective Bargaining on Teachers' Salaries in New York State,'' *Industrial Labor Relations Review* 27 (October 1973); and Robert J. Thornton, ''The Effects of Collective Negotiations on Teachers' Salaries,'' *Quarterly Review of Economic Business* 11 (Winter 1971).

30.   Jay G. Chambers, ''The Impact of Bargaining on the Earnings of Teachers: A Report on California and Missouri,'' Paper presented at the United Kingdom-United States Conference on Teacher Markets, University of Chicago, December 1976.

31.   Anthony Pascal and Lorraine McDonnell, *Unions in the Classroom: The Effect of Teacher Collective Bargaining on School Environment and Organization* (Santa Monica, California: The Rand Corporation, forthcoming).

32.   Bernard Jump, Jr., ''Teacher Retirement Systems,'' *Journal of Education Finance* 3 (Fall 1977); and Robert Tilove, *Public Employee Pension Funds: A Twentieth Century Fund Report* (New York: Columbia University Press, 1976).

33.   Dale Cattanback et al., ''Tax and Expenditure Controls: The Price of School Finance Reform,'' *School Finance Reform: A Legislator's Handbook*, ed. John Callahan and William Wilken (Washington, D. C.: National Conference of State Legislatures, 1976); Esther Tron, ''Fiscal Controls and Tax Requirements Imposed by States and Tax Options Available to School Districts,'' *Selected Papers in School Finance 1976* (Washington, D. C.: U. S. Office of Education, 1977); and John Callahan and William Wilken, ''State Limitations on Local School Taxes and Spending: A Paper Tiger?'' (Washington, D. C.: National Conference of State Legislatures, August 1977).

34.   Allan Odden and Phillip Vincent, *The Regressivity of the Property Tax: The Incidence of the Property Tax Under Alternative Assumptions of Incidence in Four States—Connecticut, Minnesota, Missouri and South Dakota* (Denver, Colorado: Education Commission of the States, 1976); and Charles E. McLure, ''The 'New View' of the Property Tax,'' *National Tax Journal* 30 (March 1977).

35.   Donald Phares, *State-Local Tax Equity* (Lexington, Massachusetts: D. C. Heath and Company, 1973). Phares is in the process of updating his study of the tax system in each of the 50 states. His revised book should provide a wealth of new information for state tax specialists by not only updating and summarizing the most current theoretical knowledge on tax incidence but also by mapping the incidence pattern of the tax systems in the 50 states for the 1976 fiscal year.

36.   John Callahan et al., ''Big City Schools: 1970–1975—A Profile of Changing Fiscal Pressures,'' mimeographed (Washington, D. C.: National Conference of State Legislatures, September 1977).

37.   The study is being conducted by the Intercultural Development Research Association in San Antonio, Texas. Robert Brischetto of Trinity University is the principal investigator.

38.   Phillip E. Vincent, ''School Finance Reforms and Big City Fiscal Problems,'' Paper prepared for the United States Committee on Taxation, Resources and Economic Development Conference, Cambridge, Massachusetts, October 1977. See also the *Levittown v. Nyquist* school finance court case in New York.

39. U.S. General Accounting Office, *Concerted Effort Needed to Improve Indian Education* (Washington, D. C: U.S. General Accounting Office, 1977); and American Indian Policy Review Commission, *Final Report* (Washington, D. C: Government Printing Office, 1977).

40. Allan Odden, *Funding Schools Financed by the Bureau of Indian Affairs* (Denver, Colorado: Education Commission of the States and the National Conference of State Legislatures, 1978).

41. National Indian Education Association, *Study of Title II of P.L. 93-638* (Minneapolis, Minnesota: National Indian Education Association, 1975); and Indian Education Training, Inc., *Report to the National Indian Education Association* (Albuquerque, New Mexico: Indian Education Training, Inc., 1975).

42. The clearest example of frictions that developed concerns the antisupplant regulation for Title I of ESEA which, as it was interpreted both by the U.S. Office of Education and the courts, prohibited states from enacting compensatory education programs designed to serve Title I eligible students who were unserved with federal dollars because of underfunding of Title I by the Congress.

43. U. S. Congress, House, Committee on Education and Labor, *Part 13 School Finance Act of 1977 and Equalization Efforts, Hearings Before a Subcommittee on Elementary, Secondary and Vocational Education on H. R. 1138*, 95th Cong., 1st sess., 1977.

44. The simulations discussed in this booklet include the one developed by the National Education Finance Project, the School Finance Equalization Management System model developed by the Education Policy Research Institute of the Educational Testing Service, the simulations designed by the ECS Education Finance Center, the simulations developed by Professor Walter Garms for the states of Oregon and Florida, and a number of simulations developed by individual states, including Florida and California.

45. Sally Bulkley Pancrazio, "State Education Agencies as Research Arenas," *Educational Researcher* 7 (January 1978), pp. 5-10.

References Not Cited

Bernstein, Charles, William Hartman, and Rudolph Marshall. "Major Policy Issues in Financing Special Education." *Journal of Education Finance* 1 (Winter 1976), pp. 299-317.

Callahan, John et al., "Maine's School Finance System: Is it Equitable?" Mimeographed. Washington, D.C.: National Conference of State Legislatures, 1977.

Lawyers Committee for Civil Rights Under Law. *Summary of State-Wide School Finance Cases Since 1973*. Washington, D.C.: Lawyers Committee for Civil Rights Under Law, 1978.

Levin, Betsy. *State School Finance Reform: Court Mandate or Legislative Action*. Washington, D.C.: National Conference of State Legislatures, 1977.

Odden, Allan. *School Finance Computer Simulations*. Denver, Colorado: Education Commission of the States, 1978.

Ross, Doris. *'76 Update: Collective Bargaining in Education*. Denver, Colorado: Education Commission of the States, 1976.

Sherman, Joel. *Underfunding of Majority-Black School Districts in South Carolina*. Washington, D.C.: Lawyers Committee for Civil Rights Under Law, 1977.

Troob, Charles. *Title I Funds Allocation: The Current Formula*. Washington, D.C.: National Institute of Education, 1977.

Vescera, Lawrence. *State and Federal Aid for Special Education*. Denver, Colorado: Education Commission of the States, forthcoming.

Urban Fiscal Studies

Philip M. Dearborn

Recent years have been fertile ones for those involved in urban fiscal analysis. First came the general revenue sharing program embodying the new concept of federal aid allocated by a formula, with the resulting entitlements free to be used virtually without restriction by local governments. Hard on the heels of revenue sharing came community development and manpower block grants, each based on formula allocations and with substantial flexibility in the use of funds vested in local governments. And of course, in the midst of the dramatic change in federal aid programs to local governments, the New York debacle created doubts about the ability of city governments to successfully manage their financial affairs. Finally, the recent economic stimulus package has directed substantial additional federal aid to local governments, and has created questions about their dependency relationship to the federal government.

The result of this series of events in the 1970s has been to focus attention on improved understanding of how cities manage their fiscal affairs, with special emphasis on the problems of analyzing current financial conditions and isolating the factors that predict future problems.

As researchers look more closely at urban finances, the dynamic process of local governmental affairs becomes apparent. Within any city, the financial situation may change abruptly as the result of changes in national and local economic trends, in population and social characteristics, and in the local political climate. Predicting the rate of inflation, forecasting local per capita income or unemployment, and speculating about elected officials' willingness to restrain expenditures or increase taxes are difficult tasks. When a study expands beyond examining one city to a comparison of a larger number of units, the challenge becomes even more difficult.

However, because of the demands for better understanding from several important areas, including the municipal bond community and the federal government, there has been a wealth of private and government studies of urban fiscal problems. Much of the attention has been directed to ascertaining the severity of current or potential financial problems in individual cities, and to comparing and ranking the financial health of all major cities. The results of these studies have been mixed.

While analysis and understanding of financial conditions in cities has improved, there is still no dependable monitoring system that can give assurance about the

Philip M. Dearborn is Vice President of the Center for Municipal and Metropolitan Research in Washington, D.C. The author wishes to thank Deborah Rodock Maiese for her assistance in the preparation of this essay.

156

health of all cities on a current basis. Nor have we isolated the underlying factors in a city, or combination of factors, that can predict several years in advance the onset of a financial crisis. Even attempts to rank the health of cities have encountered problems. A recent Treasury report lists the results of six separate rankings of fiscal strain by various researchers, including the Treasury's own ranking, which is an average of the other five. New York's hardship ranking on these studies ranged from first to seventeenth; Los Angeles was rated third, ninth, twelveth, sixteenth, and twenty-seventh; New Orleans was ranked third, fifth, eighteenth, and twenty-eighth. Clearly, the rankings are not in agreement on the question of urban strain.[1]

This paper will point out where contributions have been made to the understanding of the urban fiscal process and will consider the major difficulties that are being encountered by researchers in the areas of defining financial health, finding data, and establishing causal relationships. It will also suggest areas in which additional research may be needed.

Defining the Problem

Despite the substantial amount of thought, discussion and publication on the condition of the nation's cities, urban fiscal crisis continues to be a difficult concept to define. Opinions range on what factors should be isolated to measure the stress local governments are experiencing. Consequently, the research on cities is full of diverse definitions and characterizations of urban financial crisis.

While there is virtual unanimity that New York City has experienced a fiscal crisis, opinions differ as to whether there must be default or near default to constitute a crisis, or whether conditions such as a persistent economic decline are sufficient to constitute an urban fiscal crisis. One researcher, Dave Stanley, has suggested that there are actually two definitions of fiscal crisis, one in which the city has neither cash nor credit to meet its obligations, and the other in which there is long-term decline with deteriorating economic and social conditions.[2] Even the bond rating agencies have had trouble with definition. While they are obviously concerned with risk of default, they also hedge the definition with such language as "risk of future developments adverse to the interest of the creditors."[3]

Those who key the definition to default, either actual or threatened, have a relatively simple and observable event as an indicator. But such a narrow definition causes two problems. First, there have been almost no post-World War II default cases to use as examples, although the several threatened cases in New York State have recently added to the inventory. This makes it difficult to do statistical analysis of the factors that were present in default situations to distinguish them from non-default cases. The second problem with the narrow definition is that it seems to ignore several important policy issues, such as whether the government is meeting minimum service needs, the extent to which tax burdens are economically counterproductive, the size of the debt burden, or a large unfunded pension liability. It can be argued that the existence of these latter conditions may constitute a fiscal crisis that is as damaging to the citizens and the city's future as default.

In instances where researchers have tried to broaden the definition from default threat to broader substantive issues, troubling policy questions have been encountered. The more extensive definitions generally explain the urban crisis as a long-term development, and not a specific event. Frequently, nongovernmental social and economic symptoms, such as a deteriorating economic base or an increasingly dependent population, are used as definitions. Under these conditions, the definition is of little help in clearly segregating cities with a crisis from those that merely aren't doing too well at the present time.

In addition, different regions and cities have different tastes for urban services and different opinions on reasonable tax burdens. The assignment of responsibilities to local governments, and the ability to tax, varies between states and areas. As a result, meaningful national standards for either minimum city services or maximum city tax burdens have been impossible to achieve. Without such standards, definitions of fiscal distress based on service levels or tax burdens have been difficult to use for research purposes.

The present situation with respect to the definition of urban crisis is that most research either is anchored to the implicit threat of default, or is done in a way that avoids the need for an absolute definition. For example, many of the studies that result in rankings are concerned with relative financial health among cities, without making any positive statement about which cities in the ranking are actually in an urban fiscal crisis or about to be in one. This accounts in part, of course, for why the individual study rankings can be so disparate, without any of them being wrong per se.

Data Availability

Good research on urban fiscal problems requires timely and accurate information that relates to urban fiscal conditions. Census information is readily available for all large cities and has been heavily used by researchers. However, for the determination of fiscal crisis conditions in cities and the prediction of future problems, the use of census data has presented severe problems. The primary difficulty stems from the fact that census information about cities has been forced into a uniform system of accounting and reporting, so that national aggregated trends of government revenues, expenditures and debt can be prepared on a consistent basis. By forcing all financial information into a single format, key data and relationships are lost. For example, the sources and uses of revenues cannot be related to each other, general fund condition cannot be determined, general-obligation debt cannot be ascertained separate from revenue-supported debt, the different types of short-term debt cannot be distinguished, quasi-independent agencies are sometimes combined with the prime government, and property tax collections in relation to levies are not reported. In fact, the Census Bureau itself observed in an unpublished report that, using census data, "development of a measure of the ability of a city to deal with its problems is not possible through a purely statistical approach."[4]

The primary alternatives to using census data are financial information collected by individual states or information collected from originial sources, such as city financial reports. A recent study, *Watching and Counting*, reports that 46 states collect financial data about municipalities, and 36 of them regularly publish the information.[5] Unfortunately, the information published is not the same from state to state, and in many instances provides a basis only for comparisons of revenue, expenditure, or debt trends, and not for fiscal condition analysis. In some instances—for example, in New York State—the state-collected data have provided a basis for research on urban fiscal problems within that state. But the ability to generalize such research to other states that have dissimilar data remains questionable.

Obtaining data directly from individual city financial reports requires a substantial and sustained effort. Because of the difficulty involved in extracting this data on a comprehensive basis, this approach is usually only used by bond rating agencies and some major underwriters or investors. But even these efforts are severely hampered by the lack of uniformity in financial reporting by cities. In many instances, the cities that may be most critical to the researcher looking for fiscal crisis symptoms are the ones with confusing and undisciplined reporting. In such situations, the researcher may be forced to do case studies of individual cities merely to get meaningful data. Intercity comparisons become time consuming and virtually impossible to carry out.[6]

Bond prospectuses offer another source of original data on the financial practices of local jurisdictions. The Municipal Finance Officers Association's *Disclosure Guidelines* set forth some 137 items of information that should be included in an offering statement.[7] As a part of a National Science Foundation project on municipal credit information and quality, John Petersen and others tested the extent to which municipal bond offerings in 1975 and 1976 embodied the MFOA's *Disclosure Guidelines*.[8] They found that bond prospectuses of state and local governments on

158

the average in 1975 disclosed only 40.1 percent of the items suggested on the *Guidelines*. Six months later, the offerings included 54.5 percent of the disclosure data. Financial information was generally found to be lacking, with only a 34.2 percent compliance rate in 1976. The conclusion drawn from this study is that the informational content of disclosure statements has expanded significantly. However, the use of official statements as a source of comparative financial information is still not practical for most research.

To help remedy the problem of data availability, the Urban Institute, under contract with the Department of Housing and Urban Development, is developing a financial analysis model that identifies all the relevant financial information about a government. This instrument is designed to serve as a guide for improving data collection and dissemination. The report considers the need for financial, economic and demographic information in terms that would be helpful for the multiple users of local government data.[9] However, identifying the types of information needed will be only the first step in assuring its availability: A central point of regular and timely data collection on a national basis remains to be devised.

Timeliness of Data

Regardless of the source, most financial information about city governments is not available until well after the close of the city's fiscal year. Since most cities do not issue good interim reports on a regular basis, it is extremely difficult to determine current financial conditions in individual cities or in cities on a comparative basis.

Three of the 30 largest cities took more than nine months to issue their year-end reports and nine more took more than six months. Even in the best of situations, financial reports are seldom available within three months after the close of the year. As with the quality of the report, the slower-reporting cities are often the ones of most interest to researchers concerned with potential fiscal crisis. Ironically, New York City is one of the few cities now providing financial information promptly after the close of its fiscal year and also on an interim basis.

Improved timeliness in the financial information provided by most local governments is not likely to occur without it being required by the states or federal government, and without imposing substantial additional costs on local governments. Therefore, it may be necessary to develop more timely information from other sources. These might include information supplied to the federal government on revenue sharing, which is available reasonably promptly because failure to do so may cause a withholding of future payments; or employee income tax withholding reports filed with the Treasury. While such information may not be directly relevant to studies of urban fiscal problems, it could provide at least some insights into city financial activities on a more current basis than we now have.

Mismatched Fiscal Years

One of the data problems that continues to present niggling difficulties is the variety of fiscal years on which governments report financial information. For example, of the 30 largest cities, 13 report on a calendar year basis, 12 report on a July 1 to June 30 year, and five report on other years. To add to the confusion, the federal fiscal year is October 1 to September 30, federal grants often are on a grant year starting whenever the grant is received, and census reports on government finances are prepared for all fiscal years ending within a calendar year. The inevitable result is that comparative studies seldom compare financial results from comparable time periods.

This mismatching of fiscal periods is especially troubling when the timing of events is a significant feature of the research. For example, in considering the impact of an economic recession on the financial condition of cities, and the beneficial effects of federal antirecession measures, it is critical that there be a matching of the recession period with the cities' financial results, and with the operation of the federal program.

With the lack of uniformity in fiscal years between the governments involved, such matching of time periods is impossible, and research on such questions is extremely difficult.

Causal Relationships

At the heart of much current research about urban fiscal crises is the determination of indicators of impending crisis.[10] Historically, predicting future municipal financial performance had been mainly the responsibility of bond-rating agencies. Using some basic economic and financial ratios, together with the collective judgments of experienced analysts, the agencies compiled a good record in the post-World War II period—a time generally free from municipal defaults or other serious financial problems. The situation changed abruptly in the mid-1970s when, shortly after the bond ratings for New York were upgraded, the city was unable to sell its general-obligation securities. As a result of this event, attention was suddenly directed to the need to understand the development of the New York problem, and particularly, how the problem could have been detected based on early indicators that might be applicable to other cities.

An Advisory Commission on Intergovernmental Relations study, *City Financial Emergencies*, that had received little attention when initially released, was reassessed because it was one of the few studies available concerned with early warning signals of financial crises in cities.[11] The ACIR report identified these indicators of potential trouble: significant imbalances between revenues and expenditures, an accumulated fund deficit, short-term operating loans outstanding at the end of the fiscal year, a high and rising rate of property tax delinquency, and a sudden substantial decrease in assessed value. These indicators were obtained by generalizing from case studies of past financial emergencies, and from a theoretical model of how such emergencies might typically occur. The report concluded that the typical problem starts with a budgetary imbalance between revenues and expenditures, which if severe, results in an accumulated fund deficit that in turn must be financed with short-term loans. If these conditions continue, the city may be unable to obtain renewal of the short-term loans and thereby default. This general theory, put forth in 1973, was confirmed by the New York chain of events.

The question that really remains unanswered, however, is this: Why does the imbalance between revenues and expenditures occur in the first instance? The two ACIR indicators dealing with rising tax delinquency and falling assessments touched on this question by suggesting that the drop in revenues caused by these occurrences causes budget imbalances, but these indicators were simply derived from historical events, without exploring any underlying cause-effect relationships. In effect, the ACIR indicators only diagnose financial trouble that is at an advanced stage, and do not explain the characteristics in the government or the community that are really causing the trouble to occur.

A variety of conditions have been suggested as the underlying causes of fiscal crisis. These include such factors as high unemployment, falling population, per capita income increasing more slowly than the national average, decreasing employment, high debt per capita, underfunded retirement system, a changing mix of employment, geographical location, central-city/suburban disparities, ethnic composition, climate and quality of political leadership. And in fact, statistical analysis has shown some of these factors do have a high correlation with subjectively established definitions of fiscal crisis, and with each other.[12]

One general problem with such research has been the lack of a credible case study to explain why the linkage occurs. Another difficulty is that widespread exceptions to the cause-effect conclusions exist. For example, virtually all the underlying factors present in New York are present in other major cities, and yet similar crises in other cities are not developing as they did in New York. Even more troubling is the fact that various cities have had even worse experiences by some measures, but appear to be avoiding the New York type of crisis.

160

Newspapers and other observers have noted that management deficiencies and politics contributed to the New York City crisis. Thus, any efforts to predict future fiscal distress should take into account these two factors. To date, few studies have incorporated management and political variables due to the difficulty in quantifying and testing their relationship to urban financial conditions.[13] Consequently, most studies continue to rely primarily on economic, social and financial characteristics.

Clearly, cause-effect relationships, as they relate to fiscal crises, remain obscure and will require more intensive research than has yet been performed. Some better understanding will probably come from the very specific analysis being done on a variety of related subjects such as the future impact of retirement costs, the impacts of inflation and recession on revenues and expenditures, or the relationship of population changes to revenues and expenditures. Case studies focusing on one or several cities to discern the interworking of various internal and external factors may also contribute to better predictive models.

Impact of Federal Aid

No consideration of urban fiscal studies can be complete without mention of the need to better understand how the massive amounts of federal resources being channeled to local governments are affecting their fiscal condition. It has been suggested that because of the magnitude of the aid—over 50 percent of total revenues for some cities—there can no longer be urban fiscal crises as they have existed in the past. But a corollary of this is that, if the aid were suddenly sharply reduced, an immediate crisis would be caused in several cities. Most of such speculation has been based on inadequate information about the actual impact of various types of federal funding on individual cities.[14]

The grassroots impact of the economic stimulus programs in 48 of the nation's largest cities has recently been the subject of a Treasury Department study.[15] The research tried to discover whether these federal funds were effectively targeted to the jurisdictions experiencing the greatest fiscal stress and whether the funds have been used as a substitute or stimulus to their own municipal revenues. Because of the fungibility of these three programs, the Treasury researchers concluded that "it is difficult to determine the actual use and thus the dependency of specific local programs and services on the economic stimulus package."[16] Other problems encountered in the study and noted in the report are the lack of data at the local level, which results in tremendous dependency on national statistics, and the difficulty in developing good indicators of fiscal stress and reliance. These information problems make it virtually impossible to evaluate the impact of federal policies on individual governments, or to assess the future impact on recipient jurisdictions if federal funding levels are changed.

By the nature of municipal fund accounting, different types of federal aid have different effects on financial condition. For example, capital grants, such as for public works, mass transit or water pollution control, are segregated from local tax and operating funds and may not even be commingled with locally raised capital funds. They, therefore, have little immediate impact on the city government's finances. Over the longer term, such capital grants may reduce the long-term debt of the city and its need to pay debt service from local taxes, but these advantages to the city may be more than offset by the operating and maintenance requirements placed on the city's operating funds, as a result of the construction of federally financed facilities. The net result may be that the federal capital aid resulted in an adverse financial impact on the government.

On the other hand, because of current program pressures, general revenue sharing grants may give direct relief to the local government's operating fund, but do little to alleviate a problem in raising capital funds such as is currently facing New York.

It is unfortunate that too frequently federal aid per se has been considered the antidote to treat whatever financial problems face local governments. Federal aid may have both good and bad attributes, it may provide short-term relief or long-term benefits, and its withdrawal may be either a financial catastrophe or a matter of little concern. Until a careful analysis of all the types of federal aid being sent to cities is made in the context of the problems and financial conditions in those cities, generalizations about such aid may be misleading.

Federal Efforts to Improve Management

In 1977, the Department of Housing and Urban Development established an urban studies task force to focus on how to build local fiscal management capacity. Under discussion are the goals that should be accomplished in financial accounting and reporting and the needs of the users of the financial management system. It is expected that a final program plan will be available about August 1978. In conjunction with this work, the Advisory Commission on Intergovernmental Relations is reviewing the numerous state legal provisions which may impede widespread change in the financial practices of local government. Under contract with HUD, the ACIR will refine model state statutes that are intended to serve as a guide for legislative changes to foster improved local financial management. This effort is being guided by a committee of users and producers of municipal financial information.[17]

By targeting the state statutory basis of municipal finance, and aiming at improving financial management capacity, the Department of Housing and Urban Development has signaled new program directions for improving the capability of local governments to handle federal funds effectively and to use them to resolve local financial problems.

The best example to date of this sort of federal package deal in operation is in New York City. Following the debacle in the securities market and after great debate in the Congress, the Treasury was authorized to make short-term loans, not to exceed $2.3 billion annually, to New York City. To carry out its responsibility under the program, Treasury got involved in many local financial management activities. It was authorized to receive reports on the progress made in planning for a balanced budget and to insure that a system was put into place to more accurately monitor revenues and expenditures. Consequently, the federal government became intimately involved in shaping the future management practices of a local government, so that New York City could effectively work to solve its own problems.

Similarly, the federal government has gotten involved in financial management improvement efforts for the city of Washington, D. C.[18] This concern arose when it was learned that the city's expenditures were exceeding revenues, and that the District's financial management system had not prevented such imbalances. As a result of these problems, doubts were raised as to whether the local government's system had sufficient safeguards to permit the issuance of bonds under a new home rule charter. To remedy the problem, a $16-million financial management improvement program was undertaken, with the bill being equally shared by the federal and District governments.

To date, the new New York City financial management system is embryonic in its functioning, and the Washington system is still in a planning and design stage, but the development and operation of these systems may give important direction to federal efforts to assist local governments. If they are able to live up to the expectations that have been placed on them, they could very well serve as models.

Conclusion

Research in the urban fiscal area has many challenges yet to be resolved. There still isn't a good workable definition of an urban fiscal crisis; available data are not uniform, lack timeliness, and often are not directly relevant to the issues. Partly because of the definition and data problems, there still isn't a good understanding of the causes of urban fiscal crisis, and consequently there are no good early warning signs of such problems. In addition to these challenges, the study of urban fiscal conditions has been subjected to confusion and increased complexity by the massive increase in federal aid programs to cities.

In order of priority, the most urgent need appears to be improved financial information. This means getting more uniformity in financial reporting, more timely reporting, and data that relates to actual operating conditions in city governments. Without such improvements, statistical studies will continue to present problems; case studies will require large investments of resources for limited results; and rankings may show relative distress of the nation's cities, but not forewarn the next fiscal crisis.

A heightened awareness of the financial condition of the nation's cities is likely to continue to produce increasing demands for more urban fiscal analysis. The field is indeed fertile for new contributions that better define the problem, test predictive hypotheses, and pursue new and innovative methods.

Notes

1.   U. S. Department of the Treasury, Office of State and Local Finance, *Report on the Fiscal Impact of the Economic Stimulus Package on 48 Large Urban Governments* (Washington, D. C.: U. S. Department of the Treasury, 1978).

2.   David Stanley, *Cities in Trouble* (Columbus, Ohio: Academy for Contemporary Problems, 1976), p. 1.

3.   Twentieth Century Fund Task Force on Municipal Bond Credit Ratings, *The Rating Game,* by John E. Petersen (New York: Twentieth Century Fund, 1974), p. 46.

4.   U. S. Department of Commerce, Bureau of the Census, "Financial Environment Indicators for City Governments" (Washington, D. C.: U. S. Department of Commerce, 1976), p. 4.

5.   John E. Petersen, Lisa A. Cole, and Maria L. Petrillo, *Watching and Counting: A Survey of State Assistance to and Supervision of Local Debt and Financial Administration* (Washington, D. C.: Municipal Finance Officers Association, 1977), p. 7.

6.   Coopers and Lybrand, *Financial Disclosure Practices of the American Cities* (Ann Arbor: University of Michigan, 1976); Sidney Davidson, David Green, Walter Hellerstein, Albert Madansky, and Roman Weil, *Financial Reporting by State and Local Government Units* (Chicago: University of Chicago, 1977); Minnesota State Planning Agency, Office of Local and Urban Affairs, "City Financial Reporting" (St. Paul: Minnesota State Planning Agency, 1978); Golembe Associates, Inc., *Improving Disclosure of Municipal Securities* (Washington, D. C.: American Bankers Association, 1976); National Council on Governmental Accounting, "GAAFR Restatement Exposure Draft" (Chicago: National Council on Governmental Accounting, 1978); and Arthur Andersen & Company, *Sound Financial Reporting in the Public Sector: A Prerequisite to Fiscal Responsibility* (Chicago: Arthur Andersen & Company, 1975).

7.   Municipal Finance Officers Association, "Disclosure Guidelines for Offerings of Securities by State and Local Governments" (Chicago: Municipal Finance Officers Association, 1976).

8.   John E. Petersen, Robert W. Doty, Ronald W. Forbes, and Donald D. Bourque, "Searching for Standards: Disclosure in the Municipal Securities Market," *Duke Law Journal* (January 1976), pp. 1177–1204.

9.   Various unpublished draft chapters have been prepared by the Urban Economic and Fiscal Indicators Project of the Urban Institute, Washington, D. C.

10.   John E. Petersen, "Simplification and Standardization of State and Local Government Fiscal Indicators," *National Tax Journal* 30 (September 1977), pp. 299–311.

11.   Advisory Commission on Intergovernmental Relations, *City Financial Emergencies* (Washington, D. C.: Advisory Commission on Intergovernmental Relations, 1973).

12.   Terry N. Clark, "How Many More New Yorks?" *New York Affairs* 3 (Summer/Fall 1976).

13. Ibid.

14. Harold A. Hovey, "The Availability of Research to Support Congressional Decision Making Affecting State and Local Finances," (Washington, D. C.: Congressional Research Service, 1976).

15. U. S. Department of the Treasury, *Report on the Fiscal Impact.*

16. Ibid., p. 46.

17. Trudi C. Miller, "Current Thinking About Research Related to State and Local Fiscal Condition," (Washington, D. C.: National Science Foundation, 1978).

18. Temporary Commission on Financial Oversight of the District of Columbia, *District of Columbia Financial Management System Concept Summary* (Washington, D. C.: American Management Systems, 1978).

Productivity Improvement in the Public Sector

Nancy S. Hayward

Productivity is an economic term which identifies the *quantity* of goods or services which can be produced from a specific *quantity* of resources—manpower, capital, energy, and raw materials. As an absolute ratio, the productivity rate indicates, at a single point in time, production capability based on resource availability. Compared over time, or among similar operations, the productivity rate reflects increases or decreases in the efficiency of resource utilization.

Increases in productivity permit wages to rise without price escalation; allow more goods and services to be available without increased depletion of scarce resources such as energy; enable the individual employee to work fewer hours without reducing income; and provide the economic growth necessary to support the attainment of social objectives such as clean air and water. In short, productivity growth reduces inflation; enhances the competitiveness of U.S. products in foreign markets; and contributes to improving the quality of life enjoyed by all Americans.

Over the past decade, U.S. productivity has declined to an annual growth rate of 1.5 percent from 3.2 percent during the preceding 20 years. Meanwhile, over the past 15 years Japanese productivity has grown at the rate of 8.9 percent annually; West Germany's at 5.9 percent; and France's at 5.7 percent. The prognosis for the future decade is still worrisome. U.S. productivity is projected to grow between 2.4 percent and 2.7 percent annually, while Western Europe expects approximately four-percent annual growth and Japan anticipates a six-percent productivity growth rate. Continuation of this disparity in performance does not bode well for a dramatic reversal in the substantial U.S. trade balance deficit nor, as a consequence, for strengthening in the value of the dollar overseas.

The implications for state and local government of the U.S. "productivity crisis" are significant. The cost of delivering public services will continue to rise dramatically. Pressures to reduce the tax burden will increase as the purchasing power of the dollar declines and the relative pinch of the tax bite increases. Demand for some public services will grow as private alternatives become infeasible.

But government is not just a victim of these consequences; it is also a contributor. Low government productivity growth expedites tax hikes, which add to the costs of

Nancy S. Hayward is a Consultant and served as Assistant Director for the National Center for Productivity and Quality of Working Life.

private-sector production and service delivery; retards the expansion of necessary and desirable public services; and wastes scarce resources.

Public-Sector Productivity

In the public sector, the term productivity must be broadened to encompass both the efficiency and the effectiveness with which resources are consumed to provide services or solve problems. In the absence of a free-market system, which acts as a quality control in the private sector, the public sector must develop surrogate indicators to assure that attempts to increase efficiency do not reduce effectiveness.

On one level, productivity relates to the efficiency of governments in using resources to accomplish goals. In other words, it relates to whether more resources are required to pave the same number of streets at the same level of quality, or whether fewer resources can be consumed to achieve the same goals more efficiently.

Productivity in government also relates to whether or not the right goals are being accomplished. The question here is whether paving the streets is the appropriate goal or whether the preference of the citizenry is to build tennis courts with those same resources. The demand for private goods and services is validated by consumer choice at the marketplace. Misallocation of productive capacity in the public sector generates citizen dissatisfaction with governmental effectiveness.

On still another level, government's contribution to productivity relates to the efficient and effective allocation of resources between the private and the public sectors for services or programs which enable us to achieve a preferred mix of public and private goods for a given amount of resources. An example of this activity is the regulatory process whereby public and private dollars are allocated to reducing pollution, a societal goal the costs of which may reduce the resources that otherwise would be available for increased consumption or investments.

Mobilizing all resources to achieve professed goals is one of the responsibilities of government. The extent to which we understand the mechanism by which these resources are allocated between the public and the private sector can influence both the way we attempt to accomplish these goals and the resulting efficiency and effectiveness with which we achieve them. It can also allow us to reduce the amount of resources utilized to accomplish the same or greater responsibilities.

Sources of Productivity Growth

Increases in productivity result from using fewer resources or varying the mix of resources required to produce goods or services so that all the inputs to the production process are optimally utilized.

In government, as in all labor-intensive activities, many factors affect the extent to which manpower is effectively and efficiently utilized in the delivery of services. Among the significant influences on employee productivity are factors such as skill level, scheduling of work, availability of necessary tools and equipment, absenteeism and tardiness, health and safety, working conditions, career development opportunities, and supervision.

Even in labor-intensive operations, like most governmental services, technology can significantly increase productivity through efficiencies of time and manpower or the capability to accomplish previously impossible tasks. Technological opportunities relate not only to new innovations, but also to equipment utilization, reduction of downtime, scheduling, manning levels, and energy consumption.

Financial resources also determine the extent to which productivity can be increased. Not only do they represent the capability to acquire new technology or compensate manpower, they also generate resources through investment practices, billing and payment policies, and debt financing.

The costs and consumption of raw materials also contribute to productivity improvements. For instance, as energy becomes more expensive, it is important to look for ways to reduce energy consumption and at the same time achieve the same goals.

Similarly, land is becoming relatively more dear, especially in concentrated metropolitan areas, making it important to minimize space needs and avoid the costs associated with land acquisition and maintenance.

The methods used to organize a job also contribute opportunities for improving productivity. For example, methods which are less redundant, more logical, and smooth flowing tend to cut down on the time, equipment, and manpower needed to accomplish the tasks. Certain methods will encourage high employee performance while other procedures will frustrate and alienate the worker, resulting in lower productivity.

The environment within which the production activity is taking place must also be considered. The environment is affected by a number of factors, including regulations imposed at the federal, state or local level. Regulations can influence the types and costs of inputs to the process (equal employment opportunity, minimum wage) or the method by which the process is done (Occupational Safety and Health Administration). These regulations can negatively influence the ultimate efficiency and perhaps the effectiveness of the system. As perpetrators of regulations, state and local governments should consider the alternatives for achieving the publicly desirable goal before enforcing rigid, productivity-reducing regulations. Under the influence of regulation, government should seek, where possible, methods of achieving the social goal without adding costs or diminishing results, as some companies have done with significant benefit to their product price resulting in large gains in market share.

Lastly, government must assess whether it should be in the business of delivering some of its services. In some cases, the market mechanism may have broken down so that the private sector is not doing what it can do best. In these cases, government has a responsibility only to correct the incentives, not to deliver the product or service more expensively or less productively.

Productivity-Related Research — A Historical Perspective

From a research perspective, governmental productivity has been addressed indirectly in a number of ways. Most prevalent has been research to determine how certain goals can be achieved more effectively; in other words, how the state of the art can be advanced with regard to a specific service or function in the government. In the field of education, for example, where significant changes took place including such revolutionary ideas as the new math which was popular in the sixties, research focused primarily on greater effectiveness through new instructional techniques.[1]

Secondly, research has focused on analyzing public policy issues in terms of achieving greater equity, assigning governmental responsibility more rationally, and finding new ways to balance competing and often conflicting demands from taxpayers. In these studies, the issue of government efficiency in implementing the public policy has often been a low priority.[2]

Thirdly, research has dealt with the question of governmental structure, with the focus most recently on issues related to achieving economies of scale from regionalized government and intergovernmental contracts. This research has been mostly concerned with service delivery effectiveness, public representation and participation, and managerial control.[3]

Fourthly, research has been conducted in developing innovative technologies for the public sector to support new activities, such as pollution monitoring, or to improve upon existing equipment, such as garbage trucks, or to introduce improvements proven in the private sector, e.g., computers.[4]

While the commitment to technological research in the public sector is significantly greater than it has been in the past, it is nowhere near the level of technological research and development (R&D) associated with manufacturing and agriculture. One reason for this is the labor intensity in the public sector, which leads to the feeling that it does not lend itself to the substitution of equipment for labor to the extent, say, of agriculture, which represents only four percent of our work force. While our national productivity growth rate may only be minimally increased as a result, technology does have a significant impact on the productivity growth rates in the service industries. Pressure for research into new technologies for government have further increased as a result of significant federal R&D investment to accomplish other goals, as with the U.S. space program. State and local governments have been a prime target for adaptation of the technologies which have resulted from this program, in part because they are recipients of federal funds.

Lastly, research interest has increased in developing management systems applicable to the public environment. In these efforts—such as PPBS, MBO, program evaluation and more recently zero-base budgeting—much less emphasis is placed on specific services or functions performed by state and local government. Rather, the primary focus is on how central government management agencies can better control service delivery and how they get information on the way services are delivered.

Each of the above elements of the public-sector productivity research agenda enhances the ability to improve either the effectiveness or the efficiency of public programs. All these forms of research contribute, at least indirectly, to our ability to improve the mix of resources which are allocated to specific programs or for delivering specific services. Therefore, they have impacted the efficiency and effectiveness with which resources are used to meet citizen needs and expectations.

Current Productivity Directions

Although productivity may currently be considered a fashionable buzz word, the interest is based on the recognition of a harsh reality. That is, just doing things better is not enough because the "pie" of available resources for many governments is fixed, growing only slowly, or even diminishing. Hence, public managers and elected officials are bringing a new vigor to their search for methods of getting more from the resources we have. As a result, our new focus on government operations builds upon our previous experiences, and goes farther. It suggests that productivity improvement cannot be accomplished solely by better control through central management or by improvements in the state of the art of selected functional areas. Instead, it assumes that productivity improvement must become the responsibility of all public managers, that each manager is responsible for the entire mix of resources. This focus has defined several new, important issues for productivity research.

Motivating Managers

Managers must have incentives to change so that efficiency and effectiveness will be enhanced. They must have information on how many different mixes of resources have worked elsewhere, and how their own organization is performing in terms of unit cost and cost/benefit. They then need quantitative and analytical expertise and methodologies, behavioral knowledge to assist in gaining employee support for operational changes, and political sensitivity to ensure the support of the chief executive and the legislative branch, as well as resources to invest in technology and training. As individual departments become responsible for productivity improvement, greater cooperation on personnel, financing, and purchasing issues is required. Finally, managers need to be rewarded—through some sharing of the benefits that accrue—for the risks they have taken to accomplish the improvement.

The definition of these issues has affected the nature of some current research on productivity in government. However, while the focus has changed slightly, the significant proportion of research dollars continues to be oriented toward the management of specific governmental functions, e.g., social services and law enforcement.

Utilization of Human Resources

The fact that the majority of ongoing research relates to the utilization of human resources is not surprising inasmuch as personnel costs are predominant in governmental budgets. Research in this area has had three primary points of focus. The first has been concerned with what the employee does, how long it takes to do it, and where it fits into the process of delivering a service.[5] The second has focused on how to motivate and reward the employee.[6] Work has been done both in nonfinancial rewards and in opportunities to share the financial benefits achieved through productivity improvement. The third area has been involved with the extent to which productivity becomes an issue in labor-management relations, a natural outgrowth of increasing unionization at the state and local level. Research in labor-management relations has examined contractual productivity criteria as well as opportunities for cooperation and participation by labor through labor-management committees on issues not included in the collective bargaining process.[7] It is fair to say that increasing interest in better utilization and sharing of benefits with employees has already demonstrated actual productivity gains.[8]

Many untapped areas relating to human resources remain to be addressed. Among them is the extent to which training is available to employees at all levels, including top managers and, very importantly, middle-level managers in issues concerning technical competence and human relations, and to other employees in their specific skills areas. Moreover, progress in career development programs, which has not been as rapid as in other sectors, has a significant impact on employees' motivation and actual productivity performance.

A separate but related issue is the dearth or poor quality of the projections of the number of employees and types of skills that will be required to support public sector programs in the future. Without manpower planning programs public job security will be continually challenged, resulting in unstable labor relations and increasing the likelihood of overstaffing in some fields and manpower shortages in others. It is hoped that the work of a temporary commission created by New York State to look at employment continuity in the public sector will extend the concern for this issue to other parts of the country.

Productivity Measurement

After human resources, most productivity-related research is associated with measurement of both the efficiency and effectiveness of government activities. The traditional measure of productivity—output per man-hour—has resulted in an historical emphasis on the contribution of manpower and on the efficiency side of the productivity equation. In the private sector, the inadequacy of emphasizing the labor inputs to the exclusion of others is becoming more widely recognized. Efforts are now under way to arrive at a better measure of "total factor productivity," which would include the relative contribution of other resources, such as energy and capital.[9]

In the public sector, "total factor productivity" is equally important. In addition, with lack of a marketplace, surrogates need to be established so that effectiveness and efficiency can both be monitored.

The ability to conduct research on the measurement of productivity probably led to the misconception that for productivity to be increased it must be measurable. Measurement by itself does not raise performance. But it does provide information about where problems exist or what progress has been accomplished.

In an aggregate sense, we have no data on public-sector productivity which would allow us to determine whether productivity has been increasing or decreasing. From a purely economic point of view, government is considered to achieve one dollar of output for every dollar of input, and hence productivity is counted as zero. From a rational point of view, it is impossible to accept the premise that productivity is zero for 15 percent of the GNP and more than 12 million employees. This assumption is further reinforced by experiences of individual jurisdictions which indicate that some jurisdictions are significantly more efficient and effective than others. For example, a 1971 study prepared for the National Center for Productivity and Quality of Working Life by the Urban Institute showed that costs associated with delivering the same level of garbage collection service varied by 500 percent in two jurisdictions only 30 miles apart.[10]

Attempts have been made to measure productivity at the federal government level. With about 60 percent of the work force covered, the federal government has been achieving a productivity growth rate of approximately 1.2 percent annually for the past 10 years.[11] This is slightly lower than the average annual productivity growth rate in the private sector, which has been 1.5 percent over the past 10 years.

Current research on productivity measurement is focused first and foremost on identifying indicators of efficiency by functional category, including personnel, purchasing, police, garbage collection, and inspections. In most cases, work-load data is collected to get a handle on what employees are doing and how long it takes. In large part, jurisdictions interested in identifying the efficiency of their work force can develop adequate indicators on their own.

Research on productivity measurement has of late been turning toward the effectiveness of service delivery, including indicators of timeliness, responsiveness, and thoroughness. Because much of this information must be acquired from client surveys, a good deal of the research has revolved around methods of data collection, relevance and clarity of questions, and how surveys can be conducted within the resource limitations of individual jurisdictions. The Urban Institute has recently begun to look at the issue of the outcomes of services that are delivered by the government.[12]

Current research in the collection and analysis of comparative performance data among jurisdictions is attempting first to ascertain the extent of comparability, then pinpoint areas of greatest opportunity where different jurisdictions can look for efficiency and effectiveness improvements. However, significant problems exist, such as the lack of uniform accounting guidelines. As a result, it is difficult to ascertain similarity of services offered and the full costs of delivery.

Although the difficulty of identifying government outputs is often cited as the limitation to public productivity measurement, immediate outputs (such as food stamp applications processed, arrests surviving first judicial review, etc.) have been developed to overcome the problem of determining the ultimate output of the government service. The surrogates do not constitute single indicators of governmental productivity performance; hence a family of measures which gives the full picture of efficiency and effectiveness along with the total complement of covered activities must be developed.

Probably the greatest hindrance to greater utilization of productivity measures, as documented in a survey by the National Association of State Budget Officers in 1975, is the nonuse of available data by central management or policy-making levels of government.[13] The extent to which information is required and analyzed in the decision-making process lies at the crux of the productivity improvement and measurement problem in the governmental arena. When legislative bodies, chief executives, and budgeting and management offices do not use service productivity information in policy making, it is unlikely that interest in developing these measures and using them as part of the management function will develop among departmental managers.

Since it can be assumed that the productivity of service delivery varies significantly across governmental lines, many conclude that great improvements can be made just by raising the level of performance to that of the currently best known. In order to do this, several federal agencies have placed substantial emphasis on the importance of sharing the experiences of state and local government managers. Case studies have detailed techniques used by individual jurisdictions to increase productivity, including technological, managerial, and personnel improvements.[14] The availability of this information has encouraged others to engage in productivity improvement efforts. However, such dissemination has its limitations. Any process must be adapted to the jurisdictions which try it, and in order to make the necessary adaptation, more is required than just the availability of knowledge and experiences. It requires a local capability to modify and implement.

Developing Incentives for Change

Very little research has been done on generating incentives to change, that is, ways of motivating organizations to want to strive for greater improvements in efficiency and effectiveness. Most work in this area has focused on how central management agencies can encourage line managers, primarily through the budgeting process, to be concerned with efficiency and effectiveness. This has been a double-edged sword, however, since financial shortfalls have forced budget cuts in line agencies even though improvements in efficiency and effectiveness have been achieved. Thus, while central management pressure may be most effective in forcing a productivity concern within jurisdictions, it can also act as a disincentive to further agency improvements.

The interdependence among all levels of government as the result of the intergovernmental grant-in-aid system also presents an opportunity for a more positive incentive for increasing efficiency and effectiveness. The New York State Temporary Commission on Management and Productivity is examining the possibility of creating incentives within formula grant systems by which savings achieved by the recipient government would be shared by that level of government and the level providing the grant.[15] The federal government has attempted to experiment with a few of these concepts, such as in the housing maintenance area, where financial bonuses are being used to reward those who accomplish increased housing maintenance tasks with fewer resources.[16] In this largely untapped area, the current system, if not neutral, errs on the side of providing negative incentives for productivity improvement.

The concept of contracting the delivery of public services to private concerns or to other governments has become popular because of a belief that this would make it easier to control costs and results. The efficiency and effectiveness of these contracting provisions (which could be another government entity) do not necessarily result from reduced labor costs or better management, but may result from the characteristics of the service or the management controls built into the contract. For example, if expensive pieces of equipment are required for the delivery of the service, would it be better to have the contractor assume the costs of purchase? Or, if significant numbers or types of employees are required only for a short term, would it be better for a government not to make a long-standing commitment to accomplishing this task? Or, is performance accountability written into the contract when internal government accountability for the same service was never exercised?

The extent to which the demand and availability of public services can be more closely correlated has recently become an area of inquiry.[17] For example, what should the public role be in creating an incentive for continued private-sector service delivery? Or how much must the individual citizen be motivated to assume the responsibilities which are inherently his? In other words, how can the dependency on government in the delivery of services be reduced without abrogating the government's responsibility for achievement of certain socially desirable goals? Rationalizing demand and supply of public services has been achieved in a number of areas, including rerouting buses to correspond to ridership patterns or reducing staffing peaks and valleys by staggering permit deadline dates.

Finally, historical discussions of the growth of government have focused primarily on the federal level. We must look at growth in the state and local sector, which is proceeding at a significantly faster rate than in the federal sector. In some areas, such as regulation and income transfer, state and local governments have begun to resemble the federal government in scope of responsibilities. From the perspective of national resource availability, what is the relative benefit and contribution from the resources that are being increasingly consumed in the delivery of public services as opposed to the private manufacture of goods and delivery of services?

It should be clear that the opportunities for improving governmental productivity far exceed the current level of research in this area. The reality of fiscal pressures has placed the focus of innovation within the governments themselves. Building on this base, researchers can contribute significantly through evaluating these experiences, documenting the accomplishments and pushing forward in the politically sensitive areas.

Productivity Improvement in the Financial Functions of Government

Improvements in productivity have been primarily directed toward those services of government which are highly visible, represent the largest proportion of dollars, and are measurable. In these areas it was assumed that the benefits of improvement would be most apparent to the taxpayer, and significant savings could be reaped through simple modifications. As a result, neither financial managers nor researchers have evidenced interest in productivity comparable to that shown in police or garbage collection, for example. In many respects this is unfortunate. The opportunities are significant, and in addition, it is easier to implement improvements in an area where citizens are not likely to feel threatened by proposed changes. Furthermore, financial managers can improve the efficiency and effectiveness of their activities, as well as operations in other areas of the organization.

Nevertheless, the research and experimentation that have been undertaken in this area have identified many fruitful avenues of further pursuit and generated significant real savings. Unlike many productivity improvements in operating programs which result in reduced future costs of production, savings generated in the financial functions often produce immediate cost reductions or generate revenues and only rarely affect staffing levels. A number of improvement opportunities do not usually fall under the direct responsibility of the financial officer, but, because of the potential impact on revenues or expenditures, they should be of interest.

Budgeting

The budgeting process itself probably generates the most pervasive pressure for increased productivity in the line departments. However, unless budgetary information includes programmatic objectives along with measures of efficiency and effectiveness, it is difficult to ensure that budget cuts will be made consistent with desired service levels and consideration of the productivity potential within a specific program. The operational nature of government functions varies, and therefore different rates of improvement should be expected across departments. However, the ability of the budgeting process to stimulate productivity improvements depends directly on the extent to which policy decisions regarding budget adjustments result from analysis of the efficiency and effectiveness data provided in the budget. Simply stated, if savings achieved in one line department are allocated to another, in which efforts have not been made to improve productivity, the incentive to try again is diminished.

A significant amount of research has been undertaken on budgeting techniques.[18] Program budgeting is an important building block for improving productivity as it allows the full costs of operation to be allocated by programs. Not only does this facilitate prioritization of programs and expenditures, but it can highlight hidden overhead costs.

Cash Management

One of the prevalent areas of interest is that of cash management. Managers are addressing questions related to appropriate levels of cash to keep on hand so as to maximize the interest generated on idle funds while avoiding cash short-fall; short term/long term ratio of investments; evaluation of banking relationships; and reduction of delays in deposit and investment. A number of jurisdictions have been trying to increase the return on their investment by participation in state investment pools.

By paying more attention to cash management practices, many jurisdictions are generating "free" money.[19]

Debt Management

Similarly, interest has increased in improving governmental debt management practices. Changes in the nature and comprehensiveness of disclosure information, resulting from the New York City crisis, have already generated broad-scale reviews of financial and general management practices in many jurisdictions. These "house-cleaning" efforts have led to improvements in both the processes and policies of jurisdictional management, which have contributed to raising the bond ratings and reducing the cost of borrowing money.[20]

Collections, Billings and Deposits

Equally important is the need for efficient collection of revenues due the government. The lack of attention paid to this issue is surprisingly high. Improved management of tax collections can reduce delinquency, increase percentage of full payments, and minimize tax-exempt or nontax-producing properties. The IRS has developed sophisticated sampling techniques to maximize revenue receipts from auditing returns. Likewise, significant benefits can be achieved by reducing delays in the deposit of tax payments. Some jurisdictions are still not depositing on the day of collection, while others arrange with the bank to receive directly. The costs and benefits of these two extremes illustrate the importance of aggressive financial management. Similarly, prompt billing for licenses, permits, fines and services rendered, which in some cases is six months in arrears, will reduce government carrying costs, perhaps avoid government borrowing, and increase available cash for investment. Furthermore, old fee structures should be revised to reflect current service costs.

Intergovernmental Transfers

Within the intergovernmental grant system, opportunities also exist to improve the efficiency of financial resource utilization. Two significant issues are the speed of the transfer process and full-cost reimbursement. Proposed federal changes, including electronic transfer of funds, will reduce local government carrying costs on federally supported programs to the extent that the local government bills promptly. On the other issue, a number of jurisdictions, as a result of improved budgeting and accounting systems, realized that many allowable costs, often overhead factors, were not being charged to the funding government.[21] Careful attention to the total cost of delivery can avoid unnecessary local support to federal or state programs.

Risk Management

A number of other governmental support functions can also achieve cost efficiencies. For example, the techniques of risk management are being more widely applied to government. Through this analysis governments are attempting to minimize insurance costs by weighing premium costs against benefits and risk potential, where coverage is not mandated by law. For some this has resulted in greater self-insurance. Others are reducing insurance costs by qualifying for lower premiums. For example, monetary and nonmonetary incentives for driver safety in many public services could reduce the accident rate and therefore the insurance premiums.

Vendor Payments

Similarly, many jurisdictions are paying penalties on vendor payments that are being processed too slowly, sometimes hundreds of days later. As a result, prompt payment discounts are lost. Also basic vendor prices are often inflated, based on the historical government rate of payables, to compensate the vendor for his carrying costs. One state looked at the option, as used in some businesses, of a prepaid voucher for repetitive, routine purchases. It would facilitate the process internally and reduce the prices charged by the vendor.[22]

Purchasing Procedures

Productivity is decreased when materials are not available as a result of purchasing procedures that are not adequate to meet the needs of the operating departments. This clearly affects employee productivity as employees cannot do their job when supplies are unavailable or inadequate. It can also result in expensive emergency purchases. In the area of construction, governments must pay close attention to the issue of timing, not just in supplies, but also in services such as engineering design. Delays in these services, including zoning delays, reduce government productivity significantly. Similarly, costs of maintenance and service should be examined in the purchase of new equipment. The use of maintenance contracts for specialized equipment has benefited some jurisdictions. It is also important to look at the incidence of equipment breakdowns in terms of escalating maintenance costs and reduced employee productivity. Lastly, quantity discounts can and should be considered. However, if timed deliveries cannot be negotiated, the costs of warehousing and spoilage must be built into the cost/benefit analysis.

Capital Investment

Information on capital investment for enhancing productivity, both within the governmental organization and as it relates to private-sector productivity growth, is sorely needed. Currently, it is not known whether the low levels of capital investment in operations relate to scarcity of capital, the approval process (referenda), a lack of recognition on the part of management that investments in plant and equipment can improve productivity, or inadequate depreciation practices. While little is known about causes, the impact on government productivity is still substantial. Maintenance costs escalate, cost and energy technologies are not introduced; equipment downtime increases.

With regard to methods of financing, the Urban Institute is studying the relative impact on levels of public capital investment that results from new financing arrangements such as special tax-exempt bonding authorities and new zoning provisions.[23] Before approving new development, some jurisdictions expect the private developer to assume responsibility for building sewers, fire stations, schools, etc. In both of these cases we need to better understand the extent to which capital generation for productivity improvement is enhanced or retarded by current practices.

In a similar vein, the public sector, through roads, bridges, sewers, and other public facilities, contributes to the productivity of private-sector goods production and distribution. Knowing what the relative contribution of the existing infrastructure is to national productivity growth would help to identify targets for future investment. It would also be helpful in establishing the appropriate and necessary levels of federal, state and local support.

Conclusion

It is becoming increasingly evident that the quality of services and cost of government have an impact on both individual and corporate decisions regarding relocation. Therefore, state and local governments compete against each other. Their economic growth potential, and ability to reduce the cost of government and improve the delivery of their services, serve to increase their competitive position. To the extent that better-managed resources allow government to conduct additional programs, opportunities for job growth are increased in the public sector. To the extent the community becomes commercially and socially more attractive, private jobs are also created, resulting in further economic stability.

Clearly, productivity growth contributes significantly to our potential for economic growth, and therefore to our ability to improve our standard of living. As a nation we have become accustomed to significant strides in the quality of our life. Unless productivity is increased at a higher level than we are now experiencing, these strides are not going to be possible in the future.

Notes

1. Research in this area has been conducted by Public Technology, Inc.; the Divison of Advanced Productivity Research and Technology, National Science Foundation; and the Division of Intergovernmental Science and Research Utilization, National Science Foundation. These organizations are all located in Washington, D. C.

2. See note 1 above.

3. See note 1 above.

4. See note 1 above.

5. Patrick Manion, ''Work Measurement in Local Governments,'' *Management Information Service Report*, vol. 6 (Washington, D. C.: International City Management Association, 1974), pp. 1–21; National Commission on Productivity and Work Quality, *Improving Municipal Productivity: Work Measurement for Better Management* (Washington, D. C.: National Commission on Productivity and Work Quality, 1975); and Public Technology, Inc., *Improving Productivity Using Work Measurement* (Washington, D. C.: Public Technology, Inc., 1977).

6. John M. Greiner et al., *Monetary Incentives and Work Standards in Five Cities: Impacts and Implications for Management and Labor* (Washington, D. C.: The Urban Institute, 1977).

    National Commission on Productivity and Work Quality, *Employee Incentives to Improve State and Local Government Productivity*, based on a report by John M. Greiner, Lynn Bell and Harry P. Hatry of the Urban Institute, Washington, D. C. (Washington, D. C.: National Commission on Productivity and Work Quality, 1975).

7. National Center for Productivity and Quality of Working Life, *Labor-Management Committees in the Public Sector: Experiences of Eight Committees* (Washington, D. C.: National Center for Productivity and Quality of Working Life, 1975).

8. Greiner et al., *Monetary Incentives and Work Standards*.

9. Report of the Panel to Review Productivity Statistics of the National Academy of Sciences, under contract to the National Center for Productivity and Quality of Working Life, forthcoming.

10. Harry P. Hatry and Donald M. Fisk, *Improving Productivity and Productivity Measurement in Local Government* (Washington, D. C.: National Center for Productivity and Quality of Working Life, 1971), p. 39.

11. National Center for Productivity and Quality of Working Life, *1977 Annual Report to the President and Congress* (Washington, D. C.: National Center for Productivity and Quality of Working Life, 1977), p. 76.

12. Louis H. Blair et al., *Monitoring the Impacts of Prison and Parole Services: An Initial Examination* (Washington, D. C.: The Urban Institute, 1977); John M. Greiner et al., *Monitoring the Effectiveness of State Transportation Services* (Washington, D. C.: The Urban Institute, 1977); Harry P. Hatry et al., *How Effective are Your Community Services? Procedures for Monitoring the Effectiveness of Municipal Services* (Washington, D. C.: The Urban Institute, 1977); Annie Millar et al., *Monitoring the Outcomes of Social Services, Volume 1: Preliminary Suggestions* (Washington, D. C.: The Urban Institute, 1977); Annie Millar et al., *Monitoring the Outcomes of Social Services, Volume 2: A Review of Past Research and Test Activities* (Washington, D. C.: The Urban Institute, 1977); Alfred H. Schainblatt, *Monitoring the Outcomes of State Mental Health Treatment Programs: Some Initial Suggestions* (Washington, D. C.: The Urban Institute, 1977); Alfred H. Schainblatt, *Monitoring the Outcomes of State Chronic Disease Control Programs: Some Initial Suggestions* (Washington, D. C.: The Urban Institute, 1977); and Richard E. Winnie, *Jobs and Earnings for State Citizens: Monitoring the Outcomes of State Economic Development and Employment and Training Programs* (Washington, D. C.: The Urban Institute, 1977).

13. State and Local Government Research Program of the Urban Institute with the cooperation of the National Association of State Budget Officers, *The Status of Productivity Measurement in State Government: An Initial Examination* (Washington, D.C.: The Urban Institute, 1975).

14. National Center for Productivity and Quality of Working Life, *Improving Governmental Productivity: Selected Case Studies* (Washington, D. C.: National Center for Productivity and Quality of Working Life, 1977); Frederick O'R. Hayes, *Productivity in Local Government*

(Lexington, Massachusetts: Lexington Books, D. C. Heath and Company, 1977); and International City Management Association, *Guide to Productivity Improvement Projects, Edition 3* (Washington, D. C.: National Center for Productivity and Quality of Working Life, 1976). Also, subsequent and future editions (six issues per year) of the *Guide to Productivity Improvement Projects*, renamed *The Guide to Management Improvement Projects in Local Government*, are available on a subscription basis from the International City Management Association, Washington, D. C.

15. New York State Commission on Management and Productivity in the Public Sector, *The Application of Productivity Incentives to State-Local Aid Formulas* (Albany: New York State Commission on Management and Productivity in the Public Sector).

16. This is part of the Local Housing Authority Work Incentive Demonstration Program, Target Projects Program, of the Office of the Assistant Secretary for Housing Management of the U. S. Department of Housing and Urban Development, located in Washington, D. C.

17. Phillip Kotler, *Marketing for Non-Profit Organizations* (Englewood Cliffs, New Jersey: Prentice-Hall, 1975); Phillip Kotler, *Marketing Management: Analysis, Planning and Control* (Englewood Cliffs, New Jersey: Prentice-Hall, 1976); Christopher Lovelock and Charles Weinberg, *Marketing Cases for Public and Non-Profit Organizations* (Palo Alto, California: Scientific Press, 1977); and National Center for Productivity and Quality of Working Life, *Marketing: A Creative Approach to Citizen Participation in Government*, draft conference report (Washington, D. C.: National Center for Productivity and Quality of Working Life, 1977).

18. For a discussion of current research in budgeting, refer to the Lehan essay in this volume.

19. Ronald Forbes, *Decision Related Research in Fiscal Urban Technology: Improving State and Local Government Cash Management* (Washington, D. C.: Municipal Finance Officers Association, forthcoming); "Free Money," *Time Magazine* (June 5, 1978); Haskins and Sells, Government Service Group, *Implementing Effective Cash Management in Local Government: A Practical Guide* (Chicago: Municipal Finance Officers Association, 1977); John A. Jones and S. Kenneth Howard, *Investment of Idle Funds by Local Governments: A Primer* (Chicago: Municipal Finance Officers Association, 1973); Frank M. Patitucci and Michael H. Lichtenstein, *Improving Cash Management in Local Government: A Comprehensive Approach* (Chicago: Municipal Finance Officers Association, 1977); James C. Van Horne, "Cash Management," in *Management Policies in Local Government Finance*, ed. J. Richard Aronson and Eli Schwartz (Washington, D. C.: International City Management Association, 1975), pp. 248–262; Kurt Ronsen, "Fun with Funds; or, Deposit and Investment of Local Government Funds, *"Management Information Service Report*, vol. 8 (Washington, D. C.: International City Management Association); and "Improving Cash Management in Municipal Government," *Management Information Service Report*, vol 1 (Washington, D. C.: International City Management Association, June 1969).

20. J. Richard Aronson and Eli Schwartz, "Determining Debt's Danger Signals," *Management Information Service Report*, vol. 8 (Washington, D. C.: International City Management Association, December 1976); and Roland I. Robinson, "Debt Management," in *Management Policies in Local Government Finance*, ed. J. Richard Aronson and Eli Schwartz (Washington, D. C.: International City Management Association, 1975), pp. 229–246.

21. Dick Howard, "Random Moment Sampling: Georgia's Indirect Cost Allocation Experiment," *Innovation Report* (Lexington, Kentucky: Council of State Governments, February 1977).

22. The Vendor Payment Project (ongoing project of the Washington State Advisory Council on State Government Productivity located in Olympia, Washington).

23. The Urban Institute, "Capital Investment and Capital Stock Condition," in *Fiscal Choices for State and Local Governments*, ed. George E. Peterson (Washington, D. C.: The Urban Institute, forthcoming).